Global Leadership **Literacy**

CCBS Press

Global Leadership Literacy

Empirical analyses of cross-cultural leadership styles and practices

Amsterdam University
of Applied Sciences

CCBS-Press

First edition 2024, ISBN: 978-90-79646-53-1, NUR: 812
Editorial managers: Christopher Higgins, Aynur Doğan, Sander Schroevers
Inner and cover design: SH69T Studio, Amsterdam, Netherlands
Cover graphic: Krushon, Ukraine

Text copyright: Adi Sudradjat, Achraf Elqioin, Ajay Jaggoe, Aleyna Beyazova, Aleyna Gündoğdu, Alia Momand, Amanuel Girmay, Amaury Adriana, Amèl Loukili, Amir Helmy Hammad, Andrei Gîlceavă, Anna Krén, Annerina Tuijnman, Arian Vogelpoel, Asmae Rochdi, Berkay Akalin, Boris Havik, Britney Brako, Can Bilekirik, Catoo Creemers, Christiaan Hüner, Dafny Kelly, Danny Buskermolen, Dave Hogerwerf, Dean van Eikeren, Demi Reivers, Desiree Webster, Dexter Dekker, Direnç Kaygusuz, Dylan Sodhi, Ece Ejder, Emmilia Ekezie, Erik van Schie, Federico Hurtado Wiessner, Fernanda Barros Gomyde Porto, Ferry Ravestein, Fieras Dahoe, Fikria El Habri, Firdaouss El Azzouzi, Fiston Conte, Flo Thielen, Floris van Capelle, Francisca Owusu, Γιώργος Αθυμαρίτης (George Athymaritis), Goumana Azab, Hamza Akhloufi, Hasnaa Ziyani Choho, Ian Verkade, Ibtissam Ridouani, Ilyas Omaid, Isabel Ayseli, Isabel Burillo Alba, Isidora Valentina Vásquez Ponce, Jaden Bakker, Jaimy Loupias, Jamal Slijngaard, Jarek Witte, Jella de Boer, Je-mell Foen-A-Foe, Jenny van der Harst, John Tilburg, Joran Janssens, Jorge Davo Sainz, Jorten Löhr, Josine Haver, Julian van Affelen van Saemsfoort, Karina Leszczyńska, Kevin Soekhie, Koen Breeuwer, Laila Ekinci, Laith Shumaila, Leila Garcia, Lennart Niehof, Leyrienio Sandvliet, Lina Zaal, Lindsay Helstone, Lize-Marie Nieuwoudt, Lorenzo Bakker, Luis Pozo Gallego, Mahnaz Daneshgar, Malachi Lang-Orsini, Marciano Krasuski, Martijn Snakenborg, Masud Mobayyen, Matteo Valenteyn, Max Meinders, Max Streefkerk, Mees Strunk, Mélanie Schuit, Melle Nol, Merit Omoregie, Merna Yalda, Michelle Teuthof, Milan Bruinsma, Milan Merkx, Mohamad Skeif, Mohamed Biari, Mohamed Jbari, Mohcine Farsi, Moïse Mousa, Murat Dağli, Myangelo Poulina, Naomi Moultrie, Naomi Tshinakanudia, Nardi van Leeuwen, Nassim Aït Chrif, Nathania Van-Lare, Nelson Torres, Noureddine Boukazim, Noureddine El Ayadi El Kanfoudi, Olayah Baccai, Osman Kırbaş, Osman Kuzuoglu, Ouail El Youbari, Pau Bentgens, Quux van Luik, Rajae Sanhayi, Renske Legebeke, Rick Baas, Rina Hasani, Robin Bartelings, Roos Hafkamp, Rosaly van den Herik, Ryan Dreux, Samuel Johansson, Santiago Zapata Ramirez, Sarah Havinga, Sebastiaan Svechtarov, 추세진 (Sejin Chu), Sem Oostmeijer, Serena Darnoud, Shaed Sarwari, Shaqeel Nasibdar, Siepan Mirani, Σοφία Παπαχρήστου (Sofia Papachristou), Stella Duin, Stephanie Montero, Tarik Alouch, Tati Lintjens, Thijs van der Loo, Thimo Loos, Thyra Thomas, Tim de Rode, Tobias Ankone, Victor Regouin, Wang Hang Wang, Willem Karakaxas, Xaviero Landveld, Youri Fagel, Youssra Azzofri, Youssra El Hadouchi, Zain Sarai Edin, Zebediah Mirekuah, Zeynep Dur and Zorelly Edam.

Table of Contents

Preface

Welcome to the latest edition of our ongoing empirical cross-cultural analyses of global leadership styles and practices. The noun *Literacy* heads the title of this issue in our Global Leadership series. Literacy means competence in a specified area. We hope this edition may inspire global professionals. This book is the result of collaborative research by 152 students on the 'Cross-Cultural Business Skills' and the 'Global Business Skills' electives (minors), which are hosted by the University of Applied Sciences Amsterdam.

Over the course of a single semester, these students have empirically investigated leadership styles and practices across multiple countries, through employing a combination of research methods. More specifically, the students performed desk-based literature reviews of local scholarship, in conjunction with generating both quantitative and qualitative data through conducting a survey and interviews with thousands of local business professionals and cross-cultural scholars and practitioners. The quality of the contributions in this edited collection are thus, above all, a testament to the perseverance and collaborative work ethic of everyone involved, and, moreover, provide rich and colourful insights.

First and foremost, we would like to take this opportunity to thank all the individual co-authors for their determination to complete their respective analyses. Moreover, we also wish to extend our upmost gratitude to all the survey respondents and interviewees for being gracious enough to provide insight into the prevailing leadership styles and practices in their country. To the reader, we hope this book finds you well and perhaps, dare we say it, sitting in a convenient airport lounge waiting to board a flight to one of the countries explored in this book, with locally-informed insights into cross-cultural leadership, eager to apply them in practice.

Christopher Higgins, Sander Schroevers & Aynur Dogan

About CCBS

Since 2010, Cross-Cultural Business Skills (CCBS) has sought to educate bachelor students in both the fundamentals of cross-cultural business skills and specific research methods. CCBS/GBS are elective courses ('minor') established and taught by Prof. Dr.Hc. Sander Schroevers, Aynur Doğan MA and Christopher Higgins MA at the Amsterdam University of Applied Sciences (the Netherlands).

Educational approach

At CCBS/GBS we believe that effective learning takes place through sharing and engaging with first-hand experiences. For this reason, we challenge our students to produce new knowledge from a localised perspective. Often this involves conducting research in an unknown language, alphabet or cultural milieu, which, in turn, helps out students develop fundamental skills for the contemporary interconnected world. Our main objective is to co-create country-specific bodies of knowledge, which we generate through carrying out both expert-interviews (video and audio) with native professionals and scholars and in-depth analyses of local academic and trade literature. In order to create a truly international classroom experience, we try to host students from across the globe. Moreover, we attempt to connect our students with a broad range of representatives from the business, media and diplomatic sectors, through hosting professional symposia in the school. All CCBS-learning materials (print, digital and video) are 100% bespoke. We are honoured by the fact that we have consistently received the university's highest evaluation scores over the last ten years, and that Sander was elected as teacher of the year at the FBE-faculty.

About CCBS Global Leadership research

CCBS Global Leadership is our ongoing academic research project for the Amsterdam University of Applied Sciences, which directly informs the cross-cultural business material taught on the minor. Every six months, CCBS researchers survey C-level executives around the world. Our analytical gaze is focused on five main areas: management, meetings, leadership, recruitment and expatriates. Since conducting the inaugural international poll in 2012, the CCBS global-fact-tank has conducted interviews in 141 trade nations, with more than twenty-four-thousand professionals. Thank you!

Methodological approach

Three modes of data collection were employed to generate the insights published in this book. Firstly, insights into the cultural aspects of leadership were gathered through country-specific literature searches, in both peer-reviewed academic journals and in-country books, which served as the foundation for the subsequent research. Secondly, a global online survey on leadership was conducted with qualified respondents from each country (CCBS Survey, year). Expert sampling was used to identify the survey respondents, in conjunction with snowballing techniques, which were subsequently introduced to target a population who are often difficult to reach. In total, over 24,000 respondents participated in the CCBS survey; however almost one-third of these surveys were not used, because they were not fully completed, or their background or sometimes IP-addresses did not match our target group. The survey was created in English and subsequently translated by competent bilinguals, who were either research collaborators or supervised by them. The present study made use of translations into Arabic, Armenian, Dari, Dutch, Eritrean, Filipino, French, Greek, Krio, Pashto, Papiamentu, Serbian, Spanish, Sranan Tongo, Tagalog and surely: English. Evaluations of translation accuracy were completed by using back-translation or parallel translations, where possible. The Spanish, Dutch, English and Arabic version were rolled out in multiple countries. The questionnaire comprised 27 items, both multiple-choice and open-ended questions, which provided descriptive information on national-based views on leadership.

The respondents answered the psychometric multiple-choice questions on five or six-point Likert scales, which were anchored by terms ranging from 'not at all' to 'a lot'. All the qualitative data provided comprehensive knowledge into the topic of local leadership styles and practices. The multinational survey and interviewing were conducted between 12 October and 11 December 2024. The findings that emerged out of this research have not been presented prior to the publication of this book. Thirdly, in addition to the survey respondents, a selection of 26 leadership experts were also interviewed for the present study. These audio and video recorded interviews lasted between 15-60 minutes on average, and were transcribed verbatim (a selection of these will be published on the YouTube and Spotify channels of the CCBS minor).

Country profiles

Empirical studies have revealed that the relationship between certain kinds of motivating leadership behaviour and work outcomes systematically varies from culture to culture. As noted by the Global Leadership and Organizational Behavior Effectiveness (GLOBE) Research Program: "to date, 90 percent of leadership literature reflects US-based research and theory". The American-centric nature of extant literature is a profound problem, insofar as it fails to account for how leadership theories, styles and practices operate across national frontiers. This is important, because as the number of countries expand, so do the differences. It is for this reason that I have always been fond of Peter Drucker's quote: "Management is doing things right; leadership is doing the right things".
That is to say, leadership encompasses the human element of business, whereas management is often about systems and processes. For the purposes of writing this paragraph, I conducted a quick check on Amazon.com for the number of books with the word 'leader' in their title, which produced an incredible 60,000 results. Similarly, a quick search on ProQuest (one of the databases we recommend to students for accessing scholarly journals) resulted in almost a million hits for 'leadership'. Evidently, there is extensive research informing us of how leaders' communication styles are profoundly influenced by the geographical region in which they are operating. Regrettably, some business leaders overlook local managerial and cultural practices, and instead acquiesce to management-styles that are grounded in Western concepts, which, in turn, undermines the performance of their organisation. Given that ineffective managers risk costing organisations notably large sums of money, there is an emergent trend among both human resource professionals and senior executives to adopt more localised leadership styles and practices.

Chapter makeup

This book consists of country-specific chapters, which each describe at length the leadership styles and practices within their respective country. All country profiles were written in a standard format, in order to allow for a clearer identification of points of similarity and divergence across the different business cultures. Most of the country profiles in this book contain the following sections:

- Country introduction,
- How the indigene characterise leaders,
- Survey results and what local respondents say,
- An in-country YouTube review,
- A transcribed telephone interview with a local leadership scholar,
- A summarised video interview with a local cross-cultural trainer,
- A description of an in-country best-selling book on leadership,
- Understanding hierarchy in the chapter's country,
- How to achieve leadership empathy in that particular culture.

I will briefly introduce each of these sections in turn below.

Local leadership analysis

The more I work abroad, the more I realise that it takes more than just a survey to examine and classify national cultures. More specifically, there is too much cultural heterogeneity and nuance, which substantially impacts upon how one effectively operates in a particular country, but yet simply does not fit within prevailing academic constructs on this topic. Notwithstanding the many good Western-centric books on a variety of countries, what is invariably obfuscated in these texts is the local perspective. The need to address this lacuna in the field by prioritising localised perspectives became pivotal to our approach to investigating country-specific leadership styles and practices. This approach comprises gathering data from indigenous sources, including: (i) survey-results and what local respondents say, (ii) a local leadership scholar, (iii) a local cross-cultural trainer, (iv) and an in-country best-selling book on leadership. While having to conduct research sometimes in other languages and even scripts has proven to be incredibly challenging for some of our students, it has undoubtedly produced rich local-based data that provides insight into how leadership styles and practices are enacted in these selected markets.

Understanding hierarchy in a country

Most of the trends in Western leadership across the twentieth century were centred on moving away from hierarchical command-and-control processes. To this end, both management literature and business school education began to introduce a more egalitarian and facilitative style of leadership. For example, we started to see open-plan office architecture and 360-degree feedback. However, it is important to note that there are profound cross-cultural differences with respect to how authority is viewed. In India, for example, the teaching staff are addressed by Madam or Sir, while I also observed on occasion students standing up when their 'senior-lecturer' entered the classroom. Conversely, on my own Dutch course (CCBS - the authors of this book) local students address me by my first name, and at times feel free to contradict me in front of the class.

Relational hierarchy

Eight out of ten Swiss survey respondents (CCBS Survey, 2021) reported that employees greeted their leaders by their first name. This low-level of hierarchy results in equal and harmonious relationships between superiors and their employees, which are based on mutual trust. Being acutely aware of someone's relative level of authority is of critical importance in a country such as South Korea. This is because it determines how colleagues interact with each other, including choosing between the many different linguistic levels of politeness. For example, organisations tend to have far more levels of management compared to some other countries, each of which have their own corresponding forms of address. Hence, the informal way in which business is conducted in Australia, for example, would likely completely confuse the average Korean employee. This would especially be the case for those Korean workers who have attained senior positions within their organisations, and are wholly accustomed to VIP treatment.

Power Distance

The words Hierarchy and Power Distance are often used interchangeably. The latter can be defined as "the degree to which members of an organisation or society expect and agree that power should be stratified and concentrated at higher levels of an organisation or government" (House & Javidan, 2004, p. 12). Countries that have scored high Power Distance values in either Hofstede or Trompenaars' respective research, believe that power dispenses agreement, social order, and role stability, and, hence, should be concentrated within those in the upper echelon of organisations. In high power distance cultures, leader-subordinate relationships are characterised by paternalism, whereby a leader assumes a parental role and feels obligated to provide support and protection to subordinates under their care (Yan & Hunt, 2005). Many of the country profiles in this book reference their country's Power Distance Index score (PDI), as measured by Dutch cultural scientist Geert Hofstede. However, the value score in and of itself cannot fully explain how hierarchy operates within a particular culture. For example, despite Greece and South Korea both having equally high

11

PDI values (60), leadership is enacted in a fundamentally different way in both countries. Therefore, in this book we attempt to account for such cultural contingencies by conducting culture-specific qualitative research, including interviewing local cultural experts.

How to achieve leadership empathy

This section addresses a specific people-oriented leadership requirement: empathic soft skills. Here, empathy is defined as a leader's capacity to relate to the feelings and experiences of their employees. Empathy is an altogether broader category than sympathy, and, in fact, several researchers consider empathy to be both a key part of emotional intelligence and a critical element of being an effective leader (Bar-On & Parker, 2000). Of course, the ability to successfully build and maintain relationships has long been regarded as a fundamental managerial skill; however, in accordance with the Center for Creative Leadership, the point being made here is that, in some cultures, empathy is more important to job performance than other aspects of leadership (Gentry, Weber, & Sadri, 2016). In addition to this, the way empathic understanding is expressed varies dramatically from country-to-country. Above all, empathy touches upon a leader's understanding of role requirement. To understand its importance across different cultures, several questions in our online survey (CCBS Survey, 2020) pertained to the specific expectations that local leaders had towards empathy. Furthermore, each team attempted to interview local experts, scholars and cross-cultural trainers on the country-specific ways in which empathy is effectively utilised. To cite an example: whereas in Nordic countries empathy is partly established through low-key and modest behaviour, Latin countries prefer a warm, personal and 'simpatico' approach, while, conversely, South Koreans value a courteous leader who, above all, attempts to save face (Kibun). It is well-established that how we connect with people is dependent on our cultural background, and, as such, the ability to be empathetic is especially important for leaders working across cultural boundaries (Alon & Higgins, 2005). The results of our CCBS survey (2020) reflect this, insofar as a large majority of the respondents from the different cultures examined in this book agreed with the statement that a manager should actively spend time on the personal wellbeing of their team members. When one compares the actual country scores (Dell, Eriks, 2018), South Korea and Ukraine score significantly lower on empathy than countries such as Uruguay and Portugal, due, in part, to the fact that Ukrainian and South Korean leaders generally prefer to keep more personal distance from their employees. However, it is important to stress that having empathy for others is not the same as demonstrating empathy; this is because staff expectations may vary considerably across culture in terms of: (i) the amount of verbal attention employees require; (ii) the praise and encouragement expected by staff; or (iii) the daily routine of managers. When managers increase their awareness of the cultural context in which empathy takes place, it often has a direct impact on employee performance, the organisational climate, and the quality of the productive working relations between leaders and employees.

Concluding Remarks

It was Darwin who first showed us the supreme value inherent to diversity. With this in mind, both the increased cultural heterogeneity of today's workforce and the increasingly global footprint of contemporary organisations transforms the styles and practices through which we lead teams. This calls for leaders with an ability to decode cultural differences and adjust their leadership-style to fit the cultural milieu in which they are operating. In summary, I hope that our findings contribute to increasing the richness of extant leadership literature, alongside aiding professional leaders to recalibrate their skills and mindsets in a manner advantageous to themselves, their employees, and, above all, the organisations they serve.

de Baas

ප්‍රධාන විධායක නිලධාරී

தலைமை நிர்வாக அதிகாரி

Big-man

प्रबन्धक

Chief Executive Officer

Gerente general

Manajer umum

Generálny Riaditeľ

المدير التنفيذي

総監督

Président Directeur Général

Consejero Delegado   генеральний директор

MAIN DUDE

Afghanistan

Joran Janssens, Alia Momand, Floris van Capelle, Arian Vogelpoel, Ibtissam Ridouani, Kevin Soekhi

Afghanistan, which is often referred to as the 'heart of Asia,' is situated at the continent's crossroads, encircled by majestic mountains that define its stunning landscape. The country is almost two and a half times the size of the United Kingdom, but with a population of only around 40 million (Worldometer, 2024). This is primarily due to the rugged terrain and the fact that there are more mountains than habitable land (Dupree, 2002). This also goes some way to explaining why Afghanistan has earned the title of the 'Graveyard of Empires' because no foreign power has ever succeeded in conquering it (Machanda, 2019). Despite this troubled history, Afghanistan is a vibrant culture that is renowned for its rich traditions and warm hospitality. Indeed, its colourful bazaars, intricate art, and diverse communities reflect a history that spans thousands of years (Pamir et al., 2023). Whilst *Dari* (دري), which originates from the old persian language, and *Pashto* (پښتو,) are the country's two predominant languages, there are ten other languages spoken in the country which contribute towards its diversity. Afghan people are renowned for their loyalty and honesty. Once an Afghan makes a promise, they will uphold it, even at great personal cost. This is reflected in the business sector, in as far as leaders believe that profit can only be achieved whilst upholding strict ethical values (Ibneatheer et al., 2021). Afghanistan's historical background, intricate social structures, and the interplay between religious values and community expectations have led to the development of distinct perspectives upon leadership and authority (Kaifi et al., 2010). In particular, the emphasis upon loyalty and moral leadership is a defining factor in leadership across different regions of the country. The following chapter explores Afghan business leadership skills and practices by drawing upon both academic literature as well as survey and interview data with local professionals and experts in the country. More specifically, the chapter examines both how cultural, historical, and social factors influence leadership practices in Afghanistan and how Afghan leaders balance empathy, authority and hierarchy in order to navigate complex organisational and societal challenges.

How the Afghani characterise leaders?

In Afghanistan, leadership is deeply rooted within traditional values, religious beliefs, and a hierarchical social structure. Leaders are viewed as authority figures who provide stability and direction in a country that has historically been marked by risk and uncertainty (Mujtaba et al., 2021). This, in turn, leads to the development of leadership styles that emphasise hierarchy, where respect for formal titles is significant, and leaders' decisions are rarely questioned. The Afghan concept of *guzaara*, or cautious risk avoidance, plays a pivotal role in this specific regard, and involves leaders prioritising the safeguarding of the organisation rather than taking any unnecessary risks (Mujtaba et al., 2021). This defining feature of Afghan leadership was also discerned in the results of the CCBS Survey (2024), where two-thirds of the respondents reported that Afghan leaders are typically decisive and unlikely to reverse their decisions once they have been made, which reflects the respect for authority and decisiveness inherent within Afghan leadership. Alongside these qualities and traits, Afghan leaders also place great emphasis upon building strong relationships with their teams, a fact which was also identified in the survey in as far as all the respondents agreed with the statement that leaders should invest time in understanding their employees' personal needs (CCBS Survey, 2024). This focus upon relational forms of leadership is in broad alignment with cultural expectations of loyalty in Afghanistan, where leaders are seen as being responsible for the well-being of their communities and employees (Mujtaba et al., 2021). In addition to the authoritative dimension of Afghan leadership, our interview with Dr. Ghanshyam, a leadership consultant, also helped shed light upon the fact that Afghan leaders are also warm, authentic, and empathetic, in conjunction with emotionally connecting to their teams and being respectful in their interactions with them (27 November 2024). This approach is rooted in cultural values that emphasise care for others and respect for elders and guests, reflecting broader traditions observed within Afghan society (Mujtaba et al., 2021). Although participatory decision-making is rare, Afghan leaders are expected to acknowledge suggestions politely, even if they ultimately reject them, as a means of maintaining authority whilst fostering harmony within teams. As Dr. Ghanshyam explained, *"Leaders are emotionally connected to their teams and often prioritise empathy and respect,"* which reinforces these relational dynamics (Personal communication, 27 November 2024). Loyalty and mutual trust are also essential in Afghan leadership, with leaders often relying on close allies during times of crisis. Whilst this relational loyalty can lead to favouritism, it underscores the community-centric nature of leadership in Afghanistan (Mujtaba et al., 2021). Afghan leadership is gradually becoming more participative, particularly amongst younger leaders. The CCBS survey (2024) testifies to this shift, with younger leaders showing a greater inclination towards transformational leadership, whilst, simultaneously, balancing traditional authority with community responsibility. Younger Afghan leaders are especially inclined towards transformational forms of leadership, which are characterised by an ethical approach, fairness, and a strong commitment to supporting employees (Kaifi & Mujtaba, 2010). In so doing, these leaders bring a fresh perspective that enhances motivation and engagement within teams, in turn, helping Afghan leaders be effective even in diverse, multicultural organisations.

Afghan leaders are also known for their transformational qualities, including their ability to identify and articulate a vision, as well as stimulate intellectual creativity. Research on the Ministry of Public Works found that leaders who successfully communicated a clear vision significantly improved employee performance (Ferozi & Chang, 2021). Intellectual stimulation is another critical factor, with leaders who challenge their employees intellectually promoting creativity and innovation. This approach empowers workers to critically evaluate their assumptions about their roles and solve problems constructively, thus fostering a more effective workplace (Ferozi & Chang, 2021). The CCBS Survey (2024) also sheds light upon the fact that Afghan professionals expect leaders to possess resourcefulness, charisma, and decision-making power, with around one-third of the respondents stating that they value a 'strong charismatic personality. Despite some progress towards gender equality in the country, the survey also demonstrates that there were mixed perspectives on the issue. Specifically, one-third of the respondents agreed that men and women have equal opportunities in attaining leadership roles, whereas half strongly disagreed with this, which testifies to what Put (2022) refers to as ongoing societal challenges. This divergence suggests that the balance between traditional values and contemporary changes, such as, for example, gender equality and competition within the workplace, remains a complex issue in the context of Afghan leadership culture. Despite these aforementioned shifts towards transformational leadership, traditional values and hierarchical structures remain deeply embedded in Afghan society. Leaders continue to prioritise community welfare, loyalty, and respect for authority, but they are gradually integrating modern leadership practices to enhance effectiveness in an increasingly globalised business environment.

Survey results and what local respondents say

To gain further insight into leadership practices and preferences within Afghanistan, the CCBS survey was administered to C-level Afghan professionals, which included, amongst others, CEOs, COOs, and IT Directors. Their responses cast light upon the unique cultural and organisational dynamics that shape contemporary Afghan leadership, most notably, the dynamic between hierarchical respect, relational focus, and emerging modern influences. Below we discuss some of the most significant findings. Firstly, the survey data indicates that Afghan leaders are typically decisive, and, as such, are relatively reluctant to reverse their decisions once they have been made, as evidenced by the fact that two-thirds of respondents agreed with the statement that managers are *"not likely to change their decisions easily"* (CCBS Survey, 2024). This firm approach reflects Afghanistan's strong respect for authority and decisiveness within leadership (Mujtaba et al., 2021). However, some respondents highlighted the importance of situational adaptability, noting, *"Leadership must depend on the scenario and context to remain effective"* (CCBS Survey, 2024). Afghan leaders also place strong emphasis upon ensuring the well-being of their teams, in as far as all the respondents agreed with the statement that leaders should actively invest time in understanding the personal needs of their employees. As one CEO noted, *"Leaders who show genuine concern for their employees' challenges foster stronger loyalty and better teamwork."* This perspective aligns with Afghan cultural values, where relational leadership is critical to maintaining team cohesion and trust (Mujtaba, 2010). Secondly, hierarchical respect remains a foundation of Afghan organisational culture, as evidenced by the fact that three-quarters of the respondents strongly agreed that subordinates should address leaders by their formal titles or positions, thus emphasising the importance of rank and authority. Conversely, only one-third stated that employees may address their leaders by their first names, underscoring the formality embedded in professional relationships (CCBS Survey, 2024). Thirdly, the survey also demonstrated that Afghan leaders view competition as a tool through which to achieve better organisational outcomes, as indicated by the fact that two-thirds of the respondents stated that managers actively encourage competition within their teams (CCBS Survey, 2024). This finding is indicative of what other researchers have described as a gradual shift towards integrating result-oriented practices whilst retaining the collaborative ethos typical of Afghan work culture (Chowdhury et al., 2006). The next significant finding pertains to the fact that resourcefulness, charisma and decision-making power were regarded as key qualities and traits preferred in Afghan leaders (CCBS Survey, 2024). Interestingly, around one-third of the respondents highlighted a *"strong charismatic personality"* as being vital, while one-fifth valued intellect and fluency. This preference reflects a blend of traditional Afghan expectations, where leadership is seen as a balance of authority, intellect, and personal charm. Despite strides in inclusivity, the survey indicated mixed perspectives about the level of gender equality with respect to senior-leadership roles. Whilst one-third strongly agreed that men and women have equal opportunities to attain leadership positions, half of the respondents strongly disagreed with this statement. This divergence highlights ongoing societal challenges in achieving gender equity, even as younger generations push for change (Putz, 2022). Overall, these survey findings offer a nuanced understanding of Afghan leadership practices, emphasising respect for hierarchy, relational empathy, and evolving approaches to competition and gender equality.

Local leadership analysis

Afghan Leadership Social Media Review
Afghan views on leadership, as expressed through social media and other digital platforms, reveal diverse and evolving practices that are profoundly influenced by the country's socio-political and cultural dynamics, and thus constitute an important source of data. Leadership discussions in Afghanistan often focus upon youth empowerment, community collaboration, and addressing well-established challenges. For instance, the AYM Group emphasises practical leadership amongst Afghan youth, advocating for collaboration and skill development to create sustainable social and economic growth (Bayat, 2009). This aligns with broader global trends favouring decentralised and inclusive leadership practices. Prominent Afghan business voices highlight the importance of adaptive leadership styles in order to navigate Afghanistan's complex landscape. Commentators frequently advocate for leaders who balance cultural traditions with modern expectations, such as, for example, by promoting greater gender inclusivity within organisations and more community involvement. For example, Maryam Baryalay's research into Afghan societal norms shows a growing emphasis upon rejecting top-down governance models in favour of more participatory decision-making approaches, especially within urban areas (Putz, 2022). Similarly, Qazi Marzia Babakarkhail is dedicated to empowering Afghan women within the context of business leadership by advocating for improved education, legal reforms, and greater community engagement. Specifically, her work focuses on helping women to be strong even in difficult times (Manara Magazine Editorial Team, 2023). Her ideas about leadership are in accordance with global trends, where people want governments to include everyone and work together to make changes.

Babakarkhail stresses the importance of respecting Afghan culture whilst also making progress towards a better future for all Afghans (Manara Magazine Editorial Team, 2023). In a similar vein, Heather Barr from Human Rights Watch criticises the way governments often make decisions without listening to people. She believes that leaders should prioritise human rights and ensure that everyone, especially women, have equal rights. Barr advocates for holding the Taliban accountable for their actions and for creating laws that help Afghan women and girls regain their rights (Azadi & Siddique, 2022). These perspectives reflect a growing shift in Afghan leadership, with leaders adapting to the challenging situation whilst striving to improve inclusivity and equality. Despite ongoing political instability, Afghan leaders and influencers continue to leverage platforms like X and Instagram to promote leadership practices that emphasise inclusivity, transparency, and responsiveness. These efforts are suggestive of a broader desire amongst Afghans for leadership styles that bridge traditional values with progressive ideals.

Dr. Ghanshyam Jetta: A Leadership Consultant

Dr. Ghanshyam Jetta is a master's level graduate in leadership business administration from the University of Liverpool as well as being the co-founder of Adhrit Development Consultancy and the author of *'Be the Leader: Follow Your Inner Voice"*. In our interview with him, he provided an in-depth perspective on leadership in Afghanistan, most notably offering valuable insights into the cultural and organisational dynamics of the country (Jethwa, 27 November 2024). He began the interview by explaining that Afghan leaders are often characterised by their warmth, emotional connection, and authenticity. As he put it, *"They are emotional more than logical... they get connected very easily, which makes them authentic leaders"* (27 November 2024). This emotional approach reflects a broader cultural emphasis upon interpersonal relationships and genuine care for others. He proceeded to explain that Afghan leaders prioritise showing respect and empathy within their interactions, by inquiring about their health or family. These actions are deeply rooted in both religious principles and historical traditions, which emphasise respect for guests and caring for the community. Afghan leadership is predominantly authoritarian, with leaders expected to be decisive and firm in their decision-making. As Dr. Jethwa noted, *"I do not expect much democratic leadership there. The followers expect the leader to be strong and a quick decision-maker."* (27 November 2024). Whilst participatory decision-making is rare, leaders are expected to acknowledge suggestions politely, even if they ultimately reject them. This respectful acknowledgment reinforces the leader's authority whilst, simultaneously, maintaining harmony within the team.

Despite the prevalence of hierarchical structures, Dr. Jethwa informed us that Afghan leaders are also known for their caring nature, describing leaders as individuals who *"would do anything they can to help other people"* (27 November, 2024) This approach underscores the role of personal influence and empathy in fostering loyalty and trust within organisations. Later in the interview, he told us that Afghan organisations often mirror Western hierarchical structures with clearly defined roles, however the application of authority tends to be more rigid in practice. Dr. Jethwa observed that many leaders rely heavily on formal authority rather than personal influence. For instance, one manager he encountered struggled to balance his formal position with the need to build rapport with a more experienced team. *"He expected his instructions to be followed without question,"* Dr. Jethwa explained, *"but his team resisted, leading to frustration"* (27 November 2024). Age and seniority also play a significant role within Afghan leadership dynamics. To illustrate this, Dr. Jethwa cited the example of a younger leader whose older subordinates were reluctant to fully respect him, highlighting the cultural weight of age in commanding respect. Conversely, older leaders are respected regardless of their effectiveness, which is rooted in traditional values. In Afghan culture, open criticism and heated debates are uncommon, as they are viewed as culturally inappropriate. Instead, communication is characterised by politeness and calmness, even when addressing critical issues. Leaders are expected to articulate their decisions clearly and promptly. As Dr. Jethwa noted, *"They do not expect much democracy... The decision must be made fast, and guidance provided swiftly"* (27 November 2024). Whilst Afghan leaders excel in building relationships, Dr. Jethwa highlighted challenges in fostering participatory approaches and using personal influence effectively. These areas present opportunities for development, particularly as Afghan organisations increasingly interact with global business practices. In closing, Dr. Jethwa noted that Afghan leadership is deeply influenced by the country's religious and historical context. Respect for elders and guests, as well as a focus on community welfare, are integral to leadership practices. He explained that this cultural foundation shapes leaders to value human connections, stating, *"Business is always about people... the business benefits from relationship building"* (27 November, 2024). Despite challenges, Afghan leadership exhibits unique strengths in empathy, respect, and authenticity, offering valuable lessons for cross-cultural business interactions. As the country continues to evolve, integrating these cultural values with modern management practices could further enhance leadership effectiveness in Afghanistan.

In-country leadership bestseller

One of the most influential leadership books in Afghanistan was authored by Bahaudin G. Mujtaba in 2006and is titled *The Ethics of Management and Leadership in Afghanistan*. This work has had a profound impact upon Afghan leaders, particularly in the post-conflict era. Mujtaba, a renowned expert in leadership and management, provides a comprehensive framework that resonates deeply with the Afghan context. The book delves into various aspects of leadership, including ethical leadership, strategic thinking, and organisational culture. By blending Western management principles with Islamic values, Mujtaba offers a unique perspective that aligns with the Afghan worldview. His emphasis upon integrity, accountability, and service to the community has inspired countless leaders to strive for excellence. A central theme explored in the book is the importance of strong ethical leadership in Afghanistan. For example, he highlights how ethical leadership can directly counteract corruption—a pervasive issue in the country. By prioritising transparency and fairness, leaders can restore public trust and promote institutional stability (Mujtaba, 2006). Mujtaba argues that ethical leaders are essential for building trust, fostering collaboration, and achieving long-term success in Afghanistan. In a country marred by corruption and instability, his message has resonated strongly with Afghan leaders seeking to restore faith in their institutions (Mujtaba, 2006). Furthermore, the book underscores the significance of cultural intelligence and adaptability. Mujtaba emphasises that understanding the nuances of Afghan culture—such as the importance of tribal structures, respect for elders, and religious traditions—allows leaders to navigate complex social dynamics effectively. For instance, he discusses how leaders who demonstrate respect for Afghanistan's hierarchical and community-oriented societal values are more likely to gain the trust and cooperation of their teams (Mujtaba, 2006). This cultural sensitivity is vital in fostering strong relationships and ensuring the success of organisational initiatives. Mujtaba's insights have empowered Afghan leaders to embrace diversity, promote inclusivity, and create harmonious work environments. By offering actionable advice, such as integrating ethical decision-making frameworks and fostering participatory leadership, Mujtaba has provided Afghan leaders with the tools to create positive change in their organisations and communities (Mujtaba, 2006).

Local leadership book	
Title	*The ethics of Management and Leadership in Afghanistan*
Subtitle	-
Author	Bahaudin G. Mujtaba
Publisher	Ilead Academy; 2nd ed. edition
Year	2006
ISBN	0977421104

Afghanistan leadership YouTube review

In April 2011, Elkinser published a video with information from four researchers that was designed to serve as a training tool to help local officials in how to do business effectively in Afghanistan. According to Elkinser (2011), in order to ensure successful working relationships in Afghanistan, there are some things that professionals must know about social norms and customs. Specifically, when meeting a handshake is most common, however some people place their hands on their heart with a nod. When doing so, one should always inquire about the other person's health or their family, for example (Elkinser, 2011). The speakers then proceed to describe that business is very personal in Afghanistan and thus one should invest quality time in getting to know one's counterpart in order to establish trust. Next, the speakers go onto discuss that in Afghanistan meetings provide the means for leaders to communicate decisions that have already been made rather than being about brainstorming ideas, for example. In relation to this, the video also explains that Afghan communication style is rather indirect, and therefore that one must phrase questions intelligently and read between the lines for an answer (Elkinser, 2011)). Finally, the speakers explain that honour and shame should always be considered during meetings. To illustrate this, they describe that it is important to always express oneself in a way that is not direct or that places blame upon someone (Elkinser, 2011). The next video to be summarised is a 2021 lecture at Rana University in Kabul, Afghanistan, given by a professor specialising in business leadership (University of Business Learners, 2021). At the beginning, the professor emphasised that leadership in Afghanistan is fundamentally a group process, which resonates deeply with Afghan culture, where unity and community are highly valued. He then proceeded to note that power is a core element of leadership in the country, and that understanding this connection is crucial in the context of Afghanistan. As he put it, *"leadership involves having the power and authority to influence others."* (University of Business Learners. (2021, 12:02). However, he then stressed that effective leadership requires more than just power. Rather, knowledge, skills, and competence are equally important elements that distinguish truly impactful leaders from others in Afghanistan. Beyond these qualities, a leader must have a clear vision, one that resonates with others. The ability to connect people to this vision and inspire them to share and pursue it is what defines a successful leader (University of Business Learners, 2021). Next, the professor underscored the importance of aligning personal leadership style with cultural values in Afghan society, where strong community bonds and collective effort are key. He encouraged students to recognise that effective leadership is not only about authority but also about having the vision and skills to bring people together for a common purpose (University of Business Learners, 2021). The final video to be discussed involves a motivational speaker, entrepreneur, and business coach, who has helped individuals and organisations succeed. In this video, Pasarly (2023) reflects upon how Afghanistan, a country that has faced significant challenges, needs both strong bosses and inspiring leaders. Leaders are known for motivating others to follow them and for bringing about social change, whereas bosses follow systems and rules that are essential for creating stability and structure. In Afghanistan, where systems are still being rebuilt, having effective bosses who can implement organised approaches, as well as visionary leaders who can inspire hope, is vital. Pasarly (2023) stresses that having a personal vision is key for Afghan leaders, whilst a boss focuses on the practicalities of making that vision work. Both roles are equally important in Afghanistan's journey towards growth and stability. Later, he emphasises that there is no inherent *'good'* or *'bad'* between being a boss or a leader, as both have their strengths and weaknesses. He cites the example of Nakamura in Afghanistan, who was known for their humanitarian work, as exemplifying the impact of compassionate leadership in Afghanistan, and providing a tangible example of how leaders can transform their communities and organisations.

Understanding hierarchy in Afghanistan

Afghanistan's social and organizational structures are deeply influenced by longstanding cultural and historical values, which, in turn, shape both leadership styles and organisational practices. Traditional norms prioritise hierarchical systems, with seniority and age playing significant roles in terms of earning respect and authority within both familial and professional contexts (Ahmed-Ghosh, 2003). This characterization of Afghan leadership was corroborated by our interviewee, Dr. Ghanshyam Jethwa, who informed us that Afghan leadership is predominantly authoritarian in nature, in as far as leaders are expected to make swift, decisive decisions, whilst, it should be added, acknowledging suggestions respectfully, even if they ultimately decide not to act upon them (Jethwa, 27 November 2024). Moreover, he proceeded to explain, leaders in Afghanistan are often seen as protectors of their teams, balancing formal authority with relational empathy. This relational aspect is demonstrated by their frequent inquiries about employees' families and personal well-being, actions that are deeply rooted within cultural and religious traditions that emphasise community welfare (Jethwa, 27 November 2024). Similarly, Elkinser (2011) notes that Afghan leaders are known to go out of their way to provide emotional and material support during hardships, which, in turn, fosters loyalty and trust. Communication within Afghan organisations also reflects a balance of formal respect and indirectness, in as far as leaders use polite and subtle language to preserve honour and avoid conflict, a practice that is integral to Afghan workplace dynamics (Elkinser, 2011). This aspect of Afghan leadership was also raised by Dr. Ghanshyam Jethwa, who described meetings in Afghan organisations as often functioning as platforms to merely communicate decisions rather than engage in open discussions, reflecting a cultural preference for top-down communication (27 November 2024). However, leaders still strive to maintain harmony within teams, ensuring that their authority does not disrupt collective morale (CCBS Survey, 2019). Age is also a significant factor with respect to the organisational hierarchy within Afghan organisations, with younger leaders often facing resistance from their older subordinates, who question their authority on the basis of cultural norms that prioritise seniority (Jethwa, 27 November 2024). This dynamic creates challenges for younger managers, who often must work harder to prove their competence and earn respect (Ahmed-Ghosh, 2003). Conversely, older leaders often enjoy automatic deference, even when their effectiveness is questioned (CCBS Survey, 2019). Whilst the emphasis upon hierarchy remains strong, there is nevertheless a growing acknowledgment of participatory approaches within sectors that are more exposed to global business practices. Afghan leaders increasingly recognise the importance of personal influence and rapport-building alongside formal authority, according to our interviewee (Jethwa, 27 November 2024). For instance, they are encouraged to balance cultural expectations of decisiveness with the ability to inspire and motivate their teams, a critical factor in navigating the evolving business landscape (Mohsen et al., 2020). The organisational culture within Afghanistan also sheds light upon the tension between collectivist values and the need for individual initiative. This is because employees often prioritise loyalty to their families or tribes over organisational goals, a pattern grounded in Afghanistan's communal traditions (Monsutti, 2007). However, as workplaces adapt to international influences, there is an increasing openness to aligning personal aspirations with broader organisational objectives (Rarick et al., 2013). This shift is especially evident within family-run businesses, where leaders are learning to integrate traditional loyalty with modern management practices (CCBS Survey, 2019). In conclusion, leadership in Afghanistan reflects a unique combination of traditional authority and relational empathy, providing valuable lessons for cross-cultural business interactions. Leaders are expected to be decisive and authoritative, whilst, simultaneously, remaining deeply connected to their teams through trust and emotional support (Jethwa, 27 November 2024). As workplaces increasingly interact with global standards, Afghan organisations are gradually harmonising their cultural strengths with modern approaches to foster sustainable growth (CCBS Survey, 2019).

How the Afghans achieve leadership empathy

Successful leadership in Afghanistan is based on multiple factors, including, amongst other things, the importance of leaders having a trusting relationship with their employees and being liked and appreciated by them. This idea was corroborated in our interview with Dr. Ghanshyam Jethwa, who is a technical consultant in Kabul Afghanistan, who told us the following: *"What I saw in the leadership of Afghanistan is that they very, very much acknowledge the other person, even if they do not agree"* (27 November 2024). Afghan leaders often embody empathy through their attentiveness to personal relationships and respect for their elders. By understanding and valuing the personal needs of their team members leaders, this serves to cultivate and maintain an environment characterised by loyalty and trust (Mujtaba & Kaifi, 2010). Empathy in Afghan leadership is also often demonstrated through highly significant but ambiguous non-verbal gestures that also signal respect for the prevailing hierarchical norms (Elkinser, 2011). For example, leaders may place a hand over their heart to convey sincerity and emotional connection with employees. A slight nod, a warm smile, or maintaining respectful physical distance are other ways in which leaders express their understanding and humility towards those they work with (Elkinser, 2011). These actions serve to display empathy with their employees, whilst, simultaneously, preserving the social structure, and ensuring a balance between care and authority (Saydee, 2023). Furthermore, effective leadership in

Afghanistan requires a balance between *guzaara kaardan* (people-orientation) and *edaara kaardan* (task-orientation), which refers to the ways in which empathic leaders function as role models and uphold cultural norms and values. This form of leadership ultimately strengthens the bonds with employees (Mujtaba, 2019). Other ways in which Afghan leaders exhibit empathy is by ensuring they are accessible to their employees for personal or family-related issues, which, in turn, strengthens loyalty and solidifies their authority as protective and attentive figures. Research conducted by Wahab and Bangash (2021) underscores that inclusive leadership significantly influences employee engagement, with psychological empowerment acting as a critical mediating factor. For instance, their research highlights how Afghan leaders' inclusive approaches, such as fostering openness, availability, and accessibility, empower employees by providing them with autonomy and a sense of belonging. Psychological empowerment, as characterised in their study, includes factors such as competence, self-determination, and meaningfulness, which collectively enhance employees' engagement (Wahab & Bangash, 2021). For example, leaders who actively engage their teams in decision-making not only build trust but also instil a sense of ownership amongst their employees. This psychological empowerment leads to higher levels of employee engagement, which is particularly impactful in Afghanistan's organisational settings, where employee engagement levels have traditionally been a challenge due to socio-political complexities. Moreover, empathy in Afghanistan goes beyond a simple social connection but includes an active interest in the personal development and relationship with staff, is evidenced by the results of the CCBS Survey (2024). The importance placed upon empathy is deeply rooted within Afghanistan's cultural emphasis upon honour and loyalty (Mujtaba et al., 2021), where leaders who acknowledge and respect their employees' personal challenges are seen as more credible and trustworthy.

27

Algeria

Fernanda Barros Gomyde Porto, Pau S.A.L. Bentgens, Rina Hasani, Josine Haver, Desiree Webster & Hasnaa Ziyani Choho

Algeria, the largest country in Africa, is located strategically in North Africa along the Mediterranean Sea. Known for its cultural and linguistic diversity, this nation of 45 million people recognises Arabic as its official language, although French remains prevalent within the business and educational sectors, and English is gaining in popularity amongst the younger generations (Haddam-Bouabdallah, 2022). The age-old Algerian proverb, "اليد الواحدة لا تصفق" ("One hand cannot clap by itself" – al-yad al-wāḥida lā tuṣaffiq) nicely captures the importance of collective efforts and unity, which have profoundly shaped leadership styles and practices for generations (Kassab & Bokrouh, 2014). This sentiment reflects a nation that has long been reliant upon cooperation to overcome manifold challenges and achieve collective goals (Ramdani et al., 2017). Algeria's strategic location and abundant natural resources have made it a key player in regional economics and politics (Bendjima & Larguo, 2017). Historically reliant upon oil and natural gas, the nation is diversifying into agriculture, manufacturing, and telecommunications to foster long-term stability (Berreziga & Meziane, 2017). This cautious but deliberate approach reflects the balancing act between resource management and developmental goals (Ramdani et al., 2017). Culturally, Algeria blends traditions with modern influences, which also results in distinctive modes of leadership. For example, leadership in Algeria reflects its socio-economic dynamics and linguistic diversity, with Arabic, French, and English playing key roles in professional and educational settings (Haddam-Bouabdallah, 2022). Recent trends towards inclusivity and innovation also testify to the aspirations of the country's globally connected younger population, which is also influencing leadership (United Nations Sustainable Development Group, n.d.). This chapter explores Algeria's evolving leadership practices by reviewing academic literature and conducting survey and interview research in order to understand how Algerian leaders navigate the challenges of a changing world, whilst, simultaneously, maintaining the cultural integrity of the country.

How the Algerian characterise leaders?

In Algeria, leadership is deeply influenced by tradition, where loyalty and interpersonal relationships are of paramount importance. Hence, rather than prioritising performance metrics alone, Algerian leaders instead also emphasise dedication and trustworthiness, fostering team cohesion by promoting individuals who have demonstrated their loyalty and commitment to them over time (Samia & Rebai, 2022; Bendjima & Larguo, 2017). This approach helps to cultivate strong, united teams, instilling in individuals a profound sense of belonging and mutual support (Branine, 2017). Ethical principles in Algeria, which are deeply informed by Islamic moral values and ethical principles, subtly guide leadership practices in various respects. Although not always formally outlined, these Islamic values nevertheless subtly shape interpersonal interactions and contribute towards an atmosphere of trust and integrity within organisations (Bendjima & Larguo, 2017). For instance, the traditional Algerian saying " كل واحد يعرف مكانه " ("koul wahed ya'ref makanou"), which means *"everyone knows their place,"* is reflective of this underlying respect for order and stability that permeates Algerian leadership culture (Samia & Rebai, 2022). These principles engender a sense of responsibility and protection, in as far as leaders are often viewed by their employees as mentors who prioritise their teams' well-being (Samia & Rebai, 2022). The results of the CCBS Survey (2024) also underscore the influence of Islamic principles within Algerian business leadership. Specifically, several respondents noted that Islamic teachings emphasise fairness, humility, and compassion within leadership, which, in turn, help to guide workplace dynamics. For example, as one participant observed: "*In Algerian leadership, you see a tendency to consider the wider impact of decisions upon families and communities, which reflects Islamic values of collective responsibility*" (CCBS Survey, 2024). Leaders often demonstrate this by offering long-serving employees, promotions and recognising their contributions, which serves to reinforce the value placed upon dedication and stability within teams (Berreziga & Meziane, 2017). Majda Chekkal, a leadership coach, and CEO, who we interviewed as part of our research, also informed us that whilst loyalty is deeply valued within Algerian workplaces, this focus can sometimes sideline those high-performing individuals who lack such personal connections, thus posing challenges for their career advancement (13 November 2024). Chekkal also opined that Algerian managers often concentrate on correcting mistakes rather than offering positive forms of reinforcement, which can have a deleterious effect upon team morale. In relation to this, she proceeded to explain that employees increasingly seek acknowledgment and constructive feedback within a supportive work environment, which makes this a growing area of focus for effective leadership in the Algerian context. Ibrahim Khalil Boughambouz, a General Director of a start-up incubator near the Algerian-Tunisian border, offered additional insights into how loyalty and interpersonal relationships shape workplace dynamics in smaller, community-driven environments (Boughambouz, 13 November 2024). He noted that in regions with close-knit business ecosystems, leaders often adopt a personalised management approach, taking into account the unique needs and challenges of their employees. This serves to foster a familial atmosphere, which, according to them, strengthens long-term loyalty but may create obstacles for leaders in scaling their organisations beyond these community-based models (Boughambouz, 13 November 2024). This focus upon loyalty, incremental progress, and ethical values forms the core of Algeria's leadership style, fostering unity and stability. However, the strong emphasis upon tradition may sometimes limit flexibility, presenting challenges in an increasingly adaptive and fast-paced global environment (Ramdani et al., 2017).

Survey results and what local respondents say

The survey gathered responses from a range of C-level professionals, who shared their expertise and provided valuable insights into leadership in Algeria. The research offered a comprehensive view of local perspectives on leadership styles, hierarchy, communication preferences, and the cultural factors shaping these views (CCBS Survey, 2024). The most noteworthy survey findings will be discussed in turn below. Liza Djennane, senior internal auditor, says: "*Leadership in Algeria is shaped by a combination of cultural, political and historical factors that contribute to its distinctive character compared to leadership in other countries*". It is striking that several respondents mentioned the same three factors when asked what characterises leadership in Algeria. As one respondent opined, "*Leadership here is about empowering others to grow,*" thus underscoring the importance placed upon transformational leadership within this context (CCBS Survey, 2024). Almost all of the respondents expressed agreement with the statement that managers are expected to actively spend time on ensuring their employees' personal wellbeing (CCBS Survey, 2024). This approach reflects a shared emphasis amongst professionals with respect to fostering development and support within teams, which is in accordance with the cultural preference in Algeria for leaders who guide and encourage employees (Samia & Rebai, 2022). One unique perspective from the survey responses was the fact that local leaders are often addressed by formal titles, thus underscoring a deeply ingrained respect for hierarchy (CCBS Survey, 2024). Several respondents made mention of the fact that, in contrast to some Western contexts, interactions within Algerian workplaces tend to follow formal structures, which suggests that authority and professionalism are closely linked to respect within the context of Algerian organisations. This was corroborated by one of the respondents, Karim Brouri, CEO & Founder of a consulting and engineering company, who described Algerian leadership as paternalistic and rational, and influenced by the traditional culture in the country. He proceeded to inform us that this prevailing leadership style is a result of experiences of instability in the past, which, in turn, led older leaders to prefer caution and control (CCBS Survey, 2024). However, Karim Brouri also proceeded to note that the younger generation of Algerians entering the labour market generally prefer a more flexible, contemporary leadership style, and that "*Algerian leaders must therefore navigate between these divergent visions to evolve towards a leadership capable of integrating young recruits*" (CCBS survey, 2024). Allied with the paternalistic nature of Algerian leadership, most of the respondents also reported that although changing decisions is not uncommon, employees do like their leader to be a strong decision maker (CCBS survey, 2024). In this vein, many respondents noted a preference for direct communication styles, as evidenced by the fact that confrontations do occur during meetings. However, we should also note here that the respondents also stated that they do not mind receiving criticism about their own work during these meetings either (CCBS Survey, 2024). Next, leadership in Algeria was described by one of the respondents, Hichem Chofri, a Senior Executive Leader within a high-profile, fast-paced organisation, as being heavily influenced by the type of organisation in which it is being practiced. To illustrate this, he drew a clear distinction in terms of both mindset and management style between local private or governmental entities and international companies operating within Algeria. As they themselves put it: "*For the same country and the same local citizens, the mindset and management style differ significantly depending on whether one works for a national company or an international one with an establishment in the country*" (CCBS Survey, 2024). This dynamic reflects the unique challenges and opportunities presented by diverse organisational contexts (CCBS survey, 2024). The responses regarding perceptions of gender equality in attaining senior leadership positions demonstrated a diverse range of opinions. Whilst a notable proportion somewhat agreed with the statement that men and women have equal opportunities, there was also a significant proportion who somewhat disagreed or even strongly disagreed with this. This divergence suggests that perceptions of gender equality within the context of Algerian leadership are mixed, with many respondents recognising persistent disparities despite progress being made in some areas. With respect to the latter, Hichem Chofri informed us about the progress that has been made in relation to gender equality within leadership in Algeria. Drawing on his experience working for national state-owned companies, joint ventures, and international organisations, Chofri emphasised that since its independence in 1962, Algeria has actively encouraged women's employment and equality. *"Our society remains generally conservative, but Algeria is amongst the top countries with a high number of female engineers"*, he noted, before proceeding to add that salaries and opportunities for women and men with the same academic qualifications are equal. Furthermore, Chofri shared his personal experience of hiring a balanced workforce, with 50% women in operational and field positions, and commended the country's legal framework. *"The government policy is clear in protecting women from harassment and discrimination, ensuring that hiring processes are transparent and fair"*. Despite some societal reluctance, these policies thus demonstrate a commitment to gender equality at the national level (CCBS survey, 2024).

Local leadership analysis

Medhi Bouchetara: an Algerian leadership scholar

Mehdi Bouchetara is a scientific researcher and executive director at MDI Business School, a private institution collaborating with international institutions such as Paris Dauphine in France, HEC Montreal in Canada, and the International Management School Geneva in Switzerland. With extensive experience in leadership within the educational and research sectors, Mr. Bouchetara (13 November 2024) brings a unique perspective to Algerian leadership practices. His career has spanned roles in project management, policy consultation, and teaching, where he has overseen teams and managed complex, multidisciplinary initiatives. During the interview, Mr. Bouchetara (13 November 2024) described Algerian leadership as fundamentally shaped by the nation's socio-cultural fabric. *"Pour toute action qu'il faut mener ou bien pour n'importe quelle décision basique, il y a toujours le calcul, la réflexion par rapport à son impact social"* *("For any action to be taken or any basic decision to be made, there is always reflection and calculation about its social impact")* (Bouchetara, 13 November 2024). Leaders in Algeria often balance professional discipline with a strong emphasis upon social considerations, such as maintaining employee stability for the sake of broader social harmony. He proceeded to explain to us that this focus upon social and emotional factors is what sets Algerian leadership apart from its more economically driven counterparts, such as those in Tunisia or Europe, where decisions tend to prioritise profitability or efficiency. For instance, Algerian managers may hesitate to terminate underperforming employees, considering the impact upon their families and community, a perspective that can hinder organisational effectiveness but support societal stability (Bouchetara, 13 November 2024). Mr. Bouchetara also highlighted significant generational shifts in Algerian leadership. Younger leaders, influenced by political reforms and initiatives encouraging youth entrepreneurship, are now adopting more inclusive and collaborative approaches. He cited the establishment of institutions such as the Ministry of Start-ups and Knowledge Economy as a pivotal step in this process. This initiative has promoted entrepreneurial thinking and empowered young Algerians to take leadership roles, fostering innovation and prioritising collective success over rigid hierarchies (Bouchetara, 13 November 2024). The discussion also addressed the challenges foreign leaders may face in Algeria. According to Mr. Bouchetara (13 November 2024), understanding local regulations and social norms is crucial for building trust and credibility in the workplace. *"Les investisseurs étrangers doivent comprendre les Algériens : leur culture majoritairement musulmane, leurs traditions, et leurs dynamiques interpersonnelles."* ("Foreign investors must understand the Algerian people: their predominantly Muslim culture, traditions, and interpersonal dynamics") (Bouchetara, 13 November 2024). Algerians, shaped by historical experiences such as colonisation and the 'Black Decade,' tend to approach foreign partnerships cautiously. However, fostering personal connections and demonstrating cultural sensitivity can actually help to bridge these gaps, in turn, allowing foreign leaders to navigate Algerian workplace dynamics effectively (Bouchetara, 13 November 2024). When asked about trust and credibility in leadership, Mr. Bouchetara (13 November 2024) stressed the importance of ethical conduct and professionalism. Effective leaders in Algeria must set an example through their actions, whilst, simultaneously, maintaining open communication and exhibiting genuine empathy towards their teams. He recounted an example of a Senior Manager who would regularly visit employees' desks, personally check in with them, and ask if they needed anything. This small but impactful gesture boosted morale and illustrated the importance of human connection in leadership (Bouchetara, 13 November 2024). Furthermore, he emphasised that ethical integrity remains a cornerstone of leadership in Algeria, in as far as it is essential for earning respect and cultivating a productive organisational culture. Reflecting upon the future of Algerian leadership, Bouchetara (13 November 2024) expressed optimism about ongoing transformations. He highlighted generational and technological advancements, such as the integration of digital tools and the adoption of horizontal organisational models within private and multinational companies. These shifts, he argued, signal a move away from traditional hierarchical systems towards more dynamic, inclusive workplace environments. In conclusion,

Bouchetara advocated for leadership practices in the Algerian context that balance cultural values with global best practices, underscoring the need for ethical, empathetic, and innovative approaches to meet the demands of a rapidly changing world.

Majda Chekkal: an Algerian cross-cultural trainer

Majda Chekkal, a professional coach and the CEO of an organisation near the Algerian-Tunisian border, brings extensive expertise within leadership development and management. With a background that includes certification as a neurolinguistic programming coach and over a decade of experience in sales and training within the pharmaceutical industry, Chekkal (13 November 2024) is uniquely positioned to offer insights into Algerian leadership styles and practices. Her current work focuses upon empowering individuals and businesses to achieve excellence through structured coaching and training programmes. At the beginning of the interiew, Chekkal (13 November 2024) described Algerian leadership as traditionally hierarchical, with a strong emphasis upon vertical authority. This model, deeply rooted in the country's cultural and historical context, often results in managers prioritising direct commands over participative or demonstrative approaches. Consequently, leaders are expected to assert their authority clearly, with employees generally adhering to instructions rather than engaging in collaborative forms of decision-making. Whilst this approach has proven to be effective for maintaining organisational order, it often restricts opportunities for open dialogue and employee innovation (Chekkal, 13 November 2024). One notable challenge in the Algerian workplace, noted by Chekkal (13 November 2024), concerns the lack of recognition provided to employees. That is to say, Algerian managers frequently focus upon pointing out errors rather than highlighting achievements, a process which leaves employees feeling undervalued. *"Pour eux c'est une manière de de considération, de se remettre soi-même en question avant de jeter la faute sur l'autre"*("It is a form of consideration— reassessing oneself before blaming someone else") (Chekkal, 13 November 2024). Despite its rarity, Chekkal argued that incorporating recognition practices can be significantly beneficial. By offering praise alongside constructive feedback, leaders can create a more inclusive and motivating environment, boosting both morale and loyalty within their teams. Chekkal also underscored the cultural emphasis upon empathetic engagement within Algerian leadership, where professional and personal boundaries often blend. Leaders in Algeria frequently connect with employees on a personal level, attending family events or showing interest in their lives outside of work. This relational approach fosters trust and loyalty, in as far as it aligns with Algeria's cultural preference for leaders who demonstrate empathy and understanding (Chekkal, 13 November 2024). However, this overlap may feel unfamiliar to those from cultures where professional relationships are more strictly separated. Foreign employees in Algeria may thus encounter some challenges in terms of adjusting to these dynamics. This is not the only issue, however. Time management also tends to be more flexible than in Western workplaces, and the highly relational nature of Algerian leadership contrasts with the structured, task-focused styles that are common within other business cultures. For example, foreign managers accustomed to impersonal approaches may be perceived as distant, whilst Algerians may expect more emotional connection and relational engagement from their leaders. In discussing pathways for improvement, Chekkal (13 November 2024) stressed the importance of evolving leadership practices in Algeria to meet the expectations of modern workforces. Specifically, encouraging leaders to engage with employees more collaboratively, provide regular recognition, and integrate training programmes focused upon empathetic leadership were all steps recommended by Chekkal to help foster a more dynamic and inclusive workplace culture. This approach could bridge the gap between traditional authoritative models and the more participative styles increasingly valued by younger generations. Through her insights, Chekkal offered a nuanced understanding of Algerian leadership that underscores the balance required between maintaining cultural norms and adapting to global trends. Her perspective provides invaluable lessons for navigating the complexities of leadership in Algeria whilst advocating for practices that prioritise empathy, recognition, and open communication.

In-country leadership bestseller

"Entrepreneurship in Algeria: Reality, Challenges, and Opportunities" by Radhia Zemirli and Souria Hammache stands out as one of Algeria's most influential works on leadership and entrepreneurship. Published in 2023, the book provides an in-depth exploration of the Algerian entrepreneurial landscape, delving into its challenges, whilst, simultaneously, laying out potential opportunities for growth. Zemirli, an experienced economist and regional development consultant, offers valuable insights into the nation's socio-economic dynamics. Hammache, a professor of business strategy and innovation, brings her expertise in fostering creativity and resilience within emerging markets. Together, Zemirli and Hammache critically examine the support policies implemented by Algerian authorities and propose forward-thinking recommendations to cultivate a thriving entrepreneurial culture (Zemirli & Hammache, 2023). Overall, readers will gain a profound understanding of how leadership in Algeria is shaped by a balance of cultural, economic, and institutional factors. More specifically, the book explores

35

how leaders need to be adaptable to achieve organisational success within a context that is often constrained by bureaucratic inefficiencies and limited resources. It highlights the critical role of collaboration, not only within teams but also across public and private sectors, to overcome challenges. Additionally,Zemirli and Hammache underscore the need for a shift in mindset amongst Algerian leaders. They urge leaders and entrepreneurs to be resilient, use strategic thinking, and to adopt a long-term vision in order to ensure sustainable growth within an unpredictable and competitive business environment. Blending theory and practical advice, this bestseller appeals to a wide audience, including policymakers, academics, and aspiring business leaders and entrpreneurs within Algeria, by putting forward actionable strategies to stimulate Algeria's private sector. Recognised by local experts, *Entrepreneurship in Algeria* has gained widespread acclaim for its practical roadmap to sustainable growth and resilience for building a robust private sector capable of thriving within regional and global markets.

Local leadership book		
Title	*Entrepreneurship in Algeria: Reality, Challenges, and Opportunities*	
Subtitle	-	
Author	Radhia Zemirli & Souria Hammache	
Publisher	Our Knowledge Publishing	
Year	2023	
ISBN	10: 6206231321 13: 978-6206231325	

Algerian leadership YouTube review

Dr. Rachid Amokrane delivers a lecture at the Université Abderrahmane MIRA Béjaïa, Algeria during a conference on leadership and marketing. Addressing an audience of young Algerians, he emphasises specific business leadership values such as empathy, humility, and personal integrity. He asserts that a true leader in Algeria must inspire others by valuing their contributions and building trust, which reflects Algeria's collectivist culture (Amokrane, 2016, 13:17). This characterisation of Algerian leadership is also in line with the results of the CCBS Survey (2024), which showed that in Algeria leaders are supposed to embody humility and patience. At the start of the lecture, Dr. Amokrane encourages the audience to adopt a positive mindset and treat others with respect, stating that *"nobility in others awakens when we act nobly ourselves"* (Amokrane, 2016, 03:13). Later, he proceeds to discuss the importance of leaders fostering happiness and motivation in their teams, stressing that leadership in Algeria requires creating an inclusive and supportive environment (Amokrane, 2016, 08:59). In conclusion, he urges the audience to recognise their potential and reject feelings of inferiority, emphasising that leadership is built on self-confidence, trust, and a commitment to serving others (Amokrane, 2016, 12:45). This is supported further by the aforementioned point from Bouchetara that empathy and human connections are highly valued within Algerian leadership (13 November 2024). Next, in the *"Webinar Conseils Carrière: Le Leadership,"* Hanane Lebsis, Head of Talent Acquisition & Development at Henkel, and Yasmine Hadj-Ahmed, Communications Manager at Emploitic, discuss key leadership principles in Algeria that are tailored to organisational and cultural contexts. Conducted virtually on June 14, 2020, the webinar highlights leadership as an inclusive, adaptable skillset that is accessible to all employees, emphasising the importance of empathy, collaboration, and personal growth (Lebsis & Hadj-Ahmed, 2020, 5:24). Lebsis describes leadership in Algeria as fostering a culture of trust and open communication, where team members feel valued and motivated. As they themselves put it: "A good leader ensures that success is shared across all roles," thus reinforcing the collective approach that is so integral to Henkel's programs (Lebsis, 2020, 13:27). She proceeds to discuss that Henkel's Algerian leadership model, designed for employees at all levels, provides tailored training in multiple languages—Arabic, French, and English—thus underscoring the company's commitment to global inclusivity and development (Lebsis, 2020, 17:42). By prioritising open feedback and team cohesion, the webinar aligns Algeran leadership development with both workplace and cultural expectations, bridging the gap between individual potential and organisational success.

Understanding hierarchy in Algeria

Hierarchy in Algeria is deeply rooted in social and organisational structures, with a high-power distance reinforcing authority that flows from the top down (Bendjima & Larguo, 2017). Employees typically address their managers in a formal manner and defer to their judgment, in accordance with the aforementioned cultural respect for authority in Algeria (Samia & Rebai, 2022). Whilst, on the one hand, this top-down structure ensures accountability and direction, on the other hand, it serves to limit open communication, as junior employees may be reluctant to raise concerns or share ideas (Branine, 2017; Bendjima & Larguo, 2017). Ibrahim Khalil Boughambouz, the director of a start-up incubator near the Algerian-Tunisian border, noted in our interview with them, that in close-knit, community-driven workplaces, hierarchy often acts as a stabilising force. He proceeded to explain that this is because employees value the structure and consistency afforded by hierarchical systems, which are particularly crucial in regions where personal and professional networks are tightly intertwined. However, this deference to authority can also discourage innovation, particularly amongst junior staff, who may feel constrained by traditional expectations (Boughambouz, 13 November 2024). Similarly, Majda Chekkal, a leadership coach, observed in our interview that many Algerian managers rely heavily upon strict authority and formal communication, often preferring direct orders over collaborative forms of decision-making. Whilst this aligns with Algeria's cultural values of respect and structure, it may limit team rapport and stifle open dialogue. Chekkal underscored that this approach is particularly evident in larger organisations, where managers often focus upon maintaining control rather than fostering creativity (Chekkal, 14 November 2024). The phrase "بالمكتوب" (bel maktoub: "*what is written will happen*") reflects this cultural acceptance of slower processes and adherence to formal procedures, thus reinforcing the importance of tradition and order within Algerian workplaces (Bendjima & Larguo, 2017). Survey respondents echoed this sentiment, noting that processes within Algerian organisations often prioritise thoroughness and adherence to protocol over speed. Whilst this ensures consistency, it can hinder adaptability, particularly within fast-paced global industries (CCBS Survey, 2024). Algerian leaders also tend to retain individual control in foreign partnerships in order to safeguard local interests and preserve national identity. On the one hand, this approach strengthens authority and ensures that local values are respected, but, on the other, it can present challenges in terms of fostering trust and collaboration with external partners. As one survey respondent noted, "*In international partnerships, Algerian managers tend to prioritise stability over flexibility, which can make negotiations slower but more deliberate*" (CCBS Survey, 2024). However, generational shifts are beginning to influence Algeria's hierarchical structures. Younger leaders are gradually incorporating more inclusive practices, such as, for example, soliciting input from junior staff and fostering collaborative forms of decision-making. For example, several survey respondents highlighted a growing preference for hybrid leadership models that combine traditional respect for authority with modern team-building approaches. These shifts reflect a recognition of the need to balance hierarchical stability with the demands of an increasingly competitive and fast-changing global market (CCBS Survey, 2024). In summary, Algeria's hierarchical structures uphold respect, order, and stability, which are deeply valued within both community and organisational settings. However, this reliance on top-down authority may constrain open communication, creativity, and adaptability. A strategic blend of traditional authority and collaborative approaches could enhance leadership effectiveness and innovation, particularly as Algeria seeks to integrate within the global economy.

How Algerians achieve Leadership empathy

In recent years, empathy has become increasingly important for Algerian leaders who aim to cultivate and maintain strong, trusting relationships with their teams, especially in light of evolving workplace dynamics (Chekkal, 14 November 2024). Whilst Algeria's traditional leadership culture prioritises a formal, centralised hierarchy—where decision-making typically resides at the top—leaders are increasingly finding ways to integrate empathy, enhancing team morale without diminishing authority (Chekkal, 14 November 2024). This is in line with the results of the CCBS Survey (2024), which demonstrated that Algerian leaders are generally perceived as approachable and empathetic. For example, the majority of the respondents disagreed with the following statement, *"Do leaders retain distance from their employees?,"* thus reflecting a commitment to close interpersonal engagement. Similarly, nearly all of the respondents agreed that leaders should spend time ensuring their employees' wellbeing, which also testifies to a discernable emphasis upon empathy within Algerian business leadership (CCBS Survey, 2024). This approach is in accordance with a transformational leadership approach, which prioritises individualised consideration and encourages personal growth within teams. One respondent aptly described this approach as follows: *"Leadership here* [Algeria] *is about empowering others to grow,"* thus underscoring a shared emphasis upon development and support (CCBS Survey, 2024). Mr. Mehdi Bouchetara, a scientific researcher and Executive Director, also informed us that Algerian leadership balances professional discipline with social and emotional considerations. More specifically, leaders often incorporate personal and social factors into their decision-making, such as, for example, retaining employees for the sake of social stability. This nuanced approach reflects the interconnected nature of professional and social relationships within Algerian culture, where empathy and understanding play pivotal roles in maintaining workplace harmony (Bouchetara, 13 November 2024). By displaying open and approachable forms of communication, leaders help team members feel valued, which makes empathy a powerful complement to Algeria's hierarchical workplace structure (Chekkal, 14 November 2024). Emotional intelligence (EI) also plays a critical role in terms of empathetic leadership. Algerian leaders with high EI excel at recognising and addressing employee concerns, particularly during times of stress (Houda & Nabila, 2024). In collectivist cultures like Algeria, this alignment with societal values that emphasise family and community fosters a sense of belonging and shared purpose within teams (Larras & Kareche, 2022). Generational shifts in leadership further underscore the evolution of empathetic practices. Bouchetara observes that younger Algerian leaders are adopting more inclusive approaches, inspired, at least in part, by recent political changes and initiatives that encourage youth entrepreneurship. This shift has paved the way for leadership styles that blend traditional hierarchical respect with a modern focus upon collaboration and employee wellbeing (Bouchetara, 13 November 2024). Whilst formal respect for hierarchy remains integral to Algerian workplaces, leaders increasingly leverage democratic elements, such as, for example, soliciting input from employees. This strategy fosters inclusion without undermining the authority inherent within Algerian leadership culture (Chekkal, 14 November 2024). Feedback practices also reflect this balance, with leaders preferring to offer constructive guidance within informal settings in order to preserve harmony and respect (CCBS Survey, 2024). Despite a historical tendency to focus upon correcting errors over celebrating achievements, empathy is proving instrumental in terms of both strengthening team morale and fostering long-term commitment. As Mr. Bouchetara emphasised in our interview, trust and credibility in leadership are deeply tied to empathy, professionalism, and ethical conduct, which are essential for establishing respect and maintaining strong relationships within Algerian organisations (Bouchetara, 13 November 2024).

Armenia

Stella Duin, Isabel Ayseli, Leila Garcia, Laith Shumaila, Erik van Schie, Jorten Löhr

Armenia, also known as the "land of stones," is a South Caucasus nation where ancient traditions meet modern innovations, creating a unique cultural landscape. Despite its small size and population of only three million, Armenia is renowned for being the first country to adopt Christianity in 301 AD, a fact that still deeply influences its national identity (James, 2023). According to Raffy Semerdjian, this legacy of faith not only shaped Armenia's cultural and spiritual fabric but also established a deeply hierarchical societal structure, mirrored in its leadership styles (23 November 2024). This connection to the past is also reflected in Armenia's heritage sites, which includes the world's oldest winery, which has produced wine for over six thousand years (Harutyunyan, 2022). The nation's historical experiences have deeply impacted upon its collective psyche and leadership practices (Personal communication, November 28, 2024), as leaders prioritise stability, loyalty, and community to navigate challenges. Alongside its rich history, Armenia is also emerging as a hub for innovation, particularly within the tech sector (James, 2023). This adds to Armenia's linguistic diversity: whilst Armenian remains the main language, many Armenians also speak Russian, and English is deemed the second language (Taraday, 2024). *Aveli lav e mrjyuni glukh linel, k'an arryutsi poch' (Ավելի լավ է մրջյունի գլուխ լինել, քան առյուծի պոչ)* *("better to be an ant's head than a lion's tail")*. This proverb tells us that it is better to be a leader of a small group than to be a member of a big group. This perspective highlights the preference in Armenian leadership for managing smaller, close-knit groups, where leaders maintain direct involvement in decision-making (Taraday, 2024). Although there have been changes within Armenian leadership, as the country is still in the process of transforming from totalitarianism to democracy (Malakyan, 2013), this transformation is uneven, with urban centres like Yerevan characterised by more participatory leadership styles whereas autocratic approaches remain common in rural areas (Semerdjian, 23 November 2024). This chapter will delve further into the unique characteristics of Armenian leadership and organisational culture, examining how traditional values and modern aspirations shape leadership styles and workplace dynamics within Armenia today.

How the Armenian characterise leaders?

Armenian leadership is influenced by cultural, historical, and social factors, which creates a blend of traditional and adaptive qualities. Of particular importance to Armenian leadership are familial ties and traditional social structures, which emphasise loyalty and community. According to Kirakosyan and Sargsyan (2021), these relational dynamics create strong community ties within organisations, and reflect cultural values that are deeply rooted in Armenian society. Therefore, Armenian leaders typically prioritise loyalty, interpersonal trust, and community values. Whilst specific industries like IT and telecommunications are leading the transition towards more modern and inclusive leadership styles, traditional sectors often remain rooted in hierarchical structures. This underscores the importance of balancing cultural loyalty and trust with the adaptability required to meet the expectations of a globalised economy (CCBS Survey, 2024). Within traditional organisations and sectors, this emphasis upon close relationships often extends to familial and communal ties. The result of this is that Armenian leaders are often seen as caretakers of their community or organisational 'families' rather than, say, merely as a manager or leader within a business or workplace setting. Ultimately, leaders are expected to provide direction and security, in order to establish a sense of stability and continuity (Malakyan, 2016). This raises the question of how Armenian leaders instill trust from their employees and build loyalty? Kirakosyan and Sargsyan (2021) purport that Armenian leaders empower their employees by fostering a positive work environment. Cultivating positive work attitudes can lead to increased loyalty as employees feel appreciated and motivated. Not only cultivating a positive work environment but also empowering employees to work without continual supervision serves to give employees confidence because their leaders are exhibiting confidence in their abilities (Kirakosyan & Sargsyan, 2021). The CCBS Survey (2024) also identified other key traits for leaders to possess ad exhibit within Armenian organisations. Specifically, visionary thinking and strong decision-making skills were regarded by the survey respondents as highly valued leadership traits, with nearly one-third and just over one-quarter of them prioritising these attributes, respectively (CCBS Survey, 2024). Despite the aforementioned emphasis on collective values, Armenian leadership also exhibits a notable individualistic dimension, especially with respect to decision-making practices, according to Khzrtian and Samuelian's (2012) survey-based research. In these researchers' survey of Armenian negotiation culture, they described how a CEO of a holding company dismissed the need to consult the Board of Directors, asserting his role as the primary decision-maker. When asked to respond to this example of leadership behaviour, over 90 percent of the respondents reported that such practice was typical of Armenian leaders, thus indicating an individualistic approach to leadership within the country (Khzrtian & Samuelian, 2012). Alongside this individualistic approach, Armenian leaders often also focus on building strong relationships with their employees, emphasising loyalty and commitment to the organisation. *"Internal relationships are very important in Armenia."* (Semerdjian, 2024). They can be best described as extended family relationships, encompassing not just immediate family but also close friends and a broader network of familial connections. This loyalty-based leadership approach is especially prevalent in family-run businesses and smaller enterprises, where leaders are closely involved with employees and encourage a family-like atmosphere within the workplace. For example, leaders may frequently engage in informal conversations to understand employees' personal challenges, reinforcing a sense of loyalty and commitment to the workplace as if it were an extended family (Semerdjian, 23 November 2024). This familial atmosphere within the workplace can help to provide a lot of support and a cohesive environment for employees. However, such loyalty-based systems can also lead to difficulties in balancing professional and personal boundaries or managing conflicts of interest in family businesses (Martirosyan, 2014). For instance, many family-run enterprises prioritise hiring relatives, which, in turn, may foster favouritism and negatively impact upon overall performance (Martirosyan, 2014). Whilst these values promote a nurturing leadership style, they can complicate accountability and open communication, especially when family interests' conflict with business needs. Such dynamics may hinder objective decision-making and highlight the complexities of navigating personal and professional relationships within a culturally rich environment. In recent years, corporate social responsibility (CSR) has emerged as a growing focus in Armenian leadership, marking a shift toward aligning business objectives with broader societal values (Yegyan, 2018). Leaders who embrace CSR initiatives often adopt a community-focused approach, seeing their organisations not only as profit-driven entities but but as integral parts of society. This alignment with social values resonates with the collectivist nature of Armenian culture, where leaders are seen as stewards of both organisational and societal well-being. Leaders in progressive industries like IT are actively integrating these modern approaches, as noted by one of our survey respondents who informed us that building trust and transparency is necessary for achieving organisational success in Armenia (Personal communication, 28 November 2024). Armenian leaders are challenged to preserve core cultural values (such as community loyalty, familial ties, and interpersonal trust), whilst, simultaneously, fostering adaptability and innovation, creating a distinctive leadership style that resonates with both local and international stakeholders (Malakyan, 2016).

Armenian leaders are aware of the need for adaptability, particularly in a globalised economy where diverse management practices have become more accessible and standard (Ter-Mkrtchyan, 2008). International organisations and younger Armenian leaders are thus introducing more participatory and inclusive styles, balancing the traditional top-down approach with bottom-up feedback and collaborative decision-making. This shift reflects a gradual integration of transformational and servant leadership styles, which prioritise employee development, empowerment, and innovation within a culturally respectful framework. The latest changes reflect an increased emphasis on achieving a healthier work-life balance (Hovsepyan, 2024). As more Armenian leaders integrate modern practices, they are better equipped to manage both internal expectations and external pressures for adaptability and responsiveness.

Survey results and what local respondents say

The CCBS Survey (2024) was completed by 22 C-level executives in Armenia and offers valuable insights into the evolving leadership styles within Armenia, reflecting a blend of traditional hierarchical practices and a growing embrace of modern approaches. The most significant of these findings will be discussed in turn below. The first particularly notable finding is that nearly half of the respondents reported that managers should actively focus on their team members' well-being, thus signaling a shift towards more empathetic and people-centered leadership practices in the country (CCBS Survey, 2024). This finding is in line with the opinions of other experts on Armenian leadership, who have talked about the integration of transformational and servant leadership styles, which emphasise employee development, empowerment, and innovation within a culturally respectful framework (Hovsepyan, 2024). Despite this positive trend, hierarchical tendencies nevertheless continue to shape workplace dynamics, as evidenced by the fact that only under two-fifths of the participants stated that they do not prefer leaders to maintain personal distance from subordinates, thus emphasising approachability and trust over strict formality (CCBS Survey, 2024).The duality in leadership styles, which itself is perhaps reflective of Armenia's historical transition from a post-Soviet autocratic heritage to a more flexible and relational approach, resonates strongly with insights shared in our interview with Mr. Semerdjian. In our discussion with him, he emphasised the stark division between traditional, authoritarian leaders and the emerging new generation of leaders adopting modern, empathetic, and strategic approaches (23 November 2024). Similarly, as one respondent described, the country is navigating *"a mix of old and modern Western management systems,"* a transformation shaped by exposure to global practices and competition (CCBS Survey, 2024). With respect to the preferred leadership traits in Armenia, qualities such as visionary thinking and decision-making prowess were found to be the most valued, with just under one-third and just over one-quarter of therespondents, respectively, prioritising these attributes (CCBS Survey, 2024). Another noteworthy finding is the moderate encouragement of competition within teams; just over one-third of the respondents agreed that fostering competition helps achieve better results, whilst less than one-quarter disagreed, thus suggesting a balanced perspective regarding the role of rivalry within team performance (CCBS Survey, 2024). These findings shed light upon an ongoing transformation within leadership norms in the country, with the IT and telecommunications sectors leading the charge. Leaders in these industries often adopt progressive practices influenced by global exposure and partnerships, positioning Armenia as an emerging tech hub with a focus on innovation and modernisation (CCBS Survey, 2024). Similarly, the "Global Entrepreneurship Monitor: Armenia National Report 2019/2020" highlights the importance of knowledge-based and technology-driven business activities for Armenia's growth. According to one of our respondents: *"Being a small country, Armenian leaders* [in the Information Technology field] *are distinguished by having a strong technical expertise, leading to serve as mentors for their junior staff. Many IT leaders are actively involved in educational initiatives and collaborations".* (CCBS Survey, 204). They proceeded to explain further that, *"Armenian IT leaders are known for their versatility... places a strong emphasis on trust and personal relationships"* (CCBS Survey, 2024). Another respondent noted that Armenia was in a process of transformation, noting that: *"I believe in the nearest future other industries might also adopt and localise the Western management styles, yet there is still a lot to do to get there" (CCBS Survey, 2024).* Conversely, another participant pointed out that Armenian leadership styles remain *"a bit hierarchical,"* particularly in traditional sectors, whilst others emphasised the stark contrast between public and private leadership approaches (CCBS Survey, 2024). In a similar vein, one respondent noted that whilst Armenian leadership has made significant strides, especially in reducing bureaucracy, there is still a long way to go before achieving fully modernised and democratic leadership structures (CCBS Survey, 2024). Nevertheless, the aspiration to integrate and localise Western management styles is evident, driven by leaders' desire to elevate Armenia's global reputation (CCBS Survey, 2024). Collectively, these insights portray Armenian leadership as a dynamic hybrid, blending traditional and contemporary influences. Whilst significant progress has been made, particularly in forward-thinking industries like IT, the journey towards fully modernised and empathetic leadership practices continues across various sectors, signaling a promising yet challenging trajectory for Armenia's organisational landscape.

Local leadership analysis

Dr. Lara Tcholakian: an expert in leadership

Dr. Lara Tcholakian is a professor and lecturer at various academies and has been Chief People Officer of large corporations within Armenia. Her career also encompasses teaching about leadership and collective trauma at institutions such as the Vrije Universiteit Amsterdam, INSEAD Business School in Singapore, and the Madenna Leadership School in Armenia. Alongside this, she has also held executive positions driving cultural transformation within Armenia's corporate landscape. With over twenty years of experience in leadership roles across academic, corporate, and development sectors, Dr. Tcholakian thus offers a unique perspective upon Armenian leadership. During the interview, Dr. Tcholakian (28 November 2024) described Armenian leadership as being profoundly shaped by the country's historical experiences of trauma and its Soviet past. These legacies of the Soviet era, she informed us, continue to influence leadership today. As she put it: *"The culture is such a way that people are all to be considered guilty before proven innocent"* (Tcholakian, 28 November 2024). She proceeded to explain that this type of fear-based management discourages employees from taking the initiative or innovating within their daily practices (Tcholakian, 28 November 2024). Next, she discussed the evolving role of women in leadership within Armenia, paying particular attention to the challenges that women face with respect to being accepted as the principal decision-makers within a male-dominated organisational culture. To illustrate this, she opined: *"If a woman raises her voice in a meeting, she is seen as emotional, whereas a man doing the same is considered assertive,"* she observed, thus emphasising the double standards female leaders encounter in the country (Tcholakian, 28 November 2024). Despite these hurdles, Tcholakian informed us that there has been gradual progress in recent years, particularly in Yerevan, where women are increasingly occupying C-Suite positions. Later in the interview, Tcholakian stressed the significance of emotional intelligence (EQ) as a crucial skill for Armenian leaders to possess, going on to argue that Armenian leaders must cultivate empathy, self-awareness, and trust in order to effectively inspire and support their teams. As she stated: *"Not just technically speaking, but with the heart, because if you do not understand the people you are managing or you are leading, you will eventually fail"* (Tcholakian, 28 November 2024).

Conversely, a lack of emotional intelligence serves to hinder organisational and cultural transformation (Tcholakian, 28 November 2024). In realtion to this, she called for reforms within the educational sector in order to instill emotional awareness in future leaders from an early age. Towards the end of our interview, she brought up how generational differences are driving some of the changes observed in Armenian leadership styles in recent years. Specifically, Tcholakian (28 November 2024) told us that younger leaders, influenced by global education and exposure to Western influences, are becoming more open to collaboration and team-oriented approaches. This shift is, in turn, fostering a gradual transition from authoritarian models to more inclusive and participative leadership practices. However, she also noted that progress remains slow in this regard, in as far as many organisations still rely on subjective selection processes and prioritise hierarchical authority. When asked about how leaders foster trust and communicate with their employees, Dr. Tcholakian emphasised transparency and regular engagement with employees as being key to success. That is to say, leaders who consistently communicate organisational goals and genuinely listen to their teams build trust and loyalty. *"It has to be consistent. It has to be regular. It has to be authentic. People know when you are not being authentic."* (Tcholakian, 28 November 2024). She then proceeded to add that effective leaders in Armenia must also strike the requisite balance between compassion and accountability (Tcholakian, 28 November 2024). Reflecting upon the future, Dr. Tcholakian concluded by expressing optimism about Armenia's leadership evolution. She believes that embracing emotional intelligence, ethical practices, and inclusive decision-making will drive long-term success and cultural transformation within the country's business sector.

Mr. Raffy Semerdjian: expert in cross-cultural leadership and strategic management
Mr. Raffy Semerdjian is a distinguished professional specialising in strategy, leadership, and corporate management. He currently serves as Secretary General of the International Chamber of Commerce in Armenia and Executive Director of Management Mix. With a career spanning over thirty years across 33 countries, he combines academic rigour with hands-on expertise in order to drive organisational growth and innovation. Mr. Semerdjian provided his perspective upon Armenian business leadership, emphasiisng its deep cultural roots, historical development, and contemporary approaches. At the beginning of the interview, Mr. Semerdjian (23 November 2024) described Armenian leadership as being profoundly shaped by the country's historical and cultural context. In particular, he drew attention to Armenia's post-Soviet legacy, which has historically fostered authoritarian leadership styles. In recent years, however, this approach has gradually been

replaced by more adaptive and collaborative approaches, especially amongst the younger generation of Armenian leaders (Semerdjian, 23 November 2024). As he put it: *"The power distance in Armenia has historically been high, but the new generation is adopting a more Western, democratic approach to leadership"* (Semerdjian, 23 November 2024). Mr. Semerdjian (23 November 2024) then proceeded to explicate that Armenian leadership is marked by a generational divide. Whereas traditional leaders often operate in hierarchical, autocratic structures, their younger counterparts instead value collaboration and innovation. This evolution is supported by increasing access to education and exposure to global business practices, particularly through Armenia's extensive diaspora. Armenians succeed globally due to their adaptability, and the influence of the diaspora and greater exposure to international practices are driving this change in leadership, according to Mr. Semerdjian (23 November 2024). The IT sector, a prominent area of growth within Armenia, exemplifies this transformation. With one of the highest rates of female participation globally, it highlights the progressive mindset of new leaders in the country. In this respect, the IT sector is a shining example of progress. *"Per capita, the employees in IT, they are female. We're talking about 47, 48, 49 percent, but again, per capita."* (Semerdjian, 23 November 2024). Later in the interview, Semerdjian (23 November 2024) noted that Armenian leadership is heavily influenced by cultural norms, such as, for example, respect for hierarchy and individualism, which poses challenges, especially for foreign leaders or modern managers navigating traditional workplaces. Within traditional Armenian leadership, authority is often demonstrated through visible status symbols, whereas modern leaders focus on humility and approachability. He also underscored the importance of informal networks in decision-making and the challenges this poses for objective management. Mr. Semerdjian (23 November 2024) claimed that family and social ties often influence hiring and the decision-making process, which can hinder efficiency but reflects the relational culture within Armenia. As an illustration, he said it was important for leaders *''To take into consideration those, what I call, informal procedures in a company, not the formal procedures but the informal procedures are very important here''* (Semerdjian, 23 November 2024). Next, he moved on to discuss that communication and empathy are essential in Armenian leadership, particularly in terms of fostering trust and engagement. Modern leaders increasingly prioritise team-building and personal connection. *''How can we make you more happy? This is empathy. I call it empathy, because I am listening to them. I think the communication, in the big companies, they cannot communicate with 100 people, but the top management can divide itself and communicate''* (Semerdjian, 23 November 2024). For example, in Mr. Semerdjian's organisation, organising activities like 'Happiness Days' helps leaders connect with their teams on a deeper level. He also emphasised the need for recognition and career planning to motivate employees, again reflecting the shift towards more employee-centric leadership practices. This is because employees value recognition and the promise of career growth more than salary. This is key to building trust and loyalty according to Mr. Semerdjian (23 November 2024). *"The motivator is the recognition, the career"* (Semerdjian, 23 November 2024). When concluding, Mr. Semerdjian (23 November 2024) expressed optimism about the future of leadership in Armenia, citing the influence of the diaspora, advancements in education, and exposure to global trends as transformative factors. He believes that modern Armenian leaders are becoming strategic thinkers who balance cultural values with innovative approaches. The new Armenian leader is visionary, adaptive, and collaborative, and these traits are paving the way for greater efficiency and national progress his estimation (23 November 2024). In conclusion, Mr. Semerdjian's perspective underscores the dynamic nature of Armenian leadership. He advocates for merging cultural heritage with global practices in order to foster trust, empathy, and innovation within a fast-changing world.

In-country leadership bestseller

One of the best-selling books about leadership was written by Gor Karapetyan (Գոռ Կարապետյան) in 2024 and is called Հաջողության Թաքնված Կողմը - 181 էջ քո ապագայի մասին (The Hidden Side of Success – 181 pages about your future). Gor Karapetyan is a lecturer at the Simple Business Academy. Recently, Gor Karapetyan engaged in social activities in different regions in Armenia for the express purpose of teaching leadership develepment to young people. His book delves into essential aspects of personal growth, career development, and leadership in Armenia, with an especial focus upon the challenges and opportunities unique to young Armenians today. Karapetyan's approach is methodical yet accessible, offering a structured series of steps for those eager to take a leading role in their career some day. With a blend of personal stories, research-backed insights, and interactive materials, he guides readers to build the responsibility needed to shape a successful career and lead with impact. The author also emphasises practical, experience-driven strategies, showing young people how to approach business leadership as a means through which to serve both personal and shared goals. Rather than pushing rigid formulas, the book invites readers to take a thoughtful, individualised approach to defining and pursuing success on their own terms, empowering them to inspire and support others along the way. People who read this book will learn not to get stuck, not to get bogged down, how to set clear goals, and how to achieve them within the Armenian context (*Newmag Presents Gor Karapetyan's Book*, n.d.).

Local leadership book		
Title	Հաջողության Թաքնված Կողմը	
Subtitle	181 էջ քո ապագայի մասին	
Author	Գոռ Կարապետյան	
Publisher	NewMag	
Year	2024	
ISBN	9789939967257	

Armenian Leadership YouTube Review

In this section, we describe Christopher Dedeyan and Patrick Elliott's views on Armenian leadership and the specific leadership qualities they value. Christopher De Dayan, a leadership consultant, and advisor, focuses on fostering effective teams and advocating for diversity within the Armenian business and social sectors. His business leadership philosophy is grounded in humility, teamwork, and aligning collective goals with a shared purpose. Conversely, Patrick Elliot, a Canadian-Armenian entrepreneur, dedicates himself to sustainable development and community empowerment. He passionately bridges the Armenian diaspora with local initiatives and champions self-reliance through skill-building and principled leadership. In a conversation with CIVILNET, De Dayan underscores the critical role of humility and self-awareness in Armenian leadership. He asserts that understanding personal strengths and limitations is key to team building, stating, *"As a leader you have to position yourself to be humble and move beside your ego"* (De Dayan, 2023, 7:38). He also stresses the importance of diversity, suggesting that varied perspectives from different genders, cultures, and ideologies can uncover blind spots and improve decision-making: *"...different genders, different sexes, different ideologies, different cultures—they see things that you do not see"* (De Dayan, 2023, 7:54). Furthermore, De Dayan emphasises the necessity of aligning teams with an organisation's mission rather than individual loyalties to achieve collective success in the Armenian context (De Dayan, 2023, 8:22). Similarly, Patrick Elliot underscores the significance of a clear vision for mobilising and uniting teams. He believes leadership involves equipping individuals with practical skills like language and communication to open up opportunities, and that, *"...skills like these kickstart a lot of the prospects here"* (Elliot, 0:02:47). Elliot also ties entrepreneurship to accountability, encouraging ownership and innovation whilst upholding ethical values: *"No tolerating sliding back to the old ways"* (Elliot, 0:03:36). He advocates for learning from past experiences in Armenia in order to build resilience and maintain forward momentum, stating, *"Look at our strengths and weaknesses...so that we can construct a forward-focused mindset"* (Elliot, 0:07:43). Collectively, De Dayan and Elliot illustrate the pivotal role of humility, diversity, vision, and accountability within effective leadership in Armenia. Their insights reveal how these principles not only strengthen organisations but also empower communities to adapt and flourish in the face of challenges.

Understanding hierarchy in Armenia

Hierarchy in Armenia is influenced by cultural, historical, and globalisation contexts. Traditionally, Armenian society places a strong emphasis upon respect for authority, stability, and social order values that are deeply rooted within its prevailing leadership styles (Zhamakochyan & Hakobyan, 2013). Consequently, Armenian leaders tend to favour hierarchical structures, where decision-making is centralised and there is a clear chain of command. This top-down approach emphasises directive forms of leadership, with communication flowing primarily from the top to the bottom (Martin, 2017). This preference for hierarchical organisational structures and decision-making process is shared in both public and private organisations within Armenia. Leaders expect adherence to established procedures and routines (Ter-Mkrtchyan, 2008). This hierarchy can be discerned particularly in Armenia's traditional local business firms where decision-making is concentrated amongst senior-level management. Employees, for their part, are merely expected to adhere to directives from their superiors with little or no room for debate or input during decision-making processes (Hovsepyan, 2024). This model fosters control and stability but can sometimes stifle innovation and adaptability. However, despite the prevalence of traditional hierarchical structures in the business sector in Armenia, particularly in traditionally locally managed organisations, globalisation and the influx of modern business practices are introducing more collaborative models amongst young entrepreneurs. As aforementioned, the rise of the technology sector has catalysed a shift towards a more collaborative leadership models in the country. Therefore, Armenia's youths are increasingly adopting collaborative approaches (Yegyan, 2018). As one Executive MBA programs coordinator in Canada and Armenia noted during our interview with them, *"young leaders in Armenia are characterised by collective*

51

decision-making and reduced power distance." He proceeded to add that Higher Education and short courses have been effective in developing younger leaders' mindsets towards embracing more collaborative approaches (Semerdjin, 23 November 2024). For instance, platforms like the Entrepreneurship and Product Innovation Center (EPIC) at the American University of Armenia provide programs that focuses on team building, cross-disciplinary collaboration and innovative tech solutions, fostering a spirit of teamwork among participants (EPIC, 2024). These initiatives reflect how Armenia's youth are moving away from traditional hierarchies towards more inclusive and innovative practices. Evidence for this trend also comes from the CCBS Survey (2024), where nearly two-fifths of the respondents stated that they preferred leaders who foster trust-based relationships rather than maintaining strict formal distance. This reflects the growing influence of global business practices and a broader cultural shift towards modern management within Armenianian businesses. Despite the progress that has been made, especially within the private sector and IT sector, Armenia's leadership culture still retains strong power distance. This was evidenced by the fact that the CCBS Survey (2024) demonstrated that whilst hierarchy has been reduced in some areas, fully modernised, democratic leadership structures remain a distant goal. This ongoing tension reflects the struggle between traditional and modern leadership practices. In conclusion, whilst traditional hierarchical structures have long characterised business leadership in Armenia, there is a dicernable shift towards more collaborative and flexible leadership models. Influenced by globalisation, modern business practices, and the growing influence of young tech entrepreneurs in particular, Armenia's leadership styles are evolving. This trend is reshaping the organisational landscape, with greater emphasis on teamwork, innovation, and inclusive leadership, particularly in sectors like IT. As the country continues to balance its historical traditions with the demands of a more interconnected world, the shift towards modern, empathetic leadership is expected to accelerate.

How Armenians achieve leadership empathy

Armenian leaders achieve empathetic leadership by integrating emotional intelligence, historical resilience, and culturally rooted values that emphasise trust and relational connections, including, amongst other things, close personal involvement, community-centred approaches, loyalty-based relationships, and empathetic conflict resolution (Malakyan, 2016). Emerging from a post-Soviet legacy marked by hierarchical systems, Armenian organisations are undergoing a gradual transition towards more people-centred approaches. Indeed, one of our interviewees, Dr. Lara Tcholakian, informed us that empathy and emotional intelligence have become not only advantageous but essential traits for leaders striving to create inclusive and collaborative environments (28 November, 2024). Furthermore, Armenian business culture places significant emphasis upon group decision-making, reflecting a collectivistic approach in which the opinions of followers are highly respected. This approach not only fosters empathy but also empowers teams, contributing towards a sense of shared purpose. Therefore, leaders are expected to act selflessly, prioritising the welfare and interests of the group over personal gains (Malakyan, 2016). It I simportant to note that empathy in Armenian leadership extends beyond the workplace, reflecting the nation's cultural emphasis upon familial and community bonds. For instance, an Armenian manager might offer flexibility for an employee who is caring for an ailing family member, thus demonstrating their understanding of personal responsibilities that are deeply ingrained within Armenian culture (Poghosyan, 2021). Whilst there is clear progress with respect to leaders becoming more empathetic and inclusive within the Armenian context, particularly within innovative sectors like IT and telecommunications, Semerdjian argues (23 November 2024, Armenian leadership still contends with the legacies of hierarchical norms. The cultural significance of trust is further emphasised by our interviewee, Mr. Raffy Semerdjian, who describes empathy as the cornerstone of effective Armenian leadership. Activities such as team-building events and recognition programs help leaders connect with their employees on a deeper level, thus cultivating an environment in which team members feel supported and motivated (Semerdjian, 23 November, 2024). Contemporary Armenian leaders emphasise consistent communication, openness to feedback, and fostering trust, which aligns with the collective cultural emphasis upon group welfare and emotional connection in the country (Tcholakian, 28 November 2024). Leaders are thus expected to demonstrate genuine care for their employees through active listening and recognition of their contributions. Employees in Armenia, like in other relationship-oriented cultures, also prefer leaders who prioritise approachability and trust over strict formality, as evidenced by the fact that around one-third of of the CCBS Survey (2024) respondents stated that they value leaders who maintain close connections with their subordinates. Leaders who exemplify emotional intelligence and compassion are seen as role models, reshaping the traditional perceptions of authority and instead promoting a culture of trust and collaboration (Tcholakian, 28 November 2024). Similarly, during periods of organisational or economic difficulty, leaders often provide additional forms of support, such as mentorship or professional development opportunities, thus reinforcing trust and loyalty. Such actions align with the findings of the CCBS Survey (2024), which revealed that nearly half of the leaders prioritise employee well-being as a core aspect of their role. In conclusion, Armenian leaders achieve empathy by balancing traditional values with contemporary leadership practices. They focus upon building strong interpersonal relationships, fostering inclusive decision-making, and addressing the emotional needs of their teams, thereby creating a foundation of trust and mutual respect within the workplace.

Chile

Sem Oostmeijer and Jaden Bakker, with the support of: Jella de Boer, Noureddine Boukazim, Isidora Valentina Vásquez Ponce, Michelle Teuthof, Matteo Valenteyn

Chile, or the Republic of Chile as it is officially known, is a country located along the western edge of South America, bordered by the Pacific Ocean to the west and the Andes Mountains to the east. Spanning over 4,300 kilometers from north to south, it boasts a remarkable diversity of climates and landscapes, ranging from the arid Atacama Desert in the north to the lush forests and fjords of Patagonia in the south (Ceballos, 2014). This geographical and biodiversity has shaped the development of distinct regions, each with their own cultural and economic characteristics (Spahie & Consejo Nacional de la Cultura y las Artes, 2017). With a population of 19 million people, the capital city, Santiago, is not only the political and cultural heart of the nation but is also key economic hub in the region (Seguel, 2015). Since undergoing a process of liberalisation in the 1990s, Chile has become one of the fastest-growing economies in Latin America (Ahluwalia et al., 2005). The economy is now one of the most stable and prosperous in South America, primarily due to its rich natural resources, including copper, which accounts for a substantial portion of its exports (Nem Singh, 2012). Business leadership in Chile is also undergoing change, driven by economic shifts, social demands, and political reforms. Chilean leaders are increasingly focusing on promoting sustainability, innovation, and diversity in their organisations, reflecting global trends on more responsible corporate governance (Cabrera, 2012). Recent regulatory changes, such as labour reforms and gender equity initiatives, have also led Chilean executives to adopt participatory approaches and develop a more equitable workplace culture (ComunidadMujer et al., 2018). This chapter delves into the impact of these changes on Chile's business landscape by drawing on insights from local professionals and analysing empirical research to better understand the prevailing leadership styles and practices in the country. As one respondent aptly noted, *"In Chile, leadership is still largely hierarchical and authoritarian in many traditional companies, but there is a growing shift towards more participatory and collaborative styles, particularly amongst younger generations and in innovative sectors."* This observation underscores the evolving nature of leadership in Chile, due to cultural and generational shifts (CCBS Survey, 2024).

How the Chileans characterise leaders?

Within Chile, leadership is primarily defined by a blend of paternalistic qualities and a strong collectivist orientation. Chilean leaders are often characterised as fatherly figures who provide guidance, care, and support for their teams, thus reflecting the deep cultural values of loyalty, trust, and interconnectedness that permeate Chilean society (Littrell et al., 2013). This paternalistic style is historically rooted within Chile's familial and social structures in which leaders are expected to act not only as authority figures but rather as mentors who understand and cater to the personal needs of their employees. The collectivist nature of Chilean culture plays a crucial role in this regard in terms of shaping individual decisions, in as far as leaders are expected to prioritise the perspectives of the group, with choices frequently influenced by *"the directives of authority and the collective will"* (Charla "Liderazgo Estratégico En Chile" - Jaime Riquelme, 2018, 00:15:11). This approach serves to reinforce a sense of security and mutual respect, which is in accordance with the cultural emphasis upon group cohesion and personal relationships (Littrell et al., 2013). Despite the continued influence of these traditional expectations, Chilean leadership has undergone significant shifts in recent years due to globalisation and the increasing influence of Western business practices in the country. In contemporary Chile, there is a growing trend towards a more individualistic and formal leadership style, particularly within both urban-based corporate settings and new start-ups (Jordán et al., 2014). This shift is characterised by a focus upon performance metrics, individual employee growth, and the adoption of systematic management approaches, which, in turn, are designed to drive efficiency and embed transparency within decision-making processes. However, as positive as these changes are, Chilean leaders nevertheless remain inclined towards charismatic forms of leadership, where inspirational figures take centre stage and cultivate a vision that resonates with employees at an emotional level (Jordán et al., 2014). Furthermore, leaders in Chile are expected to be accessible and approachable, thus embodying a humanistic leadership style that fosters open communication and team inclusivity (Huidobro, 2008). This is corroborated by the results of the CCBS Survey (2024) which shows that three-fifths of Chilean managers consider it highly important to actively dedicate time to ensuring the well-being of their team members, highlighting the human-centered and paternalistic aspects of leadership in the country. Hence, caring for employees plays a key role in fostering a harmonious and productive work environment (CCBS Survey, 2024). This style is regarded as being essential within a society where personal bonds and relational harmony are valued (Huidobro, 2008). The expectation is that Chilean leaders should not only guide but rather actively involve employees within the mission of their organisation, thereby creating a shared sense of purpose. This human-centered approach is embodied by leaders who admit mistakes and seek input from their teams, which, in turn, reinforces an environment of humility and collaboration (Huidobro, 2008). However, whilst Chilean leadership retains many paternalistic elements, there is also an increasing presence of transactional leadership frameworks, especially within larger organisations. Within these settings, leaders often delineate clear roles and expectations for their subordinates, thus minimising individual responsibility in favour of a structured hierarchy where decisions flow from the top down (Huidobro, 2008). Employees, in return, expect their leaders to set and uphold this vision, whilst they themselves focus upon fulfilling their designated roles within the broader organisational framework. As Arnaldo Canales, Executive Director of Fundación Liderazgo Chile, explained to us in our interview with them, *"In Chile, 80% of organisations still function based on fear and distrust, often relying on a punitive approach rather than fostering autonomy and a sense of purpose within their teams"* (Canales, 12 November 2024). This observation aligns with the traditional top-down leadership style prevalent within many Chilean companies, where directives are handed down with limited room for individual initiative. Nevertheless, Canales proceeded to inform us that there is a gradual shift towards integrating more human-centered practices within some organisations, though the change remains uneven in practice (12 November 2024). These adaptations reflect Chile's journey towards a balanced integration of paternalistic and modern leadership principles, which allows more room for flexibility and adaptation (Huidobro, 2008).

Survey results and what local respondents say

The CCBS Survey (2024) was conducted in order to obtain detailed insights into leadership styles and practices in Chile. Over 16 professionals, including C-level executives and managers with significant experience within the Chilean workplace, participated in the survey, providing valuable perspectives into the evolving nature of leadership in the country. The most notable findings from the survey are outlined below. Firstly, the results show that Chilean leaders are often admired for their charisma, resourcefulness, and intellectual capabilities, as well as their ability to build strong professional networks. In fact, these traits are seen as essential for inspiring teams and achieving organisational success in the country (CCBS Survey, 2024). The respondents also underscored that leaders are expected to be powerful decision-makers who also act as good listeners, thus emphasising the importance of both technical competence and relational skills. This aligns with observations that personal relationships within the workplace are as critical as professional ones, as one participant noted: *"In Chile, the personal relationship is as important as the working relationship"* (CCBS Survey, 2024). Secondly, whilst traditional hierarchical structures remain influential within the business sector, according to our findings, Chilean leaders are beginning to adopt more inclusive and empathetic approaches, as the majority of the respondents reported that managers should actively invest time in the personal well-being of their team members, signaling a cultural shift towards more human-oriented forms of leadership, as discussed by Huidobro (2008). One respondent articulated this perspective stating, *"Before being a good leader, you should be a good person. So, human skills are being valued much more"* (CCBS Survey, 2024). Another key finding is that direct criticism is often avoided within Chilean workplace culture, largely because open confrontation is perceived to create tension. However, this trend is changing, with younger leaders coming to embrace honest and more collaborative communication styles. As one respondent observed, *"Chilean leaders are bad at saying things directly, but the new generations of leaders understand the benefit of honest and collaborative conversation"* (CCBS Survey, 2024). Finally, the survey shed light upon significant gender disparities with respect to senior leadership roles within Chilean organisations. However, female leaders, whilst still underrepresented, are gaining visibility and are often celebrated for their ability to foster inclusive and empowering work environments. As one female leader stated, *"I admire leaders who create a work environment, delegate responsibilities effectively, and allow their team members to showcase their potential"* (CCBS Survey, 2024). These findings point towards a Chilean leadership culture that is rooted in traditional values but increasingly adapting to prioritise collaboration, empathy, and inclusivity.

Local leadership analysis

Chilean leadership social media review:

Leadership in Chile is undergoing profound transformation, as traditional hierarchies are blended with more modern, collaborative approaches in order to meet the demands of a rapidly changing world. Carlos Muñoz highlights this shift towards decentralised leadership models, where trust, empowerment, and addressing societal challenges like inequality and sustainability play a pivotal role. According to Muñoz, leaders in Chile must embrace adaptability in order to balance local traditions with global innovation, thus fostering an environment where teams feel both autonomous and accountable (Muñoz, 2022). Empathy and authenticity are increasingly recognised as essential traits for effective leadership. Ana María Núñez Torres, on her LinkedIn page, emphasises the importance of leading from the heart, stating that true leadership enables deeper connections and inspires others to thrive. She notes that leaders who approach their roles with genuine care and emotional intelligence unlock limitless possibilities for their teams (Núñez Torres, 2024). Inclusivity also plays a central role in terms of leadership development within Chile. Initiatives like Lucía Vilariño Fiore's mentorship program are driving efforts to promote diversity and equity in traditionally male-dominated fields, such as firefighting. Her LinkedIn profile shows how these programs provide personalised guidance, tools, and networks that empower a new generation of leaders to challenge existing norms and create more inclusive spaces. Vilariño Fiore's work illustrates the growing push in Chile for leadership that reflects broader societal values, including equity and fairness (Vilariño Fiore, 2024). Courageous decision-making is another key aspect of impactful leadership in the country. Sofia Tenreiro underscores that challenging the status quo often signals effective leadership. She asserts that making bold, sometimes unpopular decisions demonstrates a leader's commitment to progress and long-term goals, even when faced with resistance. This approach is particularly relevant in the Chilean context, where leaders frequently navigate polarised environments and complex challenges (Tenreiro, 2024). These perspectives collectively reveal a leadership style in Chile that prioritises collaboration, empathy, and inclusivity. By addressing the unique complexities of their social and cultural context, Chilean leaders are redefining leadership to better align with the values and aspirations of their society.

Arnaldo Canales: a Chilean cross-cultural trainer

Arnaldo Canales is the Executive Director of *"Fundación Liderazgo Chile,"* and has an extensive background in leadership and emotional education. With qualifications in engineering, psychology, and a doctorate in education, Canales has dedicated his career to fostering socio-emotional competencies in children, adults, and professionals. His work spans from advocating for emotional education legislation in Chile to acting as a leadership consultant and cross-cultural trainer. Towards the beginning o four interview with them, he reflected upon his journey, Canales noted, *"Leadership is not just about guiding and directing but understanding how our temperament and behaviour impacts upon others on an emotional level"* (Canales, 12 November 2024). When asked about the evolving demands of leadership in Chile, Canales shared his insights into how economic transformations and the shift toward a knowledge-based economy are reshaping traditional leadership structures in Chile. He proceeded to explain that the longstanding hierarchical and fear-based management style in Chilean organisations hinders both employee engagement and productivity. He opined: "In 80% of Chilean businesses, fear and distrust are the dominant emotions. Statements like, *'If you do not like it, you can leave,'* or, *'This is what you are paid for,'* reflect thid punitive style of management that fails to foster autonomy and purpose" (Canales, 12 November 2024). Later in the interview, Canales discussed the importance of emotional intelligence in leadership, advocating for a shift toward more horizontal, inclusive structures. He argued that emotionally intelligent leaders not only create positive organisational cultures but also enhance productivity and well-being. As he himself put it: *"A leader's emotional state is always present in their interactions—it shapes the workplace climate,"* he explained, highlighting the urgency of integrating emotional education into leadership training from an early age (Canales, 12 November 2024). In response to a question about workplace culture, Canales criticised the pervasive use of sarcasm and irony within Chilean organisations, which he believes fosters a toxic environment. He stated, *"Sarcasm is not constructive feedback; it creates disconnection and erodes trust. Leaders need to learn how to give feedback that empowers, rather than diminishes, their team members"* (Canales, 12 November 2024). This sentiment resonates with younger generations, who increasingly reject traditional hierarchical structures and seek workplaces that value inclusivity and well-being. Towards the end of the interview, Canales reflected upon the future of leadership in Chile, emphasising the need for leaders to develop socio-emotional skills such as empathy and adaptability. He warned that technical expertise alone is insufficient, stating, *"We are often hired for our skills, but fired for our behaviour. Emotional intelligence must become a core focus of leadership development"* (Canales, 12 November 2024). In conclusion, Canales' insights underline the transformative potential of emotionally intelligent leadership. His work highlights the critical role of self-awareness, empathy, and positive organisational culture in terms of fostering both individual and societal growth. As Chile navigates its way through an economic and cultural evolution, Canales' approach offers a compelling blueprint for the leaders of tomorrow.

In-country leadership bestseller

"Liderazgo Real: De los fundamentos a la práctica" is an influential book on leadership in Chile, written by Rodrigo Jordán and Marcelino Garay. Published in 2014, this book adopts a unique approach to leadership by intertwining both academic theories and the authors' profound real-life experiences. Jordán, a well-known Chilean leader in both corporate and mountaineering worlds, and Garay, who has a background in social and organisational development, wrote the book

to redefine the meaning of leadership within complex and high-stakes environments. The book critiques traditional 'great man' leadership theories, advocating instead for collective strength and teamwork. In "*Liderazgo Real*," the authors introduce the Delta Leadership Model (MLD), which places values at its core. According to Jordán, values are fundamental to effective leadership in Chile in as far as they form the foundation upon which Chilean teams can build a sense of shared purpose and resilience. This model emphasises practical, actionable leadership skills that transcend hierarchy, making it especially relevant and accessible to leaders across all organisational levels in Chile. Additionally, the book provides a deep dive into theories like situational leadership, emotional intelligence, and adaptive leadership, applying these concepts to practical scenarios in diverse Chilean industries, from corporate boardrooms to the country's extreme outdoor challenges. For instance, Jordán illustrates how adaptive leadership was crucial during a high-stakes mountaineering expedition in Antarctica, where unpredictable weather conditions required the team to continually reassess their strategies and roles to ensure both progress and safety. This real-world application underscores the relevance of these theories in dynamic and high-pressure environments. A key highlight of *"Liderazgo Real"* is its focus on fostering leadership within a group rather than an individual focus, which is particularly significant in the Chilean cultural context. The authors argue that effective leaders in Chile should develop self-leadership and guide teams through empowerment rather than authoritative command, thus aligning with the collaborative values of Chilean society. As they explain, successful leadership requires building and maintaining connections, being present for team members, and fostering an environment where everyone's contributions are valued. The practical approach of Jordán and Garay's work makes "*Liderazgo Real*" not just a book but a toolkit, designed for anyone aiming to lead teams through complex situations in various sectors. This book is ideal for leaders in crisis management, as it addresses how to harness collective strength and build resilience, key elements within both personal and professional settings. For readers interested in a practical, values-based perspective on leadership that goes beyond traditional paradigms, "Liderazgo Real" is a must-read.

Local leadership book	
Title	*Liderazgo Real*
Subtitle	De los fundamentos a la práctica
Author	Rodrigo Jordán & Marcelino Garay
Publisher	Vertical S.A.
Year	2014; 2nd edition
ASIN	B00NA915NE

Chilean leadership YouTube review

This review summarises key insights from two YouTube lectures on leadership in Chile, delivered by Dr Jaime Riquelme and Maven Lomboy, which provide a detailed exploration of the unique dynamics characterising Chilean leadership culture. Both speakers emphasise that Chile operates within a "vertical, collectivist society," where leadership is defined by strong hierarchical respect and group consensus (Charla "Liderazgo Estratégico En Chile" - Jaime Riquelme, 2018, 00:11:55; Chile, De La Autoridad Al Liderazgo – Maven Lomboy, 2024, 00:17:00). Dr. Riquelme, a Chilean academic with a background in the military, highlights that Chilean leaders often adopt an authoritarian style, rooted in a paternalistic approach. Similarly, Maven Lomboy discusses how this paternalism serves to position leaders as 'father figures' who unilaterally enforce decisions, fostering a top-down hierarchy that limits subordinates' initiative (Chile, De La Autoridad Al Liderazgo – Maven Lomboy, 2024). This leadership style is further reinforced by the collectivist nature of Chilean culture, where decisions are shaped by authority and the collective rather than individual autonomy (Charla "Liderazgo Estratégico En Chile" - Jaime Riquelme, 2018). Both speakers observe that this reliance upon collective approval often results in reactive decision-making due to the country's high uncertainty avoidance. As noted by Dr. Riquelme, *"strategic decisions are often reactive and lack a long-term vision"* (Charla "Liderazgo Estratégico En Chile" - Jaime Riquelme, 2018, 00:20:18). Maven echoes this sentiment, emphasising that avoiding ambiguity hinders innovation as well as the development of proactive, long-term strategies (Chile, De La Autoridad Al Liderazgo – Maven Lomboy, 2024). However, both speakers also identify opportunities for growth with respect to Chilean business leadership. Dr. Riquelme and Maven Lomboy argue for a transition from traditional paternalistic leadership to a more horizontal, collaborative approach within Chile. Maven Lomboy introduces the concept of 'adult-to-adult' relationships, encouraging leaders to foster autonomy and collaboration whilst respecting individual contributions (Chile, De La Autoridad Al Liderazgo – Maven Lomboy, 2024). Dr. Riquelme underscores the potential for Chilean leaders to harness opportunities within international markets and innovation, calling for strategic leaders to embrace change and adapt to global demands (Charla "Liderazgo Estratégico En Chile" - Jaime Riquelme, 2018; Chile, De La Autoridad Al Liderazgo – Maven Lomboy, 2024). Ultimately, both lectures underscore the need for Chilean leaders to evolve beyond traditional authoritarian models by embracing inclusivity, fostering a culture of innovation, and adopting long-term strategies. These changes are deemed essential for navigating the complexities of the contemporary world and ensuring Chile's sustainable development within an increasingly interconnected global environment (Charla "Liderazgo Estratégico En Chile" - Jaime Riquelme, 2018; Chile, De La Autoridad Al Liderazgo – Maven Lomboy, 2024).

Understanding hierarchy in Chile

Chile's hierarchical structure is deeply rooted in both its national and organisational culture, where hierarchy often dictates interactions, decision-making, and organisational dynamics. This structure is notably influenced by the country's history of economic development, political shifts, and traditional values. Within Chile, hierarchy within organisations is generally high, reflecting a top-down approach in which authority is concentrated at the upper levels, and decision-making is often centralised (Schneider, 2009). For instance, research by Littrell and Cruz Barba (2013) underscores that Chilean leaders tend to adopt a 'Parental Leadership' style, where they are seen as nurturing yet authoritative figures. This leadership style is valued in Chile, where managers are expected to provide guidance and support to their employees, reflecting a somewhat paternalistic approach that reinforces the hierarchical order within organisations (Littrell et al., 2013). Further support for this comes from the results of the CCBS Survey (2024), in as far as many respondents characterised Chilean leadership as hierarchical, with leaders maintaining a significant degree of authority and personal distance from their subordinates (CCBS Survey, 2024). Similarly, in an interview with Arnaldo Canales, a leadership expert in Chile, he observed that this style often includes a focus on maintaining formality and a sense of control, whilst, simultaneously, still being approachable enough to offer emotional support and guidance. Canales emphasised that this approach is deeply tied to the socio-emotional competencies leaders are expected to demonstrate in their interactions (Canales, 12 November 2024). In this context, managers maintain a personal distance from their subordinates, enhancing the perceived hierarchy and formality of the workplace. Furthermore, in studies on Chilean leadership preferences, it was found that leaders were expected to exercise authority decisively, with limited need for justification or consultation from lower levels, thus affirming the hierarchical nature of the organisational structure (Rodriguez et al., 2009). Another aspect of Chilean organisational hierarchy is the emphasis on titles and formal roles, which helps to reinforce authority and respect for position. The results of the CCBS Survey (2024) indicate that subordinates typically address leaders by their titles, such as 'Director' or 'President,' both in verbal and written forms of communication. This practice is seen as crucial for maintaining respect and formality within organisations (CCBS Survey, 2024). Moreover, having an academic title on business cards or email signatures is common, further solidifying hierarchical structures (CCBS Survey, 2024). As described by Abarca et al. (1998), employees within Chilean firms generally do not challenge decisions made by their superiors, as questioning authority may be perceived as a lack of respect. This cultural inclination towards maintaining harmony and respect within hierarchical relationships often discourages open criticism or questioning of decisions, which is regarded as essential to preserving the chain of command (Abarca et al., 1998). Moreover, Chile's business environment is characterised by 'hierarchical market economies,' which is where diversified business groups and multinational corporations operate within a highly structured, top-down framework. This environment not only reflects hierarchical patterns in corporate governance but also reinforces the limited autonomy and empowerment granted to employees. According to Schneider (2009), Chilean businesses tend to be organised around a few dominant entities that hold significant control over capital, labour, and technological resources, creating a hierarchical market structure that further solidifies the power distance within organisations (Schneider, 2009). This was also reflected in the CCBS Survey (2024), as the respondents reported the preference within Chile for highly centralised decision-making processes and limited delegation of authority, especially within traditional and large-scale organisations. We gained further insight into the reasons for these preferences within Chile in our interview with Arnaldo Canales, who informed us that this lack of autonomy stems from a deeply entrenched culture of mistrust and fear within many organisations. He noted that leadership styles in Chile often prioritise control and oversight over employee empowerment, which can hinder innovation and team dynamics (Canales, 12 November 2024). Ultimately, the Chilean organisational culture supports a rigid hierarchical structure, where respect for authority and adherence to the chain of command are essential components. Managers are viewed as decision-makers who rarely delegate significant power, and employees are expected to comply without extensive input. This deference to hierarchy is reflected within both public and private sectors and is seen as a defining feature of the Chilean organisational culture.

How the Chileans achieve leadership empathy

Chileans approach leadership empathy through a unique blend of cultural values and a strong commitment to collective success, which emphasises the role of leaders as facilitators of group harmony and resilience (Littrell et al., 2013). Chile's leadership style can be described as 'nurturing' within a 'Parental Leadership' framework, wherein leaders are both caring and supportive, establishing an environment that feels inclusive and enjoyable for all team members (Littrell et al., 2013). This approach to leadership not only creates a positive work culture but also builds rapport and loyalty, in as far as employees feel personally valued and understood in their roles. Within Chilean leadership, empathy is also achieved through a deep-rooted emphasis upon teamwork and shared goals. Rodrigo Jordan's Delta Leadership Model, for example, places adaptability and values at its core, where leaders see their role as guiding teams through challenges, whilst, simultaneously, remaining attuned to individual needs (Jordán et al., 2014). This cultural emphasis upon shared experiences in turn strengthens interpersonal connections and deepens trust. Furthermore, although Chilean organisational culture values professionalism, loyalty, and a certain degree of hierarchy, leaders are also expected to exhibit flexibility and openness to new ideas within these boundaries (Rodriguez et al., 2009). This balance allows leaders to be both approachable and directive, creating an environment where empathy is shown through active listening and attentiveness to employees' well-being (Littrell et al., 2013). For instance, Chilean leaders tend to spend time engaging directly with employees to understand their personal and professional challenges, ensuring that their well-being is prioritised (CCBS Survey, 2024). This is evident in the way leaders frequently check in with their teams, offer support and foster an open dialogue about workplace concerns. Whilst leaders maintain a certain degree of professional distance to respect organisational hierarchy, they balance this by cultivating trust through regular interactions and by being visibly present and approachable during key moments (Rodriguez et al., 2009). This aligns with the Delta Leadership Model outlined by Rodrigo Jordán, which emphasises adaptability and values-based leadership as critical components for building trust and fostering a cohesive team environment. Jordán underscores the importance of aligning personal and organisational values, which strengthens interpersonal bonds and enhances collective performance (Jordán et al., 2014). This is also supported by the results of the CCBS Survey (2024), where Chilean leaders were also reported as prioritising employees' well-being, with many respondents noting that leaders actively create spaces for collaboration and personal support. Jordán further supports this by arguing that effective leadership involves creating climates of respect and mutual support, where professional boundaries coexist with personal investment in team members' growth and well-being (Jordán et al., 2014).

This dual approach—maintaining professional boundaries whilst investing in their team's well-being—exemplifies the empathetic leadership style that is central to Chilean organisational culture (Rodriguez et al., 2009). Ultimately, Chilean leaders cultivate empathy by balancing collective objectives with individual understanding. By fostering open communication, demonstrating resilience, and engaging with their teams on a personal level, Chilean leaders build lasting bonds based upon mutual respect and cultural alignment (Littrell et al., 2013). This empathetic approach not only strengthens internal cohesion but also aligns leadership practices with the broader values of Chilean society, making empathy a cornerstone of effective leadership within Chile (Rodriguez et al., 2009).

Dominican Republic

Adi Sudradjat & Youri Fagel, with the support of: John Tilburg, Dafny Kelly & Marciano Krasuski

Nestled in the heart of the Caribbean, the *República Dominicana* (Dominican Republic) occupies two-thirds of the island of Hispaniola which it shares with Haiti, a former French colony. Affectionately known as *Quisqueya*, which means '*Mother of All Lands*,' the nation boasts a rich tapestry of influences drawn from Taíno, African, and Spanish heritages (Rivera & Torres, 2013). Indeed, Santo Domingo, the capital city, holds the distinction of being the oldest inhabited Spanish settlement within the Americas. Moreover, it is a World Heritage Site that is home to the first university in the New World, which serves to testify to the Dominican Republic's pivotal role within the region's colonial history (Jiménez, 2010). Economically, the Dominican Republic has the largest economy within the Caribbean and Central American regions, which derives, in part, from its diversification into tourism, tobacco production, and mineral exports (Cabrera, 2017). The nation is also globally renowned as the leading exporter of premium cigars, which is a testament to its thriving tobacco industry, in addition to being the sole source of larimar, a rare blue gemstone often referred to as the 'stone of Atlantis' (García & Peña, 2016). In conjunction with these economic achievements, the Dominican Republic is also the birthplace of an impressive number of Major League Baseball players in the US, which is also a considerable source of national pride (Vargas, 2019). Societally speaking, the Dominican lifestyle is grounded in a profound appreciation for family, community, and social bonds. This collective ethos extends into the nation's organisational landscape, influencing its leadership styles. As Sánchez and Rodríguez (2014) observe, Dominican leadership embodies a balance between traditional values such as *familismo* (family-centredness) and *personalismo* (relationship-centred leadership), and modern aspirations for regional economic integration. Ultimately, these traits define how Dominican leaders interact with those they lead within their organisations.

How the Dominicans characterise leaders?

Leadership within the Dominican Republic is deeply influenced by its cultural heritage, familial values, and historical traditions. Within the Dominican Republic, the authoritarian legacy of past regimes has left an indelible mark upon leadership styles and practices, fostering a culture characterised by both hierarchical structures and caution. Known as *caudillismo* (strongman rule), this tradition has ingrained a wariness within Dominicans, who often view others with caution and are generally sceptical about others' motives within professional settings (Diaz, 2011). Unsurprisingly, research shows that Dominicans tend to favour autocratic management styles (Cropanzano et al., 1999). Related to this, Dominican leaders are often seen as paternalistic figures by their employees, a point which reflects the family-centric nature of many businesses within the country. This familialism is also espied in the fact that leadership roles frequently pass from generation to generation, thus prioritising loyalty, and interpersonal relationships over formal qualifications (Badia, 2011). As a respondent in the CCBS Survey (2024) noted: *"Most companies are family-owned and therefore passed down to children without taking their skills into account, which proves to be an obstacle for companies to achieve their full potential."* This approach underscores a preference for relational trust, or *confianza*, as the foundation of professional interactions. Notwithstanding this, Dominicans also tend to favour leaders that balance authority with warmth and empathy, with leaders expected to be assertive and motivational whilst maintaining harmonious interpersonal relationships. *Personalismo* encourages this people-oriented management style where leaders are approachable and involved in the lives of employees (De La Sota & Zaino, 2018). Furthermore, Dominican leaders often rely upon a high-context communication style, where non-verbal cues and implicit understanding play key roles. This preference aligns with a societal tendency for avoiding direct confrontation, in order to ensure harmony and mutual respect within workplace interactions (Montesino, 2002). The Dominican population is predominantly Catholic, and, indeed, the very first cathedral in the Americas was built in Santo Domingo. Both religion and the country's colonial past have played a pivotal role in terms of how the country's business landscape has developed over time, especially religion, which has contributed towards a leadership culture that values discretion and adaptability (Diaz, 2011). In conclusion, leadership within the Dominican Republic reflects a dynamic interplay of traditional values and modern practices, rooted in familial loyalty, interpersonal trust, and an evolving adaptability to contemporary North American influences.

Survey results and what local respondents say

Dominican executives with multiple years of leadership experience within Dominican organisations participated in the CCBS Survey (2024) in order to enrich our understanding of leadership dynamics within the country. This section presents key findings emerging from the responses of over 70 respondents. In order to enhance both the generalisability and validity of the findings, we have opted to draw upon data from a previous period of data collection (CCBS Survey, 2017) as well as this year's survey data (CCBS Survey, 2024). The most significant findings will be discussed in turn below. The first key finding from the survey is that the respondents confirmed the hierarhical nature of leadership within the Dominican Republic, whilst, simultaenously, still maintaining a people-oriented focus (CCBS Survey, 2024). This is in accordance with the research of Montesino (2002), who also argued that a top-down leadership approach prevails within the country. One of the respondents elaborated upon this, noting that: *"the Dominican Republic has a paternalistic management style, whilst still maintaining a high level of respect and hierarchy, as leaders maintain a very formal relationship with their subordinates, also outside of the work floor."* This formal dimension to leadership in the Dominican Republic was also confirmed by the fact that the respondents were in broad agreement over the importance of subordinates addressing leaders by either their titles or positions (CCBS Survey, 2024). Further support for this comes from the fact that 25% of the respondents indicated that a strong charismatic personality is the most important trait for Dominican leaders to possess, whilst 56% of the respondents indicated they do not prefer to hear criticism in an indirect manner, outside of staff meetings. This sentiment was shared by one of the survey respondents, who explained that: *"Criticism in general and specifically personal criticism is not tolerated; it is not appreciated and is seen as a personal attack and public humiliation."* The next noteworhty finding pertains to the people-oriented nature of Dominican leadership, which was evidenced by the fact that the vast majority of the respondents reported that it is very important for leaders to spend time actively ensuring the well-being of their team members. This aspect of Dominican leadership was also illustrated by Victor Mendez (CCBS Survey, 2017), a senior Audit Manager, who opined: *"leadership in the Dominican Republic is evolving, with trends differing from other cultures. The emphasis upon fostering a close relationship between staff and their manager is seen as highly important"*. The third significant finding emerging from the survey results concerns the importance placed upon decisiveness in leaders' decision-making processes. This was evidenced by the fact that the majority of the respondents agreed that once a manager makes a decision, they are unlikely to easily alter it (CCBS Survey, 2024). This indicates a preference for firm leadership as well as respect for authoritative decision-making processes, which is in accordance with Montesino´s (2002) framing of leadership in the Dominican Republic. The final key finding is that there is a strong emphasis upon adhering to deadlines within the Dominican Republic, with failure to do so being perceived as tantamount to failure (CCBS Survey 2024).

Local leadership analysis

Hayrold José Ureña Espaillat: a Dominican leadership scholar

In order to gain deeper insight into leadership within the Dominican leadership, we conducted an interview with Hayrold José Ureña-Espaillat, a Dominican scholar, who wrote the research paper entitled *"Knowledge and innovation management in agribusiness: A study in the Dominican Republic"* (Ureña-Espaillat et al., 2022). In that paper, he discusses the impact of knowledge management as an integrating element for sustainable development. Alongside his scholarship, Mr. Ureña-Espaillat is also the Director of fuels at the Dominican *"Ministerio de Industria, Comercio y Mipymes"* (Ministry of Industry, Commerce and MSMEs). He specialises in project and social management, and completed his PhD in Management Sciences at the *Universidad Politécnica* in Cartagena (Ureña Espaillat, 24 April 2024). At the start of our interview, Mr. Ureña-Espaillat explicated that the Dominican Republic, despite its small size, is the third most popular tourist destination within Latin America, and is a highly smart and dynamic country with its own particular rhythm. This, combined with the level of migration occurring in the Dominican Republic at this juncture, has had a profound impact upon business leadership skills and practices within the country. In response to a question about what distinguishes leaders in the Dominican Republic from their international counterparts, he responded that they have extensive cultural knowledge (Ureña Espaillat, 24 April 2024). Next, he proceeded to explain that because of these cultural differences, leaders have to regularly deal with an extensive array of different communication styles. In light of this, Dominican leaders have had to develop excellent communication skills, and, most importantly, become more empathic in their approach; that is to say, they respect everyone for who they are (Ureña-Espaillat, 24 April 2024). Later in the interview, Mr. Ureña-Espaillat moved onto discuss the issue of hierarchical structures within the Dominican Republic, noting that: "U*nfortunately, and from the perspective of organisations in the past, the leader was a hierarchical figure*" (Ureña-Espaillat, 24 April 2024). However, today, the hierarchy is more horizontal than it was in previous years, in as far as everyone collaborates with one another and employees trust each other, albeit there are still clear rules that must be followed. Next, when asked about what specific characteristics Dominican leaders possess, Mr. Ureña-Espaillat responded that Dominican leaders are assertive, clear, honest, and, most importantly, serve as a source of motivation for their employees. As he himself put it: *"To be able to create an environment that is not a work environment. But when people sit down to do tasks that are not so routine, that they can promote creativity, there is that internal [and] external motivation that has to be operationalised"* (Ureña-Espaillat, 24 April 2024). He proceeded to inform us that although Dominican leadership is transformational in nature in that they are clear, grounded, and result-oriented, knowledge, creativity, training, and motivation are also essential attributes that must be present within any Dominican company. Having said this, he also concluded by telling us that the truth about Dominican leaders is that just like all people, they are all different: *"If I told you that there is a rule of thumb for this, I would be lying to you"* (Ureña Espaillat, 24 April 2024).

Social Media Review

Social media within the Dominican Republic underscores the evolving nature of leadership, with both leaders and organisations using various platforms to inspire change, share insights, and shape narratives around Dominican leadership development. Ligia Bonetti, CEO of Grupo SID, exemplifies this by emphasising, *"Leadership is not synonymous with popularity but with conviction"* (Bonetti, n.d.). Her advocacy for transformative practices reflects how Dominican leaders must strike the requisite balance between global challenges and local needs. Platforms like Instagram and YouTube also serve to amplify grassroots perspectives, such as, for example, *Impulsa Tu Liderazgo RD*, which promotes transformational leadership by inspiring future leaders and fostering inclusivity (Impulsa Tu Liderazgo RD, 2023). On LinkedIn, Francisco Javier García illustrates how strategic leadership within tourism has propelled the Dominican Republic's economy to regional prominence (TurismoRD, 2023). Social media also celebrates cultural identity. Figures like Gwendolyn Siegel reflect upon family values, resilience, and community as key constitute elements of their leadership journeys, thus demonstrating how cultural authenticity fosters a sense of belonging and trust with those one leads (Siegel, 2024). Through these digital platforms, Dominican leaders showcase their ability to collaborate, and inspire, thus providing a window into a leadership culture that is both locally grounded and globally engaged.

In-country leadership bestseller

"El espíritu del emprendedor dominicano y factores que lo construyen" (*The spirit of the Dominican Entrepreneur and the factors that shape it*), written by Barna Management School, is the culmination of five years of research. This collaborative effort involved contributions from various members of Barna's academic community, including, amongst other figures, the rector, professors, and master's students. The book sets out to inspire the nation's youth and provide a roadmap for the Dominican Republic's development. Throughout the course of the book, Dominican entrepreneurs are portrayed as bold, persistent, risk-taking, and deeply passionate about their respective entrepreneurial ventures. These qualities, in turn, enable them to overcome obstacles and navigate the manifold challenges of entrepreneurship within an environment often characterised by uncertainty and resource limitations. Optimism and self-confidence are the defining traits of these individuals and are reflective of their belief in their ability to succeed. This positive mindset empowers them to confront difficulties head-on and persevere, even in the face of tremendous adversity. Moreover, their self-assurance fosters trust amongst stakeholders, whether they be customers, investors, or business partners. Fernando Barrero, a professor, and the academic director at Barna Management School, asserts that in the era of the Fourth Industrial Revolution, prosperity lies within fostering research and cultivating an ecosystem that empowers more entrepreneurs and students to become future leaders. This perspective aligns with findings from Deloitte, as highlighted by senior consultant Cameron Diaz, which emphasise that strong leadership is the cornerstone of entrepreneurial success. Leaders who inspire trust, and foster collaboration are essential for navigating the challenges of an ever-evolving global landscape. By nurturing such leadership, the Dominican Republic can not only empower its entrepreneurial spirit but also shape a future generation of visionaries who are capable of driving progress for the nation.

Local leadership book		
Title	*El espíritu emprendedor Dominicano*	
Subtitle	Los factores que lo construyen	
Author	Barna Management School	
Publisher	Barna Management School	
Year	2019	
ISBN	9789945096248	

Dominican Leadership YouTube Review

Alongside academic research and primary data, YouTube also offers unique insights into Dominican leadership, showcasing how local leaders balance collaboration, adaptability, and tradition. This section reviews videos that shed light upon the strategic approaches that define leadership within the Dominican Republic. Raúl Burgos is the founder of the initiative *"Dominicana se Transforma"* (The Dominican Republic Transforms). He joined the Dominican talk show *Esta Noche Mariasela* (2023), where he and the host Mariasela talked about what makes a good leader and what specific traits and attributes are required within the Dominican context. In this video, he shares that good leaders in the Dominican Republic must not only work with their teams, but also influence and inspire them. Hence, the characteristics of what makes a good Dominican leader are being knowledgeable, which, in turn, helps influence their teams, in addition to always staying positive: they should never make excuses or complain. As he put it: *"Nadie quiere seguir a alguien que se esté quejando [y] que esté haciendo excusas"* (*"No one wants to follow someone who complains and who makes excuses"*). Dominican leaders should also possess and be able to communicate to others a clear vision along with exhibiting a contagious passion for this vision, never settling but rather always striving for ways to improve further. Notwithstanding the importance of these aforementioned attributes and behaviours, Burgos also stated that leaders need good teams behind them, before then proceeding to explain that before one becomes a leader, one must first be a follower, in order to watch and learn and implement these best practices in the future (Esta Noche Marisela, 2023). The second interview to be summarised here is another interview with Raúl Burgos, this time on the Super7fm (2023). In this interview, he stated that if leaders within the Dominican Republic do not show their vulnerability, and, in other words, who they really are inside, then they are not empathic and they will never inspire people: *"Eres un líder porque te dieron la posición y ejerces esa actividad, pero no eres un líder en el sentido real de la palabra"* (*"You are a leader because you were given the position and you exercise that activity, but you are not a leader in the real meaning of the word"*). He then proceeded to delineate that a true Dominican leader is someone who wants to develop you as a person and, as such, is followed by people voluntarily. More specifically, this must be someone who has a vision and a sense of direction, and who allows their subordinates to help them create the path to achieving their vision. His perspective thus highlights the adaptability of Dominican leaders, which complements the aforementioned collaborative approach.

Understanding hierarchy in the Dominican Republic

The Dominican Republic's leadership approach is deeply rooted in its cultural and historical foundations, which emphasise respect for authority and hierarchy. Influenced by its Roman Catholic heritage—which also underscores respect for authority—as well as the legacy of *caudillismo* (strongman rule), Dominican society has developed a culture characterised by centralised forms of decision-making and caution within leadership practices (Betances, 2004). Historically, the Catholic Church's alignment with political power embedded hierarchical values within society, which remain discernible within organisational structures today (Bedggood, 2016). Indeed, leaders within the Dominican Republic are viewed as authority figures, whilst respect for their position is deeply ingrained within workplace culture. Interestingly, this hierarchy is not always overtly observable due to the friendly and casual nature of the interactions between individuals of different levels of seniority. However, it becomes evident during decision-making processes, where the opinions of those in higher positions carries significantly more weight than those of their subordinates (CCBS Survey, 2020).

Communication is often indirect, particularly with respect to sensitive matters, which reflects the cultural preference for subtlety and discretion (Montesino, 2002; Becker, 2011). Hofstede's Power Distance Index provides a useful lens through which to examine these dynamics. With a Power Distance score of 65, the Dominican Republic demonstrates a strong preference for structured authority, where leaders are seen as paternalistic figures who foster loyalty and a familial atmosphere within their teams (Lebrón Rolón, 2008). This hierarchical inclination is reinforced within family-owned businesses, which are the cornerstone of the Dominican economy. These enterprises thrive upon loyalty and trusted group ties, reflecting the collectivist nature of the culture (Díaz, 2011). A study by PUCMM University demonstrated that 22% of Latin American employees surveyed accepted preferential treatment for family members within business settings, thus underscoring the role of familial loyalty within workplace dynamics. Professional titles also hold significant weight within Dominican workplaces. As Dávila and Elvira (2005) observe, titles such as *Licenciado* or *Ingeniero* are essential for establishing authority and respect within workplace relationships. This aligns with the findings from question 16 of CCBS' Global Leadership Survey, where a large majority of the respondents either strongly or somewhat agreed that *"it is important for subordinates to address leaders by their titles"* (CCBS Survey, 2024). These formalities, in turn, influence decision-making, communication styles, and interpersonal dynamics, thus reinforcing the organisational hierarchy. Whilst a participative management style is beginning to gain some traction in the country, particularly within multinational corporations, many organisations in the Dominican Republic retain traditional hierarchical structures. Hence, leaders accustomed to centralised authority may find the evolving demands of a globalised market challenging, in as far as participative leadership styles foster diversity and encourage open communication channels (Badia, 2011). Despite these changes, the dominance of high power distance and authoritative management styles continue to present challenges to inclusivity, particularly with respect to women's ability to attain leadership positions. However, some progress is evident as female representation is continuing to grow across various sectors, thus seemingly reflecting a gradual shift towards greater gender equity in the country (World Trade Press, 2010). This balance between tradition and modernity continues to define the hierarchical landscape of Dominican organisations. Dominican leaders must demonstrate resilience and adaptability to navigate the challenges the country faces, whilst, simultaneously, implementing innovative strategies. Within this high-context culture, communication remains deeply nuanced, relying on non-verbal cues and implicit understanding rather than direct statements. These subtleties underscore the importance of balancing respect for tradition with adaptability in order to thrive within an increasingly interconnected world.

How the Dominicans achieve leadership empathy

Dominican leadership combines traditional hierarchical influences with a growing emphasis upon empathy and participative management approaches. Montesino (2002) observes that managerial styles within the Dominican Republic often reflect authoritarian tendencies that are deeply rooted within cultural respect for authority. However, there is a discernible shift at the present juncture, with empathy emerging as a crucial element in terms of enhancing both employee morale and loyalty. Leaders who can strike the requisite balance between authority and gaining an understanding of their employees' personal needs, will secure higher levels of workplace engagement (Montesino, 2002). Moreover, leaders are encouraged to adopt a "ground-up" approach, as Sepulveda de Jesús explains: "*When you start too high in the career ladder, you do not acquire the skills to work with people at lower levels*" (23 March 2017). This philosophy underscores the importance of Dominican leaders taking the time and possessing the skills that are needed to understand the challenges faced by their employees across all levels of the organisation, in as far as it enables them to foster genuine connections and empathy with their subordinates. The historical preference for the paternalistic approach also means that empathy has always featured as a critical component of Dominican leadership. Leaders who take the time to understand the unique needs and motivations of their employees can provide tailored incentives, in addition to building greater trust within their teams. As José Guzmán, a digital marketing leader, noted, "*Leadership is about people's care, both professional and personal. Taking care of your team and leading by example is the most powerful tool*" (CCBS Survey, 2024). Similarly, Gustavo (2024, October 3), a Mexican leadership expert, opines that Dominican leaders are defined by a unique blend of energy, closeness, and empathy, which, in turn, enables them to connect deeply with both their teams and communities. The article "*El nuevo liderazgo dominicano: Un modelo caribeño que inspira*" discusses the evolution of leadership within the Dominican Republic, underscoring a shift towards a more empathetic and inclusive approach in recent years. This empathetic leadership style has, in turn, led to increased employee engagement and organisational success, thus serving as an inspiring model within the Caribbean region. This emphasis upon interpersonal relationships is also reflective of the warmth and informality of Dominican culture more generally, where conversational slang such as "*¿Qué lo qué?*" (what's going on?) reinforces a sense of closeness (Suriel, 2023). The importance of empathy is also observed by Vázquez (2010), who, in his talk

"La felicidad en el trabajo" (Happiness at work), stresses that investing in employee happiness is essential for achieving successful outcomes. Vázquez argues that characteristics such as confidence and autonomy are more impactful than technical skills, thus purporting that Dominican leaders should prioritise understanding their teams. He draws a direct correlation between employee satisfaction and customer satisfaction, asserting that internal workplace harmony is often reflected externally within business success. This approach fosters inclusivity and collaboration (Vázquez, 2010). In conclusion, Dominican leadership empathy is characterised by respect for cultural values, and a deep commitment towards personal and professional care. This distinctive blend of *simpatico* attentiveness and resilience ensures that Dominican leaders know how to drive success within their organisations.

El Salvador

Youssra Azzofri, Isabel Burillo Alba, Laila Ekinci, Shaqeel Nasibdar, Nelson Torres, Ian Verkade

República de El Salvador (The Republic of El Salvador) is the most densely populated nation within Central America. The name "El Salvador" itself, which refers to *"The Saviour"* in English, is a direct reference to God, thus reflecting the nation's deep Christian roots; approximately three-quarters of Salvadorans identify as Christian (*El Salvador - United States Department of State*, 2023). This Latin-American country exhibits a diverse ethnic composition, with the majority of the population identifying as *Mestizo*, a heritage reflecting a blend of European and Indigenous ancestry. The largest minority group in the country white, whilst the remainder of the population includes Indigenous tribes such as the *Izalco* and the *Pancho* (Aizpurua-Iraola et al., 2023). The Salvadoran people are widely recognised for their sociable, easy-going, and hospitable nature. These qualities also extend to their business leadership styles, which often take on a paternalistic inflection in which leaders prioritise the welfare and protect their employees, thus fostering a supportive and nurturing work environment (Sanchez, 2000). As El Salvador has undergone rapid economic development, the country has come to place greater emphasis upon cultivating its future leaders.

One example of a notable economic milestone took place in 2021, when President Nayib Bukele announced that El Salvador, and its population of 6.4 million people, would become the first nation in the world to adopt Bitcoin as its official national currency (Alfaro et al., 2024). In the same year, this Spanish-speaking country experienced significant economic growth and has maintained a steady upward trend in GDP ever since (*El Salvador Overview*, 2024). To support the advancement of leadership skills and practices within the country, educational initiatives such as the *Líderes Inspirando Futuro y Éxito* (LIFE) program have been introduced. This program specifically aims to enhance the current management competencies and cultivate conditions to improve leadership for future generations of Salvadorans (Schmalenbach et al., 2022). In this chapter, we will examine in-depth the nuances of Salvadoran leadership styles through recourse to reviewing academic literature and analysing survey and interviews data with local leaders, scholars and experts.

How the Salvadorans characterise leaders?

According to Flores-Hernández et al. (2022), a significant proportion of businesses in El Salvador are family-run. Their research highlights that these enterprises often employ an autocratic and centralised decision-making style. In practice, this leadership approach involves a hierarchical structure in which decisions are predominantly made by senior-level figures with minimal input from lower-ranking members of the organisation (Flores-Hernández et al., 2022).

This characterisation of Salvadoran leadership was corroborated by the results of the CCBS Survey (2024), which demonstrated that leadership styles in El Salvador are primarily autocratic and paternalistic in nature. Flores-Hernández et al. (2022) explain that this autocratic tendency is deeply embedded within the cultural context of Salvadoran family businesses, where loyalty to the family is prioritised and intertwined with business operations. The presence of multiple generations working within these family enterprises, coupled with the inclusion of non-family managers, creates additional challenges, however. Specifically, non-family managers often have limited influence over strategic decision-making processes. In contrast, non-family organisations, such as those in the Maquila factory sector, tend to prioritise more task-oriented outcomes and short-term efficiency, which, in turn, also leads to centralised forms of decision-making (Soler et al., 2016).

The GLOBE study provides additional insight into Salvadoran leadership by virtue of underscoring the country's strong collectivist cultural values, where leaders are expected to prioritise group and community welfare over individual goals (Segundo, 2022). Above all, these collectivist norms emphasise respect for hierarchy and authority. Leaders who exhibit transformational leadership styles can thus gain appreciation from their employees if their approach aligns with these cultural expectations. However, this is complicated further by the fact that any efforts to reduce the level of power distance between leaders and employees within organisations in El Salvador, by, for example, fostering informality or closeness with subordinates, may be perceived as a sign of weakness on the behalf of leaders (Segundo, 2022).

This is because, generally speaking, leaders are expected to project strength, decisiveness, and confidence, reflecting the cultural preference for maintaining clear power dynamics. Thus, leaders who attempt to minimise this distance by adopting a more casual or informal demeanour risk undermining their authority (Kallmer, 2024). Consequently, Salvadoran leaders face the challenge of balancing transformational leadership techniques that resonate with collectivist values while maintaining the authoritative presence expected by their followers. This self-protectionism is also echoed in the fact that Salvadoran leaders are often resistant to criticism expressed outside formal settings. Despite this, however, the results of the CCBS Survey (2024) also demonstrate that Salvadoran leaders tend to invest time in ensuring the personal well-being of their teams, albeit the results of the survey also showed divergent preferences amongst the respondents regarding the degree of personal distance leaders should maintain from their employees (CCBS Survey, 2024), which again points to the aforementioned balancing act that Salvadoran leaders need to negotiate (Segundo, 2022). Finally, data from the LAPOP project conducted by Vanderbilt University indicates that Salvadorans ultimately tend to value leaders who uphold order, security, and respect for established authority figures (Córdova Macías et al., 2013). Especially during periods of uncertainty, Salvadoran leaders are expected to make decisive choices that promote stability within their communities and organisations.

This expectation reinforces a preference for strong, directive leadership and top-down management styles, which was also found in the CCBS Survey (2024), as over half of the respondents expressed a preference for leaders who possess powerful decision-making capabilities. Collectively, these traits frame Salvadoran leadership as diverse, encompassing a blended style that merges authoritarian tendencies with a community-centred approach. Leaders are expected to both serve as role models, uphold familial and community values, and act as anchors of stability.

Survey results and what local respondents say

Sixty-four Salvadoran C-level executives and managers provided their insights on leadership styles and practices in El Salvador by completing the CCBS Survey (2024). The findings below offer valuable perspectives upon the prevailing leadership approaches adopted within the country. To examine various dimensions of leadership in El Salvador, the respondents were asked to reflect upon the factors that distinguish Salvadoran leadership from that of other nations. The results indicate that leadership in El Salvador remains predominantly influenced by hierarchical and authoritarian models. However, with the rise of younger generations, this dynamic is evolving. As one respondent noted, "*En El Salvador, en las generaciones de +50 años, muchas veces existe un liderazgo muy vertical, con el objetivo de que haya respeto, no obstante, esto está cambiando y las generaciones millennials estamos propiciando un liderazgo más horizontal, involucrando en la toma de decisiones*" ("*In El Salvador, amongst individuals over the age of 50, leadership is often characterised by a vertical structure, with an emphasis on maintaining respect. However, this dynamic is shifting, as the millennial generation is advocating for a more horizontal leadership approach, which involves greater participation in the decision-making process"*) (CCBS Survey, 2024). Equally important in this regard is the emphasis that the respondents in this survey placed upon prioritising the personal well-being of their subordinates. Overall, 96 percent of the respondents agreed with the statement that managers in El Salvador should dedicate time to actively ensuring the personal well-being of their team members (CCBS Survey, 2024). As one respondent observed, *"Generalmente, los líderes en El Salvador nos destacamos por tener un enfoque de integración y cohesión del equipo, para que todos se sientan valorados y lograr sacar lo mejor de cada miembro"* (*"Generally, leaders in El Salvador are distinguished by their focus on team integration and cohesion, ensuring that all members feel valued and helping to bring out the best in each individual"*) (CCBS Survey, 2024). Furthermore, the relationship between leaders and subordinates appears to reflect a degree of informality between leaders and their employees, in as far as 80 percent of the respondents indicated that employees are permitted to address their leaders by their first names. However, when asked about the importance placed upon the use of formal titles, only 56 percent disagreed with the necessity for them to be used, which perhaps is indicative of a gradual shift towards more approachable leadership styles and enhanced team cohesion. With respect to the traits and qualitie preferred in leaders, the vast majority of the respondents agreed that leaders are expected to be strong decision-makers. Further support for this comes from the fact that more than half of the respondents indicated that once a manager has made a decision, they are unlikely to change it (CCBS Survey, 2024). Furthermore, leaders are expected to possess a range of other qualities, including being good listeners, visionary thinkers, and having a strong, charismatic personality, high level of commitment, high intellect, and access to valuable networks (CCBS Survey, 2024). Notwithstanding these qualities, leaders are also expected to actively promote the personal well-being of their employees, motivate them, and create an environment in which all team members feel welcome and at ease. In recent years, the number of female leaders has also increased, albeit there are ongoing debates amongst Salvadorans regarding whether men and women truly have equal opportunities in attaining leadership positions, which was echoed in the survey results also. This division may also reflect differing perspectives upon leadership styles, as stated by one of our respondents, Vanessa Lara, a CEO, who stated: *"El liderazgo femenino es más cercano, inclusivo y enfocado en resultados, la gente se cohesiona más"* (*"Female leadership is more approachable, inclusive, and result-oriented, leading to greater cohesion among people"*). In conclusion, it is evident that assuming a leadership role in El Salvador is not an easy task, and not accessible to everyone. In this context, it is the employees who select their leader, rather than the leader selecting their employees. This dynamic was exemplified by one respondent, a CEO, who articulated the essential qualities of a Salvadoran leader as follows: *"Leadership in El Salvador often combine adaptability and strong community ties. Leaders are accustomed to navigating challenges with limited resources and emphasise personal connections to build trust and loyalty. This approach, shaped by social and economic realities, distinguishes Salvadoran leadership with its practical and people-first focus"* (CCBS Survey, 2024).

Local leadership analysis

Mauricio Umana: A Salvadoran leadership scholar

Dr. Mauricio Umana, a distinguished scholar from El Salvador who holds a PhD in Business Competitiveness and Economic Development from the University of Deusto in Spain, has devoted numerous years to studying business leadership. With extensive experience in corporate environments, policymaking, and lecturing at prestigious institutions such as Harvard University, Dr. Umana provides a unique perspective on the evolution of leadership in El Salvador as well as the cultural dynamics that shape it. At the beginning of the interview, Umana reflected upon what defines a 'typical' business leader in El Salvador, ultimately, identifying two primary leadership archetypes in the country: the *'transformational leader'* and the *'anti-leader'* (15 November 2024). He explained that transformational leaders are characterised by their clarity, integrity, and widespread recognition, both domestically and internationally. He stated that *"Este líder íntegro, a quien llamo el "líder de la transparencia", se caracteriza por ser profundamente transformador gracias a su honestidad y valores sólidos"* (This leader of integrity, whom I call the 'leader of transparency,' is characterised by their honesty and strong values and is profoundly transformative") (15 November 2024). In contrast, he argued that anti-leaders, whilst often successful in accumulating power, tend to erode trust through unethical practices such as corruption and manipulation (Umana, 15 November 2024). This dichotomy underscores a broader tension between authentic leadership and self-serving opportunism within the country. Dr. Umana then proceeded to stress that Salvadoran leaders are profoundly influenced by their cultural context, with many Salvadorans exhibiting common characteristics within their communication, thinking, and behaviour. He noted that these shared traits foster a sense of unity, but also contribute towards a rigid, fixed perspective (Umana, 15 November 2024). He moved onto say that approximately 80 percent of leaders in El Salvador continue to adopt an autocratic leadership style, which is consistent with the hierarchical structure prevalent within most organisations. The continued persistence of autocratic leadership can be attributed to the entrenched organisational frameworks. However, Dr. Umana expressed his dissatisfaction with this approach, arguing that it hinders the introduction of innovative ideas as well as the ability to adapt in a constantly evolving global landscape. Furthermore, when foreign leaders assume roles in El Salvador, Dr. Umana (15 November 2024) emphasised the importance of understanding local expectations. He identified three key attributes for success: respecting cultural norms, demonstrating humility, and maintaining a polished appearance (Umana, 15 November 2024). In relation to this, he noted that Salvadorans appreciate approachable yet professional leaders and view arrogance or disregard for local traditions as significant missteps. Later, Dr. Umana (15 November 2024) discussed that he has observed a gradual, albeit slow, shift towards more inclusive and empathetic leadership approaches. Whilst traditional, top-down hierarchies continue to dominate, more leaders are experimenting with models that prioritise collaboration and transparency. These emerging practices align with global leadership trends, focusing on fostering empathy and empowering teams. When asked about gender equity, Dr. Umana (15 November 2024) noted some progress with respect to the expanding leadership roles for women. However, he stated that challenges such as favouritism and superficial judgments based on appearance persist. He asserted that genuine meritocracy requires dismantling these biases and ensuring that skills and competencies take precedence over superficial attributes (Umana, 15 November 2024). When asked about empathy, Dr. Umana highlighted that it is a cornerstone of effective leadership and stressed the importance of leaders establishing genuine connections with their teams, maintaining open communication, and valuing diverse perspectives. He argued that leaders who prioritise these relationships can build cohesive, resilient teams even within hierarchical structures (Umana, 15 November 2024). However, Dr. Umana also cited the rigidity of traditional Salvadoran organisational structures as representing a major barrier to progress, arguing that the 'top-down' leadership style that is upheld by longstanding educational and workplace norms, undermines innovation and collaboration. To remain competitive, he advocates for flatter, more transparent organisational models that empower teams and encourage continuous learning (Umana, 15 November 2024). In conclusion, Dr. Umana underscored the importance of making leadership development more accessible, and that by sharing knowledge and best practices, El Salvador can inspire leadership transformations not only within the country but also on a global scale (15 November 2024).

Guillermo Felix Dardano: a Salvadoran cross-cultural trainer

Guillermo Felix Dardano, a certified cross-cultural coach, possesses extensive expertise in corporate and executive training, including within El Salvador. Drawing upon his broad professional experience across Central America, Europe, and the United States, Dardano analyses leadership through a historical lens, exploring its influence on leadership models in the region. With qualifications as an Intercultural Coach and over a decade of experience in sales and marketing within the agricultural sector in El Salvador, Dardano provides valuable insights into Salvadoran leadership styles. At the outset of the interview, Dardano (21 November 2024) noted that Salvadoran leaders exemplify resilience and adaptability, shaped by historical challenges like the Civil War and struggles with gang violence. Despite these adversities, El Salvador boasts strong business leaders who play a crucial role in the nation's progress. Dardano noted that leadership in El Salvador is undergoing significant transformations, particularly under the influence of President Nayib Bukele (21 November 2024). He further emphasised that Salvadoran leadership, whilst deeply rooted in Latin American cultural traditions, has begun to integrate modern Western management practices. In contrast to the often-impersonal leadership styles seen in certain European or U.S. contexts, Salvadoran leaders maintain a visible and respected presence, cultivating strong relationships with their teams (Dardano, 21 November 2024). When asked about empathy in leadership, Dardano stated that *"It is a cornerstone of Salvadoran leadership"* (21 November 2024). He proceeded to explain that leaders engage closely with their employees, demonstrate genuine concern for their well-being via both small gestures, such as inquiring about their families, and broader initiatives that support their professional and personal lives. However, Dardano (21 November 2024) emphasised that leaders must exercise impartiality to avoid fostering divisions within their teams. Nonetheless, Dardano (21 November 2024) stressed that many Salvadoran companies remain entrenched within traditional, family-dominated leadership structures, where decision-making is centralised amongst family-led boards or tightly knit management groups. Whilst this model provides stability, it often stifles innovation and limits opportunities for employees in lower positions to contribute towards decision-making processes. A lack of investment in employee development is another significant obstacle, according to Dardano, as companies are reluctant to fund training programs due to concerns about high turnover rates. Consequently, talented individuals frequently seek opportunities abroad, resulting in a brain drain. However, improved safety conditions in the country and government support have begun to attract skilled workers back to El Salvador. Later in the interview, Dardano (21 November 2024) stated that there was a growing presence of women within leadership roles, particularly in sectors like agroindustry and textiles, since they often serve as primary income earners in single-parent households. According to Dardano (21 November 2024), this shift reflects gradual progress in prioritising merit and performance over traditional family ties. Furthermore, he stated that *"La era digital está transformando profundamente el liderazgo en El Salvador. La adopción de Bitcoin y la influencia de las redes sociales han transformado la dinámica del lugar de trabajo y dotado a las generaciones más jóvenes de herramientas innovadoras"* (*"The digital age is profoundly reshaping leadership in El Salvador. The adoption of Bitcoin and the pervasive influence of social media have transformed workplace dynamics and empowered younger generations with innovative tools"*. He underscored the resilience of Salvadoran workers, which has driven advancements in sectors like aviation and international business. As businesses transition from traditional agricultural models to more diversified and globalised operations, leaders are adapting to meet new demands. Whilst challenges persist—particularly in fostering innovation and retraining skilled employees—leadership in El Salvador is evolving positively. Dardano (21 November 2024) concluded that Salvadoran leaders must balance respect for their cultural heritage with the need to adapt to a globalised world. Leaders who embrace empathy, innovation, and inclusivity will play a pivotal role in the country's growth. By building trust and empowering its citizens, El Salvador has the potential to establish a distinctive and successful model of leadership on the global stage.

In-country leadership bestseller

Juana Bordas' *The Power of Latino Leadership: Culture, Inclusion, and Contribution* (2023) is a best-selling work that provides a perspective on leadership through the lens of Latino culture and experience. This book offers the first comprehensive leadership model grounded in the values and traditions of the Latino community. Bordas, who emigrated from Nicaragua to the U.S. at a young age, draws extensively from her personal journey to explore the factors that shaped her leadership aspirations. As the president of Mestiza Leadership International, a firm specialising in leadership development, diversity, and organisational transformation, Bordas integrates her own professional expertise. Her narrative examines the formative impact of her upbringing upon her leadership philosophy and the questions that drove her to pursue leadership. (Brunner, 2023). *The Power of Latino Leadership* provides an in-depth examination of leadership principles rooted in Latino culture. The book highlights the distinctive attributes and values that Latinos contribute towards leadership, advocating for a framework that is inclusive, community-focused, and socially conscious (Publishers & Bordas, n.d.).

Bordas outlines ten core principles that exemplify the unique and impactful qualities of Latino leadership, not only exploring how to lead as a Latino but also examining its cultural origins. Central to her discussion are fundamental values such as family, community, and mutual care, which are emphasised as cornerstones of effective leadership. The book underscores how these principles foster inclusive and impactful leadership styles, grounded in collaboration and cultural pride (Peace Corps Worldwide, n.d.). The book also examines essential traits such as mentorship, resilience, the rich heritage of activism within Latino communities and the importance of such qualities which can help someone become a better *'Latino'* leader. This book resonates with leadership perspectives in El Salvador, particularly those reflected within initiatives like the LIFE program, which was implemented by universities in the region to promote the social-emotional development of university students in El Salvador via specialised courses on transformational and servant leadership (Schmalenbach et al., 2022). Furthermore, research investigating the mediating role of leadership in El Salvador and Nicaragua underscored that *"leadership is a process of collective social influence, in which leaders and followers are partners"* (Moriano León et al., 2009, p. 669). These perspectives resonate with the themes explored in Bordas' work, particularly her focus on cultivating the most effective and inclusive forms of leadership in the region.

Local leadership book	
Title	*The power of Latino leadership*
Subtitle	Culture, Inclusion and Contribution
Author	Juana Bordas
Publisher	Berret-Khoeler Publishers
Year	2023
ISBN	9781523004089

Salvadoran leadership YouTube review

Juana Bordas actively disseminates her knowledge to inspire and empower others in becoming effective Latino leaders. In the podcast *'Deep Leadership'* (2023), hosted by leadership author Jon S. Rennie, Bordas discussed the underrepresentation of Latino leaders and shares her perspectives on related topics. She began the discussion by defining her concept of leadership as follows: *"Leaders create a society that takes care of its people"* (Bordas, 2023, 08:59). Bordas then proceeded to stress the importance of community within Latino leadership, emphasising that in Latino culture, leadership is collective rather than individualistic in nature. This is reflected in the way that Latinos treat others with respect, irrespective of their social or professional standing. Furthermore, Bordas underscored that Latinos constitute a culture, not a race, positioning them as a model for diversity and inclusion. As a multicultural paradigm, Latino leadership embodies inclusivity, where all individuals are regarded as equals, and the identity of the leader is not always readily apparent. Whilst elders are respected, they are also considered equals within the group. Bordas asserted that *"every person can learn Latino leadership; you just have to open your corazón (heart) to it"* (Bordas, 2023, 16:21). The perspective Bordas shares about Latino leadership, appears to resonate with the wider Salvadorian community. For instance, the CCBS survey (2024) indicates that approximately seventy percent of the respondents align with the view that leadership in El Salvador typically emphasises strength, decisiveness, and confidence. These traits reflect the cultural preference for clear power dynamics and focusing upon the well-being of employees. However, it is essential to note that not all organisations or leaders adhere to this model. For example, in our interview with Dr. Umana, he remarked, *"In El Salvador, approximately 80 percent of leaders still follow an autocratic leadership style, which aligns with the highly vertical structure of most organizations"* (15 November 2024). This illustrates that, whilst leadership practices are evolving, many companies continue to uphold traditional, hierarchical approaches to leadership. In a separate podcast led by Jenn De Wall (Weaving Influence, 2023), Bordas emphasised two fundamental principles of leadership. The first principle is that the leader is equal. One of the primary challenges in creating an equitable society is the tendency for individuals to seek dominance. Equal leadership, Bordas argues, requires leaders to treat everyone with respect, demonstrating kindness, taking time to ensure the well-being of others, and fostering a safe and open environment. When leaders adopt this approach and focus on developing their people, a second transformation occurs: *"Leadership by the many"* (Weaving Influence, 2023). This concept suggests that individuals begin to see themselves as leaders, recognising their own potential to lead. As a result, an authentic organisation is formed, where individuals are motivated to work diligently and willingly (Hastings, 2023). This concept aligns with the perspective of Dardano, who stated that empathy is key to leadership in El Salvador and that leaders engage closely with their employees and demonstrate genuine concern for their well-being (21 November 2024). This perspective is further supported by the CCBS Survey (2024) in which one CEO remarked: *"El liderazgo comprende el acompañamiento continuo y comunicación con el equipo para mantenernos en sintonía con los objetivos que deseamos alcanzar. Un diferenciador es el trato al equipo el mantener un ambiente armonioso y colaborativo haciendo partícipes a todos con sus opiniones y sugerencias"* ("Leadership includes continuous support and communication with the team to stay in tune with the objectives we want to achieve. A distinguishing factor is the treatment of the team, maintaining a harmonious and collaborative environment, and involving everyone with their opinions and suggestions"). This quote reinforces the essential leadership qualities that Bordas identified as pivotal to success within the region.

Understanding hierarchy in El Salvador

Leadership in El Salvador is characterised by an autocratic style, where organisations operate within rigidly vertical systems and centralised decision-making frameworks. This hierarchical approach reinforces a culture of respect but often stifles innovation and limits organisational progress (Umana, 15 November 2024). According to Sayes (2015), this structure presents both challenges and opportunities for effectiveness, in as far as managers typically adhere to a top-down model, with authority concentrated amongst senior-level leadership. Consequently, employees often prioritise compliance over creativity, hesitating to challenge decisions or propose new ideas out of fears over being reprimanded or job insecurity (Sayes, 2015). With respect to the gendered nature of organisational hierarchies, disparities persist. This was corroborated by the results of the CCBS Survey (2024), where respondents expressed divided opinions over the question of gender parity in senior-leadership roles. However, one of our interviewees, Dardano (21 November 2024) emphasised that there has been some progress in this regard, due to the fact that women dominate leadership positions within certain sectors. As he remarked, *"In many industries in El Salvador, women are leading many jobs, particularly in fields like agroindustry and textile maquilas"*. However, family-run businesses play a significant role in terms of perpetuating hierarchical systems within the Salvadoran corporate landscape, by virtue of the fact that leadership positions are frequently passed down through the generations, with authority often confined to familial lines (Umana, 15 November 2024). Dr. Umana informed us that whilst the first generation may build a business on the back of their vision and determination, subsequent generations sometimes lack the necessary expertise or drive, which, in turn, leads to organisational stagnation (15 November, 2024). One of the responses from a respondent in the CCBS Survey (2024) adds additional weight to this argument, in as far as they indicated that traditional leaders often rise to power due to their familial ties and prominent surnames. These entrenched structures extend beyond family-run enterprises to shape labour relations across the country. Hierarchical dynamics delineate clear dependencies between employees and employers, fostering organisational order but also amplifying workplace conflicts. The rigid framework, combined with economic pressures, exacerbates dissatisfaction over wages, job security, and working conditions. Delays in resolving disputes further heighten tensions, with management practices reinforcing this top-down culture (Perspectiva Laboral El Salvador, 2011). In relation to this, Dr. Umana stated: *"Approximately 80 percent of leadership positions are assigned based on familial or personal ties rather than on professional competence. This preference often elevates connections, appearance, or reputation above technical skill and honesty"* (15 November 2024). Despite these challenges, there is a growing minority of organisations, particularly multinational corporations, that are adopting more horizontal leadership models. These companies emphasise transparency, participatory practices, and team collaboration. Unlike traditional Salvadoran enterprises, these organisations are typically managed by professional leaders rather than founders or family members. However, as Dr. Umana highlighted, *"Organizations with horizontal structures still represent a minority in the Salvadoran business context"* (15 November 2024).

How the Salvadorans achieve leadership empathy

Salvadoran leaders achieve empathy by fostering meaningful interpersonal connections with team members and promoting a culture of open communication. This leadership style reflects the nation's cultural emphasis upon family and social unity. By prioritising personal relationships, leaders enhance trust and collaboration within professional settings (Flores-Hernández et al., 2022). The CCBS Survey (2024) corroborates this perspective, as one CEO highlighted that leadership in El Salvador often combines adaptability and strong community ties, emphasising personal connections to build trust and loyalty. Leaders who prioritise emotional development values, such as, for example, optimism, fellowship and compassion, create a workplace environment that subsequently motivates and engages employees (Soler et al., 2016). Similarly, around 60 percent of our survey respondents expressed a preference for maintaining close relationships with their employees, asserting that such connections do not compromise respect (CCBS Survey, 2024). According to one of the interviewees, Dardano, a leadership consultant, stated: *"La empatía surge de forma natural porque el empleado salvadoreño medio es bastante responsable.*

89

Los salvadoreños se esfuerzan por agradar y, a su vez, reciben la benevolencia de sus líderes" ("*Empathy arises naturally because the average Salvadoran employee is quite responsible. Salvadorans strive to please and, in turn, receive kindness from their leaders*")(Dardano, 21 November 2024). Similarly. Effective leaders must actively listen, explaining that leadership is about exerting influence and serving others: *"Para ser un líder eficaz, hay que escuchar el doble de lo que se habla"* (*"To be an effective leader, you must listen twice as much as you speak")* (Umana, 15 November 2024). Additionally, Zivkovic (2022) notes that empathy in leadership promotes a culture of responsibility and care, which, in turn, inspires creativity and drives innovation. This perspective aligns with the findings of the CCBS Survey (2024), where Arteage, an independent consultant, also specifically stated that leaders in El Salvador are known for focusing on team integration and cohesion, ensuring that everyone feels valued to bring out the best in each member within the workplace. Further support for this perspective stems from the fact that around 95 percent of the survey respondents agreed with the statement that managers should actively spend time ensuring the personal well-being of their team members (CCBS Survey, 2024). Dardano (21 November 2024) also adds additional weight to this, noting that Salvadoran leaders increasingly recognise the importance of inquiring about employees' well-being: *"De este modo, la empatía se convierte en una pequeña pero esencial herramienta para un buen líder"* (*"In this way, empathy becomes a small yet essential tool for a good leader").* Furthermore, Dardano highlighted government efforts to prioritise workplace relationships, observing that *"Muchas empresas fueron multadas por no hacer las contribuciones pertinentes a los programas sociales... Esto ha servido como una llamada de atención a las empresas privada para que se pongan a la altura de los nuevos estándares más humanos"* (*"Many companies were fined for failing to make social program contributions... This has served as a wake-up call for private enterprises to align with more human-centered standards")* (Dardano, 21 November 2024). This shift illustrates the growing recognition of empathy and relational leadership as integral components of effective management within El Salvador.

Greece

Jamal Slijngaard, Stephanie Montero, George Athymarits (Γιώργος Αθυμαρίτης), Noureddine El Ayadi El Kanfoudi, Sofia Papachristou(Σοφία Παπαχρήστου), Jenny van der Harst

Greece, which is considered by many to be the cradle of Western civilisation and democracy, possesses a rich historical legacy that continues to influence the contemporary business sector, particularly with respect to leadership practices. Officially known as the Hellenic Republic (Ελληνική Δημοκρατία, Elliniki Dimokratia), Greece's strategic location at the crossroads of Europe, Asia, and Africa has made it a vital gateway for global trade and commerce. The Port of Piraeus, one of the busiest in the Mediterranean (Dedola Global Logistics, 2024), and the country's maritime infrastructure generally has made Greece a leader in international shipping and logistics, with Greek shipowners controlling the largest maritime merchant fleet in the world (HETCO| Hellenic Trade Council, 2024). Whilst deeply rooted in its classical heritage, modern Greece has expanded beyond its shipping industry to include other key industries such as tourism, energy, and agriculture. The Mediterranean diet—often marketed as the key to longevity and wellness (Gerber & Hoffman, 2015) — has helped Greece gain global recognition. Tourism, driven by Greece's diverse geography and cultural splendour, remains the cornerstone of its economy (Papatheodorou & Arvanitis, 2023). Since joining the EU and adopting the Euro in 2001, Greece has undergone significant economic and political challenges. Despite this, however, Greece has invested in renewable energy projects and strategic pipeline connections to secure its position as an energy hub (Stonenews, 2024). Greece is home to one of the oldest Indo-European languages, Modern Greek, which remains the official language of the country. Greek culture is rich with proverbs and sayings, reflecting the country's deep philosophical traditions. For example, Socrates' famous quote, "ἓν οἶδα, ὅτι οὐδὲν οἶδα" (*What I certainly know is that I know nothing*), continues to shape modern education and philosophical thought (Omilo, 2023). Greece's intellectual legacy, rooted in the philosophies of Socrates, Plato, and Aristotle, shapes modern business practices also through a paternalistic leadership style that values strong family ties, clear communication, and structured environments to minimise uncertainty (Richard, 1995). This mirrors Plato's philosopher-king model and Aristotle's emphasis upon balanced, rational decision-making, as Greek leaders act as ethical mentors who prioritise integrity, trust, and employees' well-being (Shaw, 2022). The following chapter explores Greek leadership styles further through academic literature, surveys, and interviews with local managers and experts.

How the Greek characterise leaders?

Within Greek culture, leadership is viewed as a position of significant responsibility and honour, rather than a title that is accorded to someone by mere virtue of their hierarchical status. Rather, true leadership status in Greece is earned through the demonstration of values and behaviours that align with deeply rooted cultural ideals (Papalexandris & Galanaki, 2012). Key traits such as integrity, wisdom, and a commitment to justice are deeply influenced by Greece's philosophical heritage. Ancient philosophers, notably Plato and Aristotle, provided the foundational concepts for Greek leadership with, amongst other things, a strong emphasis upon ethical governance. Plato's *The Republic* emphasises ethical leadership through the concept of philosopher-kings—leaders who rule with wisdom and justice (Shaw, 2022). Aristotle's virtue ethics promotes balanced decision-making within leadership (Horak, 2021). This philosophical influence persists in modern Greek business culture, where leaders are expected to prioritise ethical behaviour and fairness. According to one of our interviewees, a Greek academic specialising in leadership dynamics, business in Greece has traditionally been tied to a specific mentality—one that individuals either inherently possess, develop through personal experience, or acquire within a family setting (Anonymous, 20 November, 2024). This cultural approach to leadership stresses deeply rooted values, such as trust and interpersonal connections, which align closely with the concept of *philotimo*. Philotimo, which embodies respect, trust, and honour, is a defining quality of Greek leadership, a fact which was supported by the CCBS Survey (2024), in as far as charismatic and resourceful leadership traits were identified as key qualities for Greek leaders to possess. *Philotimo* instills a self-imposed code of conduct rooted in fairness and integrity (Papalexandris, 2007), a trait that is especially valued within Greek society, where assertiveness and independence are prevalent. As our Greek scholar (2024) explained, *philotimo* fosters teamwork and dedication within leadership and business, but it can also be misused. Leaders or organisations may exploit this value by demanding excessive effort or loyalty, especially during crises, in turn, leading to potential burnout or unfair practices. This dual nature of *philotimo*—as both an asset and a source of potential exploitation— adds complexity to its role in Greek leadership. Alongside *philotimo*, decisiveness is a key trait expected of Greek leaders, who must demonstrate confidence, clarity, and resolve, particularly during times of change or uncertainty (Commisceo Global, 2023). The CCBS Survey (2024) reinforces this characterisation, in as far as the vast majority of the respondents agreed that leaders rarely change their decisions once they are made, highlighting a strong preference for decisiveness. Moreover, the respondents identified being a powerful decision-maker as the strongest indicator of an effective leader (CCBS Survey, 2024). This blend of decisiveness and *philotimo* is exemplified during critical moments, such as the 2008 financial crisis, when many Greek business leaders prioritised the well-being of their employees and communities whilst making tough decisions to uphold ethical commitments. Similarly, in family-owned Greek businesses, leaders often choose long-term partners over higher bidders, demonstrating *philotimo* through their focus on trust and loyalty, which reinforces the integrity central to Greek business culture (Karageorgiou & Selwood, 2020). Another essential trait is trust and loyalty, which is rooted in the legacy of *proxenia*. The ancient role of *proxenia*, similar to modern intermediaries or middlemen, has had a lasting impact, shaping a business culture centered on strong networks and loyal partnerships (Creanza, 2024). This tradition has cultivated a preference for having strong networks and loyal partnerships built on mutual trust, which remains a core aspect of Greek business practices today. In addition, the influence of the Greek Orthodox Church has shaped a strong moral foundation in Greek business practices as religion and family are central to the Greek identity. Today, around 97% of Greeks identify as Orthodox Christian, and this religious influence extends into modern business practices, where leaders are often guided by a strong sense of moral responsibility and community duty (Papalexandris, 2007). Family dynamics are equally foundational, providing both financial and emotional support. This creates loyalty and trust within organisations, with business dealings often taking place within close-knit networks of family and friends (Thanailaki, 2021). Whilst family-centered leadership fosters trust and loyalty, the scholar we interviewed highlighted the lack of meritocracy within Greek organisations, where hiring often favours familial networks over qualifications. This practice builds strong personal bonds but hinders merit-based growth and innovation (Anonymous, 20 November, 2024). Reflecting this family-centered nature, leaders often adopt a paternalistic approach, acting as guardians and mentors within the workplace. In this capacity, leaders are expected to take a personal interest in their employees' well-being, supporting both their professional and personal growth. As Broome (1996, pg.79) notes, *"in Greece, you must manage persons, not personnel."* This paternalistic style in turn creates a sense of trust and loyalty (Giousmpasoglou, 2014). Competence is another highly regarded trait, with experience being the most frequently cited quality of successful managers. Approximately 30% of Greeks emphasised managerial experience in 2012, alongside traits like intelligence, decisiveness, and administrative ability (Papalexandris & Galanaki, 2012). The CCBS Survey (2024) reinforces this focus on competence, with organisational experience remaining a top priority, whilst also highlighting a growing appreciation for market expertise, technical competence, visionary thinking, and charisma (CCBS Survey, 2024). With respect to demographic preferences in Greek leadership, research shows that older managers value a humane orientation and strategic vision, whereas younger managers prioritise people development and adaptability. Successful Greek leaders are those who can balance these qualities, adapting their approach to unite diverse perspectives under the pursuance of shared goals (Papalexandris & Galanaki, 2017).

Survey results and what local respondents say

The CCBS Survey (2024) aims to explore the key traits, values, and practices that define effective leadership in Greece. By gathering insights from C-level executives and experienced professionals, the survey demonstrates how Greek leadership blends traditional values like hierarchy and decisiveness with modern priorities such as team well-being and relational leadership. This section summarises the most noteworthy findings. Firstly, the CCBS Survey (2024) found that being a powerful decision-maker is considered the strongest indicator of an effective leader, reflecting the cultural emphasis on stability, confidence, and the ability to lead with clarity and resolve (Commisceo Global, 2023). Employees also value leaders for their organisational experience, market expertise, and technical competence, alongside personal traits like charisma and resourcefulness. Charisma and professional networks are especially significant in this regard, whilst family connections are seen as less important, thus indicating a shift away from traditionally inherited advantages towards professional competence (CCBS Survey, 2024). Furthermore, research by Chatzivamvaki (2016) highlights how Greek leaders often leverage their charisma to foster a sense of belonging and loyalty, thus blurring the lines between formal authority and personal connection. The results of the survey also reveal a preference amongst Greek employees for a structured hierarchy, where senior leaders are formally addressed, which reflects prevailing cultural norms. This was corroborated by one of our interviewees, who noted that interactions with senior leaders in Greece tend to be more formal than in other countries. As he explained: *"In meetings, people may speak to the senior in a more formal manner, unlike the more relaxed interactions seen in other cultures"* (Anonymous, November 20, 2024). This aligns with the survey findings, where more than half of the respondents emphasised the importance of maintaining visible symbols of leadership, including formalities within communication. At the same time, the vast majority of the respondents reported that it is acceptable to address leaders by their first names, thus apparently signaling a gradual shift towards a more relational leadership style in the country (CCBS Survey, 2024). Team well-being also emerged as a key leadership priority, in as far as over 80 percent of the respondents identified it as being critical. This aligns with Greece's paternalistic leadership style, where leaders act as mentors who care for the personal and professional growth of employees (Giousmpasoglou, 2014). Echoing these findings, our other interviewee, Mrs. Palla, stressed the importance of maintaining a balance between authority and inclusiveness, fostering trust, and ensuring team members feel valued. As she observed: *"Greek leaders excel in fostering trust, loyalty, and collaboration through personal relations whilst balancing authority and accountability."* (Mrs. Konstantia Palla, November 29 2024). However, Greek leaders tend to prefer indirect confrontation, with only 17 percent reporting that they are willing to address issues directly in meetings, thus reflecting a cultural preference for maintaining harmony and respect (CCBS Survey, 2024). The importance of hierarchy is further reinforced by the value that is placed upon visible symbols of leadership, such as, for example, status-representative spaces and transportation, with more than half of the respondents emphasising their significance. Time management also plays a key role within Greek leadership, with more than half of the respondents framing missing deadlines as being synonymous with failure. However, 24 percent of them expressed a more flexible view, reflecting a balance between structure and adaptability (CCBS Survey, 2024). These findings, combined with the broader cultural value of *philotimo*—which emphasises trust, respect, and honour—highlights the evolving nature of Greek leadership. Whilst rooted in tradition, Greek leadership is increasingly adapting to contemporary workplace demands, blending stability with relational and flexible leadership practices.

Local leadership analysis

Dr. Anonymous: a Greek leadership scholar

Dr. Anonymous is a Greek professor and migration expert with extensive knowledge of cultural and organisational dynamics within Greece. With a strong academic background in anthropology, sociology, and geography, he has held research and teaching positions at prestigious institutions across Europe. His work focuses on how cultural, social, and economic factors intersect to shape organisational and leadership practices within the Greek context. His expertise provides valuable insights into how Greek leadership is influenced by historical, cultural, and societal frameworks. According to Dr. Anonymous, effective Greek leaders must possess foresight, the ability to plan strategically, and the skills to inspire and motivate their teams. He underscored the importance of fostering a positive organisational culture, listening actively to diverse viewpoints in order to make balanced decisions (20 November 2024). However, he noted that traditional expectations of hierarchy and strong authority figures still profoundly shape leadership perceptions in Greece. Dr. Anonymous described Greek workplaces as *"traditionally hierarchical, often limiting subordinates' ability to voice opinions"* (Anonymous, 20 November 2024). However, this dynamic is gradually shifting as younger, internationally experienced employees advocate for more open and collaborative work environments. They proceeded to explicate how the hierarchical and formal nature of Greek organisations constitutes a challenge for foreign professionals. As they put it: *"In Greece, there is often a more top-down organisational structure, and interactions with senior leaders can be formal, contrasting with the more relaxed approaches seen in other countries"*. This hierarchical culture, combined with unclear career pathways, can frustrate newcomers (Anonymous, 20 November 2024). Moreover, he observed a shift from valuing experiential and familial knowledge towards prioritising technocratic and professional expertise. Historically, Greek business leadership relied heavily on the experience that was gained through practice or family-run businesses. As they explained, *"Traditionally, leadership was seen as something you developed through practice or familial connections"* (Anonymous, 20 November 2024), before then proceeding to acknowledge that this approach has been criticised for lacking professionalism. However, they pointed out that Greece is increasingly adopting a more meritocratic mindset. Later in the interview, they also explained that Greek Orthodox values promote strong community bonds and loyalty in leadership, but they can also reinforce patriarchal and authoritarian tendencies, limiting openness and merit-based practices in some cases (Anonymous, 20 November 2024). Additionally, Greek leadership is deeply influenced by cultural concepts such as *philotimo*—a value rooted in honour, selflessness, and commitment to collective goals. As they themselves informed us: *"Philotimo inspires individuals to prioritise the common good, but it can also be exploited in crisis situations when employees are pressured to overextend themselves"* (Anonymous, 20 November 2024). He also pointed out how Greece's historical emphasis upon classical values, such as community and democracy, continues to resonate within contemporary leadership styles, albeit it is used more symbolically than practically (Anonymous, 20 November 2024). Reflecting on recent changes, they concluded by discussing that there was a growing inclination amongst Greek leaders toward global markets, internationalisation, and merit-based hiring practices. In realtion to this, they expressed optimism about the potential for further modernisation, but acknowledged that hierarchical structures and informal hiring practices remain persistent challenges within the Greek context.

Mrs. Konstantia Palla: a Greek cross-cultural trainer

Mrs. Konstantia Palla is a distinguished sociologist, Certified Professional Coach, and Certified Mentor with credentials from the International Coaching Federation. She is the founder of Field of Law Greece and a former President of ICF Greece, bringing over twenty-five years of experience in business and leadership coaching. Specialising in team coaching, leadership development, and organisational behaviour, she strives to help leaders and teams succeed by utilising her approach of active listening, emotional intelligence, and coaching techniques. Her experience across diverse cultural contexts provides valuable insights into the influence of empathy, hierarchy, and societal values within Greek leadership culture. According to Mrs. Palla,the main difference between Greek leadership and other countries is based upon societal values. *"Philoxenia, Meraki, and Philotimia. You will not find that anywhere else!"* (Mrs. Konstantia Palla,

29 November 2024). Greek business culture is predicated on principles that promote hospitality (*philoxenia*), care (*meraki*), and honor (*philotimia*), values that are also discernable amongst most Greek leaders and daily depicted in their work. Furthermore, there are several leadership traits and practices that differentiate Greece from other countries. The most evident difference is flexibility, and strictness when it comes to leading a group, as Greek leaders have been socialised within a more laid-back culture. Besides this, philanthropy(*philanthropia*, promoting people's welfare) has increasingly become a focus of Greek leadership, in as far as leaders strive to become mentors and supporters at the same time, placing both the commitment and future of their teams above everything (Mrs. Konstantia Palla, 29 November 2024). Notwithstanding these societal values, our Greek leadership expert also informed us that other traits are equally important, most notably: *"Emotional intelligence and empathy is the foundation for every leader"* (Mrs. Konstantia Palla, 29 November 2024). These elements strengthen the bonding of the team, create a supportive working environment, and naturally strengthen trust which is highly regarded in Greece. A she herself put it: *"We are a highly communicative people"* (Mrs. Konstantia Palla, 29 November 2024), before then proceeding to explain that empathy helps leaders to better understand the needs and concerns of their members, thus formulating the conditions of cooperation, mutual trust, and communication. When leaders blend their empathy for the personal challenges and needs of employees, with the appropriate directiveness and support, they create an environment that encourages cohesion and efficiency within the group, leading to long-term success (Mrs. Konstantia Palla, 29 November 2024). Greek leaders view authority as a way to direct, motivate, and include their team in achieving communal goals, which can be achieved via the right blend of coaching skills, authenticity, and decisiveness. An equally important aspect of Greek business culture are personal relationships, team bonding, and open communication. As Mrs. Palla told us: *"We [Greece] excel in fostering trust, loyalty, and collaboration through personal relations but also balancing authority and accountability"*(Mrs. Konstantia Palla, 29 November 2024). Greek leaders strike the right balance between their use of authority, inclusiveness as well as the commitment of their team, which, in turn, positively impacts upon leadership effectiveness. Later, Mrs. Palla stressed the need for stability, structured decision-making, and careful risk assessment, as this approach helps Greek leaders respond quickly to highly dynamic business environments, focus on continuous learning and adapt to unknown conditions. As she put it: *"it is all a part of our flexible leadership approach"* (Mrs. Konstantia Palla, 29 November 2024), thus referring back to her previous comments about the preference for the transformational style within Greek leadership. To end this insightful interview, Mrs. Palla provided her own definition of leadership and outlined what she would like Greek leaders to aspire to, stating: *"Leadership is the power of inspiring others to believe in their potential and walking with them by building a culture of collaboration and elevated respect. When the team*

feels supported and recognised, success naturally follows..." (Mrs. Konstantia Palla, 29 November 2024).

In-country leadership bestseller

One of the best-selling books on leadership in Greece is *The Timeless Leaders (Leadership Lessons from Ancient Greece)* by Thomas Katakis (2024). This book draws leadership insights from Ancient Greek history and mythology, offering lessons on succession, team building, vision, business ethics, vulnerability, and humility. Katakis, a seasoned business executive with over twenty years of experience in multinational companies, integrates historical wisdom with contemporary business practices to make leadership lessons universally relevant (Εκδόσεις Κάκτος, 2024a). The book emphasises storytelling as a core teaching tool, using the deeds of Ancient Greek heroes to illustrate leadership principles. According to Katakis, storytelling conveys values and principles in a vivid, memorable way, making leadership concepts more engaging and applicable (Εκδόσεις Κάκτος, 2024b). Katakis structures his leadership philosophy around three key pillars. First, he focuses upon vision and purpose, drawing inspiration from Greek heroes who led with clear goals and motivated their followers through shared purpose, much like contemporary business leaders who articulate a compelling company vision to align and inspire their teams. Second, he highlights empowerment and team dynamics, stressing the importance of trust, open communication, and collaboration. This mirrors modern organisational strategies where leaders delegate effectively, foster innovation, and create a culture of psychological safety. Third, he stresses the importance of ethics and authenticity, advocating for leaders to practice humility and integrity, by reflecting on mythological figures like Odysseus, and build credibility with their employees by prioritising transparency, such as through reflective practices like 360-degree feedback, and ethical decision-making within an increasingly accountability-driven environment (Ekorinthos, 2024). One key takeaway from the book is the prioritisation of Greek business leaders *leading with purpose and clarity*. Katakis illustrates how ancient Greek leaders, such as Pericles, inspired their followers through a shared vision and well-defined goals. Contemporary business leaders, he argues, can emulate this by fostering a clear sense of direction and aligning their teams with a common purpose. Another lesson is the *importance of empowering teams and building trust*. Drawing from stories of Greek generals and warriors, Katakis shows how collaborative leadership that values diverse perspectives strengthens both morale and organisational effectiveness. Finally, adapting leadership to the cultural context is a recurring theme, as Katakis stresses the importance of cultural intelligence, such as tailoring decision-making styles to align with diverse team dynamics within global organisations. By integrating his professional experiences with these global business examples, Katakis demonstrates how timeless lessons from Greek history can be applied to meet the needs of modern organisations. These takeaways make *The Timeless Leaders* a practical, culturally rich guide for leadership development, bridging ancient wisdom with contemporary applications across industries and cultures.

Local leadership book		
Title	*The Timeless Leaders*	
Subtitle	Leadership lessons from Ancient Greece	
Author	Thomas Katakis	
Publisher	Kaktos	
Year	2024	
ISBN	9786182152072	

Greece leadership YouTube review

In this insightful YouTube video titled *"Leadership through the eyes of leaders,"* there is an interview between Katerina Manu, Regional General Manager for the Balkans, and Vasilis Rabat, Consultant at Xerox Hellas, who engage in a thoughtful discussion on Greek leadership. The discussion sought to explore the challenges and opportunities faced by leaders in Greece, offering insights into their personal experiences and philosophies. The conversation began by defining leadership from their own perspectives: for Katerina, leadership is about inspiration and motivation, whilst Vasilis focused on what leadership is not—specifically, poor communication and self-isolation, such as, for example, leaders locking themselves away in their offices. Katerina then proceeded to discuss the traits of ineffective leaders, highlighting arrogance, conceit, and exclusion from decision-making, which can demotivate teams and hinder performance (Manu, 2017, 0:17). Vasilis proceeded to add that a lack of trust within a leadership team, authoritarian behaviour, and failure to promote merit-based decision-making are significant pitfalls for Greek leaders (Rabat, 2017, 0:44). He believes that a visionary leader should foster a positive, inclusive environment that empowers individuals and enables the organisation to achieve success. The interview then shifts to the personal influences on their leadership journey, highlighting the leaders who had a profoun impact upon their lives. Katerina credits Mark Dixon, CEO and founder of Regus, when noting: *"The person who comes to mind is the founder and active CEO of Regus. Mark Dixon leads the company strategically, yet he stays in touch with operations on a daily basis. What he also does, which is very important to me, is to keep the spirit of continuous innovation and the approach to challenges arising from an ever-changing environment."*(Manu, 2017, 1:25). Katerina, after acknowledging Vasilis's extensive experience in leading a company, asked him for advice for young, aspiring Greek leaders, to which Vasilis responded: *"If someone is starting as a leader, I would advise them to carve out their own strategy, to look at the past, get to know the people, the company's history… Naturally, they need to have people they trust by their side, and they need to build a team of people who are, if possible, even more capable than themselves. This team will lead them to success because, as we know, we should not be afraid to have competent people by our side."* (Rabat, 2017, 2:29). As Katerina revisited the question about leaders who have left a lasting impact upon their lives, Vasilis reflected upon the impact of his uncle, whose perseverance and ambition shaped his understanding of leadership (Rabat, 2017, 3:33). He also recalled his early Director, whose confidence in him allowed him to become the youngest CEO in Europe at the time (Rabat, 2017, 4:13). In conclusion, Vasilis emphasised the importance of remaining authentic, understanding a company's history and building a strong team within Greek leadership. He stressed the significance of leading by example, quoting Ray Kroc, the founder of McDonald's: *"The quality of a leader is reflected in the standards they set for themselves"* (Rabat, 2017, 3:24). Katerina, inspired by John Quincy Adams and quoting him, ended by encouraging young leaders to embrace growth and ambition: *"Dream more, learn more, do more, and become more"* (Manu, 2017, 5:10). The insights shared by Vasilis Rabat and Katerina Manu provide valuable guidance for the next generation of Greek leaders.

Understanding hierarchy in Greece

Within Greek culture, the term "leader" often implies more than just a person in a senior-level position; rather, it often refers to someone who possesses unique qualities or a charisma who naturally inspires others. However, when used in a formal context, such as "the leader of the party," then it typically refers to a person's rank within a hierarchical structure (Papalexandris & Galanaki, 2012). Although Greek business culture is characterised by a hierarchical structure, it nevertheless places strong emphasis upon close interpersonal relationships across all levels, in turn, creating a family-like atmosphere that promotes loyalty. Building upon this perspective, Mrs. Palla, one of our interviewees, emphasised the importance of balancing authority with inclusiveness within Greek leadership. As she observed, *"Greek leaders excel in fostering trust, loyalty, and collaboration through personal relations whilst balancing authority and accountability"* (Mrs. Konstantia Palla, 29 November 2024). Greek leaders build loyalty by forming personal connections with their subordinates, often integrating them into a trusted "in-group," which blurs the lines between a formal hierarchy and an extended family (Haran, 2015). This aligns with the broader cultural principle of collectivism and in-group loyalty, principles that naturally extend into workplace dynamics (Hofstede Insights, 2023). A common Greek proverb, "Η εμπιστοσύνη είναι σαν βάζο: όταν σπάσει δεν μπορεί ποτέ να είναι ίδια" ("*Trust is like a vase; once broken, it can never be the same*"), reflects the deep cultural importance placed upon trust and loyalty as essential foundations in both hierarchical and business relationships. Reflecting this, Greek leadership combines respect for authority with approachability and personal involvement. Whilst hierarchy is valued, there is also an expectation that leaders should be accessible, communicative, and protective of their teams, as evidenced by the fact that Greece scores relatvely low on Hofstede's power distance scale (Hofstede, 2023). This blend of hierarchical respect and leader approachability is closely aligned with Plato's philosopher-king ideal (Shaw, 2022) and Aristotle's concept of balanced decision-making (Horak, 2021), where leaders prioritise both organisational goals and the well-being of their people. Greek leaders often adopt a paternalistic style, blending professional authority with familial loyalty. This is exemplified by Spyros Kyriakopoulos, the CEO of a Greek shipping firm, who said, "*In Greece, we work with our heads, but we lead with our hearts*" (Safety4Sea, 2023), which testifies to how leaders balance company control, whilst, simultaneously, providing emotional support, embodying a leadership style that is both hierarchical and compassionate. Moreover, one of our interviewees explicated how the hierarchical nature of Greek organisations shapes subordinates' perspectives. Historically, limited job opportunities and economic instability forced employees to comply with rigid systems, creating a culture where subordinates were hesitant to challenge authority (Anonymous, 20 November 2024). This preference for a structured, stable hierarchy extends to Greek family-owned businesses, where leaders typically choose to reinvest profits rather than take on debt for rapid growth (Thanailaki, 2021). Senior figures, often family heads, prioritise stable and predictable environments to ensure the company's long-term security. This risk-averse strategy is consistent with Greece's high score for uncertainty avoidance, thus indicating a cultural inclination towards structured, stable decision-making (Hofstede Insights, 2023). Similarly, the results of the CCBS Survey (2024) demonstrate that half of the respondents associated missing deadlines with failure, thus underscoring a cautious approach to reliability and structure. However, a significant proportion believed that missing deadlines does not equate to failure, thus highlighting a balance in Greek leadership between maintaining stability and allowing adaptability within decision-making (CCBS Survey, 2024). The scholar we intervieweed also linked Greece's risk-averse leadership approach to structural factors, such as, for example, the absence of a robust welfare state and limited safety nets. This cautious mindset has historically prioritised stability over innovation. However, there are notable exceptions, such as the shipping industry, which showcases the potential for bold risk-taking within certain sectors. As economic conditions evolve, this cautious approach is gradually giving way to more innovative and dynamic leadership practices (Anonymous, 20 November 2024). Whilst this risk-averse approach reflects a preference for stability, it does not diminish Greece's strong entrepreneurial spirit, which is evident in the widespread preference for self-employment. As our leadership consultant stated in our interview, *"Greek leaders place value on careful risk assessment, maintaining a predictable course for the company"* (Mrs. Konstantia Palla, 29 November 2024), thus highlighting the need for stability and flexible leadership spirit. Nearly half of the workforce is self-employed and around 90% of businesses employ fewer than 10 workers (Papalexandris, 1997). Within these small, family-run firms, leadership usually falls to a senior figure or owner, who holds decision-making power. Additionally, the emphasis upon Higher Education as a route to social status and economic success reinforces these hierarchical distinctions, as many leaders come from prestigious educational backgrounds (Papalexandris, 2007). The scholar we interviewed also raised the challenges that hierarchical structures, inefficiencies, and long working hours may present for international professionals in Greece, but also noted the positives of a highly social and relational workplace culture that fosters strong connections and solidarity (Anonymous, 20 November 2024). These dynamics capture both the rigidity and warmth of Greek workplaces. Overall, hierarchy within the business sector combines deep-rooted cultural values with a commitment to relational loyalty and stability, which makes Greek workplaces unique in terms of their blend of respect for authority and a familial, connected approach to leadership.

How the Greek achieve leadership empathy

Greek leaders excel in empathetic leadership by combining emotional intelligence, ancient philosophical insights, and deeply rooted cultural values that emphasise community well-being. In the absence of rigid systems or structures, many challenges in Greek organisations are managed through interpersonal relationships rather than formalised procedures. As a result, qualities like emotional intelligence and empathy are not just beneficial but rather absolutely essential for leaders to effectively handle day-to-day situations (Anonymous, 20 November 2024). This was supported by our other interviewee, Mrs. Palla, who informed us that Greek leaders often adopt a transformational leadership style, blending flexibility with structured mentorship to inspire their teams (29 November 2024). Emotional intelligence and empathy are foundational in this respect, in as far as they create a supportive working environment and strengthen team cohesion. This approach ensures that employees feel valued, thus fostering a positive culture that aligns personal growth with organisational goals. As Mrs. Palla stated: *"Empathy helps leaders better understand team needs and create conditions for cooperation and mutual trust, which are critical for achieving long-term success"* (29 November 2024). Leaders with strong emotional intelligence manage their own emotions and those of their team, fostering a supportive environment where employees feel understood and included (Koutoula, 2022). Broome (1996), notes that a successful Greek manager is expected to show genuine concern for their employees' needs, including personal and family matters, thus reflecting the cultural significance of family within Greece. For instance, a Greek manager may accommodate an employee's request for flexible working hours to care for an elderly parent, demonstrating a deep understanding of the importance of family obligations. Similarly, during times of personal hardship, such as illness or financial strain, Greek leaders might provide support through additional leave or financial assistance, further strengthening the trust and loyalty that define workplace relationships (Broome, 1996). This commitment to supporting employees reflects the family-oriented values that are so central to Greek culture, where empathy in leadership is firmly grounded in building strong interpersonal connections. This characterisation of Greek leadership was also corroborated by the results of the CCBS Survey (2024), where three-quarters of the respondents agreed to some extent that prioritising team well-being is a central aspect of Greek leadership. Whilst Greek leadership fosters strong interpersonal bonds, more than half of the respondents also reported that maintaining a respectful personal distance from employees is equally important (CCBS Survey, 2024). This balance reflects a leadership style that combines professionalism and authority with a consultative and relational approach, encouraging employees to feel both supported and involved in decision-making (Chatzivamvaki, 2016). This relational focus blurs the lines between formal hierarchy and a family-like atmosphere, where leaders integrate subordinates into a trusted "in-group," thus reinforcing the sense of belonging and loyalty (Haran, 2015). As Mrs. Palla eloquently stated in our interview, *"Leadership is the power of inspiring others to believe in their potential and walking with them by building a culture of collaboration and elevated respect. When the team feels supported and recognsed, success naturally follows"* (November 29 2024). The empathetic nature of Greek leadership is also influenced by the philosophical teachings of Plato and Aristotle. Virtues such as moderation and integrity guide leaders in making balanced decisions that uphold ethical standards whilst, simultaneously, caring for employees' well-being (Koutoula, 2022). Whilst traditional hierarchies might sometimes limit open dialogue, effective empathy within leadership helps to bridge these gaps, building organisational loyalty and motivating employees to work towards shared goals (Chatzivamvaki, 2016). Our interviewee also noted the importance of effective empathy within the beginning of the interview *when stating: "Greek leaders who are empathetic can increase cohesion, efficiency and results within the group" (Mrs. Konstantia Palla, November 29 2024).* In conclusion, Greek leaders blend emotional intelligence, philosophy, and cultural values to create an empathetic style that balances hierarchy with genuine care, fostering loyalty and a strong sense of community.

Nigeria

Tobias Ankone, Boris Havik, Quux van Luik, Victor Regouin & Merit Omoregie

Nigeria, which is often referred to as the 'Giant of Africa,' is renowned for its vast cultural and economic significance upon the continent. With over 200 million people and more than 520 languages spoken, Nigeria represents one of the most linguistically diverse countries in the world (Kori-Siakpere et al., 2024). This diversity is also reflected within the country's complex social and economic fabric. Nigeria is home to Nollywood, the world's second-largest film industry, which produces around fifty films weekly, thus testifying to its creative and cultural reach (Van Gelder, 2017). The country is also well-known for its colourful culture and festivals like FESTAC'77, which serves as further evidence of its diverse history (Ojukwu, 2020). Nigeria also has the largest economy in Africa, primarily due to the oil sector, which makes it a key player in global markets (Abubakar et al., 2022). Agriculture is also an influential sector, contributing around one-quarter of GDP, with the potential to generate sixty-five percent of employment and half of export share if fully harnessed (Erumebor). The structure of the Nigerian economy is typical of an underdeveloped country. The oil and gas sector is the primary economic driver, generating the vast majority of export earnings and government revenue. Conversely, the industrial and manufacturing sectors make up only a small part of GDP (Chete et al., 2014). Despite its economic potential, Nigeria faces manifold challenges, including sharp socio-economic inequalities, with under half of the population living below the poverty line (Abubakar et al., 2022). This juxtaposition of wealth and poverty is a recurring theme in Nigeria's development. The country's historical and contemporary leaders have been instrumental in shaping Nigeria's path. Figures such as Oba Rilwan Akiolu symbolise a mixture of traditional and modern leadership approaches (Oolasunkanmi, 2023). Recently, Oba remarked *"And things are going to get better. We should learn to get close to the Almighty"*, combining economic insights with religious convictions (Kasali, 2024). Nigeria's unique blend of traditional and contemporary leadership styles will be explored in this chapter, through a detailed analysis of academic literature, and survey and interview data from local leaders (*'Ogas'*) and experts.

How do the Nigerians characterise leaders?

Within Nigeria, leadership often adopts a hierarchical structure, prioritising respect for authority and seniority within organisations (CCBS Survey, 2024). Leaders are perceived as strategic thinkers and decision-makers, who are expected to embody specific qualities, such as, for example, resourcefulness, organisational experience, and technical expertise. As one of the respondents in the CCBS Survey (2024) noted, *"leadership in Nigeria is more of hierarchy than collective interests,"* which serves to illustrate the culturally ingrained preference for clear leadership structures. Nigerian leaders are also respected for their ability to compromise and maintain fairness, fostering trust within their teams. This approach aligns with the cultural emphasis upon accountability and the importance of age and professional accomplishments in establishing leadership authority (CCBS Survey, 2024). Leaders who offer equal opportunities to people from all social and ethnic backgrounds are fair and embody the inclusiveness of Nigeria's diverse cultural fabric. These qualities contribute towards the establishment of courteous, motivated, and harmonious work environments (Ejimabo, 2013; Hassan & Lituchy, 2016). Nigerian leadership styles also generally lean toward autocracy, with leaders often making decisions independently within strict hierarchical structures, a tendency that is profoundly shaped by the nation's risk-averse culture, where leaders are expected to provide a clear vision and be attentive, albeit subordinates rarely influence key decisions (CCBS Survey, 2020; Sokoya, 1998). Ejimabo's (2013) findings were also supported by the results of the CCBS Survey (2020), where over half of the respondents stated that traditional values also play a pivotal role in leadership perceptions, where elders embody natural authority as a result of their wisdom and experience, which makes them respected figures, both within community and organisational settings. Empirical research further underscores the cultural roots of leadership styles within Nigerian organisations, particularly within small and medium enterprises (SMEs). For instance, Lawal et al.'s (2014) study of 268 Nigerian SMEs found that an autocratic leadership style prevailed, with significant power gaps between owners and employees. This approach restricts employee involvement and mirrors the broader cultural norm in which hierarchical and autocratic structures are common across various sectors (Lawal et al., 2014). Interestingly, research by Ojokuku et al. (2013) found that there was no significant relationship between leadership style and organisational effectiveness in Nigeria, which appears to indicate that whilst autocratic styles are prevalent, they do not necessarily have a direct impact upon employee performance. This insight is in accordance with findings from Ukaidi (2016), who noted that autocratic leadership can yield high production levels within certain contexts, albeit this often depends heavily upon the leader's presence. The connection between leadership and cultural values in Nigeria extends beyond business into traditional social structures. Nigerian communities often derive authority from hierarchical positions, with elders typically responsible for decision-making. Leaders within such settings are expected to provide direction, sparingly delegate tasks, and uphold cultural norms like respect for elders, collective decision-making, and the preservation of peace. Through these practices, leaders maintain their role as custodians of tradition, foster community cohesion, resolve disputes, and impart cultural values, often using storytelling as a tool for transmitting wisdom (Adedokun, 2008; Igwe & Ateke, 2019). Consequently, elder figures naturally occupy key leadership roles within Nigerian organisations also, whereas younger members respect and adhere to the decisions set forth by their seniors (Ejimabo, 2013; Iguisi, 2014). Despite the dominance of traditional autocratic styles, a gradual shift toward more inclusive, transformational leadership is emerging, driven by challenges such as economic instability. According to one of our CCBS Survey (2024) respondents, Ughulu, transformational leaders inspire their staff to go above and beyond by exhibiting qualities like charisma, vision, and empathy. In actuality, they inspire teams by providing individualised assistance, outlining objectives clearly, and promoting creativity by motivating staff members to assume responsibility for their jobs. They prioritise innovation and socio-economic progress and are increasingly advocated as means of addressing these challenges by aligning organisational goals with broader societal needs. This shift reflects a broader move towards integrating Nigeria's cultural heritage with modern governance principles, suggesting a future vision for Nigerian leadership that is both adaptive and progressive in nature (Nwankwo et al., 2019).

Survey results and what local respondents say

The CCBS Survey (2020-2024) was completed by a range of Nigerian executives (*top ogas*) across various industries, offering valuable insights into the challenges and expectations of leadership within Nigeria. In order to enhance the generalisability of the data, we drew upon survey data from two different periods of data collection. The most significant of these findings are discussed in turn below. Firstly, according to the survey respondents, Nigerian leaders operate within an environment marked by significant socio-economic obstacles, including, amongst other things, the country's vast ethnic heterogeneity and complex cultural dynamics. These factors, in turn, demand that Nigerian leaders possess resilience and adaptability to navigate the complexities of their roles. Alongside resilience, the respondents also unanimously agreed that strong decision-making skills and visionary thinking are essential qualities for Nigerian leaders to possess (CCBS Survey, 2020). At the same time, the respondents identified areas where Nigerian leaders might fall short, pointing out notable differences between Nigerian leadership practises and what one sees in other countries. For instance, the respondents indicated that Nigerian leaders often emphasise maintaining strict control over their subordinates rather than prioritising a service-orientated approach. This management style can, in turn, result in leaders who do not consistently model desired behaviours and are sometimes perceived as being overly authoritative (CCBS Survey, 2020). This was illustrated by one of the respondents, Appolo Goma, a CEO, who stated: "*a lot of people do not practice what they preach* [in Nigerian leadership]" (CCBS Survey, 2020), thus underscoring that leaders' actions may not always align with their words. The next key finding is that the majority of the executives felt that leaders should dedicate time to understanding and addressing their subordinates' well-being. Additionally, two-thirds of the respondents preferred not to maintain a rigid personal distance from their subordinates. This is in line with the work of Udegbe (2012), who posited that love, trust, and respect are foundational elements of Nigerian leadership culture. However, one respondent, Adedeji, observed that "*leadership in Nigeria is hierarchical in structure. It is more about hierarchy than collective interests*" (CCBS Survey, 2024), whilst another respondent, Uduma, noted that leaders "*actively spend time ensuring the personal well-being of their team members*" whilst still encouraging competition within their teams to achieve optimal results (CCBS Survey, 2024). The respondents were also in agreement over the fact that fostering healthy competition within teams can drive employees to excel (CCBS Survey, 2020). Another notable finding was that most respondents assumed that their subordinates would follow established rules, albeit some acknowledged that circumstances might sometimes justify flexibility. As Ehidiamen Olanrewaju Eromosele explained, "*the rules are there as a guide, but initiatives that lead to better outcomes are encouraged*" (CCBS Survey, 2020). Finally, the survey revealed that it remains uncommon to address leaders by their first name in Nigeria, but that this practice is gradually becoming more accepted, especially in organisations with younger staff. As communications manager Obabayi Fagade observed, "*this is a growing trend, particularly in companies with a young workforce*" (CCBS Survey, 2020). Another change concerns gender equality, a relevant issue throughout Africa and in Nigerian business circles. According to the respondents, female leaders often need to prove themselves more than their male counterparts, working harder to gain respect and credibility. However, there is an increasing acceptance of female leaders within Nigerian organisations (CCBS Survey, 2024).

Local leadership analysis

Dr. Olanrewaju Olasupo Ariyibi: a Nigerian leadership scholar

Nigerian leadership is influenced by a distinct blend of contemporary influences, hierarchical systems, and traditional beliefs. Dr. Olanrewaju Olasupo Ariyibi, a lecturer at Lagos State University provides insightful commentary on this changing paradigm within Nigerian leadership. His observations emphasise how cultural customs and the requirements of modern leadership interact (Ariyibi, 30 November 2024). At the beginning of our interview, Ariyibi informed us that Nigerian leadership is distinguished by its goal-orientedness. That is to say, he proceeded to tell us, leaders emphasise compliance and directive authority, placing the attainment of company goals above all else. With well-defined channels for communication and decision-making, hierarchical organisations predominate (30 November 2024). Because it is prohibited to skip tiers in this structure, respect for leadership authority and organisational order is thus reinforced. Furthermore, leadership is heavily influenced by age and experience, which, in turn, reflects a culture that values elders and their judgement (Ariyibi, 30 November 2024). In Nigeria, leadership styles frequently correspond with societal standards of group conformity. Leaders anticipate that staff members will follow instructions designed to help them accomplish shared objectives. The senior leader, known as the '*Oga*,' is highly respected, and their choices are rarely challenged. Although this method guarantees efficient organisational operations, authority can occasionally be confused with unbridled power (Ariyibi, 30 November 2024). Navigating the Nigerian corporate climate can thus at times present unique hurdles for international managers. Acculturation, or adapting to local languages, cultures, and market-specific dynamics, is one of the main challenges. Despite English being the official language, local dialects and Pidgin English often hinder communication. Furthermore, Ariyibi proceeded to explain, employees frequently oppose foreign policies that are imposed without taking local cultural circumstances into account, which emphasises the necessity of adaptable leadership techniques (30 November, 2024). Later in the interview, Ariyibi explicated that an essential component of good leadership within Nigeria is establishing trust. Building trust amongst employees requires transparency within one's decisions and actions. Therefore, leaders are required to keep lines of communication open, fulfil their commitments, and acknowledge accomplishments quickly. Empathy is also important in this regard, Ariyibi explained, in as far as leaders are urged to foster inclusive workplaces and include staff members within decision-making processes. This strategy boosts staff engagement and morale, whilst, simultneously, promoting alignment with company objectives (Ariyibi, 30 November 2024). Next, Ariyibi told us that over time, Nigerian leadership methods are beginning to incorporate influences from around the world. The adoption of inclusive and cooperative approaches has been aided by exposure to global best practices. To be successful, these tactics must be modified to fit Nigeria's cultural and economic realities, Ariyibi pointed out. Leaders are better able to negotiate the intricacies of the Nigerian business environment when they strike a balance between local customs and global perspectives. Additionally, as leadership in Nigeria evolves, there is a nascent understanding of the necessity of putting employee welfare before company objectives (Ariyibi, 30 November 2024). In summary, a dynamic fusion of tradition and modernisation defines Nigerian corporate leadership. There is a move towards more open, compassionate, and inclusive behaviours, even whilst cultural norms and hierarchical institutions still play a significant part. This development emphasises how crucial it is to strike a balance between corporate goals and worker welfare and to modify leadership techniques in accordance with regional circumstances. For local and international CEOs hoping to succeed in Nigeria's commercial environment, such strategies offer a strong foundation.

Emmanuel Emielu: a Nigerian cross-cultural trainer

Emmanuel Emielu is a Nigerian leadership expert, consultant, and public speaker who specialises in organisational transformation and leadership development within Nigeria. With extensive experience in both local and international business environments, Emielu has collaborated with various organisations, helping them navigate the unique challenges of the Nigerian market. According to Emielu (21 November 2024), understanding Nigerian leadership requires a nuanced grasp of the country's broader business context, which is shaped by distinct cultural, social, and economic dynamics. A key theme Emielu underscored in the interview concerned the entrenched role of hierarchical leadership within Nigeria. Traditionally, Nigerian organisations have been characterised by a top-down structure, with centralised decision-making processes and authority resting with senior-level leaders. As Emielu explained, *"In Nigeria, it is a matter of positional leadership, where the boss has the final say upon important matters"* (Emielu, 21 November 2024). Although this model still dominates in local businesses, Emielu informed us that there has been a shift within multinational corporations and progressive Nigerian companies, where more inclusive leadership styles are emerging, promoting collaboration and shared decision-making. Emielu also stressed the importance of ethical values within Nigerian leadership. In relation to this, they drew a clear distinction between leaders who prioritise integrity and those who do not. Nigerian leaders must embody a combination of empathy, credibility, and competence: *"A good leader must not only guide their team toward organisational goals but also understand their employees' personal challenges"* (Emielu, 21 November 2024). Personal traits such as honesty, integrity, and effective communication are also essential for success, Emielu argued, particularly in a country where economic hardship can impact upon employees' lives. Another emergent trend within Nigerian businesses is corporate social responsibility (CSR). Emielu observed that leaders who prioritise the welfare of their employees build trust, motivation, and loyalty. As they put it, *"A leader who can understand and connect with the personal lives of their employees builds trust, which is essential for motivation and loyalty"* (Emielu, 21 November 2024). Empathy has become a cornerstone of effective leadership, helping leaders navigate Nigeria's complex business environment. The influence of globalisation has also profoundly shaped Nigerian leadership. Emielu noted that Nigerian leaders are increasingly exposed to international best practices, which, in turn, has led to the modernisation of their leadership approaches. However, he stressed the importance of adapting these global insights to the local context: *"Global leadership influences have brought about new ways of thinking, but Nigerian leaders have to adjust these ideas to suit our own unique challenges"* (Emielu, 21 November 2024). This blending of global strategies with local cultural values reflects the evolving nature of leadership within Nigeria. Emielu highlighted opportunities for foreign businesspeople, noting that success in Nigeria depends upon understanding and adapting to the local culture. *"Foreigners who are willing to understand the culture, adapt, and build local relationships tend to succeed more than those who come with a strictly Western mindset"* (Emielu, 21 November 2024). He also pointed to the rising influence of women within Nigerian business, particularly in sectors such as technology and finance, which marks a positive shift in leadership dynamics. Finally, Emielu stressed the importance of moral values within Nigerian leadership. Integrity, humility, and self-control are essential for building trust and inspiring teams. *"If we do not apply values like integrity and humility, we will not have the ability to inspire and guide people effectively"* (Emielu, 21 November 2024).

In-country leadership bestseller

One of Nigeria's *ogbonge* (best-selling) books on leadership is *Effective Leadership in Nigeria*, written by Onyema Nkwocha, an accomplished leader and academic with a deep understanding of the unique challenges Nigeria faces. Published in 2012, the book provides a thoughtful examination of the Nigerian leadership landscape, focusing on the political, social, and economic issues that shape the nation's needs. Nkwocha argues that Nigerian leaders must balance traditional values with modern principles, advocating for integrity, accountability, and ethical governance in order to build public trust in a country where corruption and institutional distrust are prevalent. As Nkwocha states, *"a [Nigerian] leader is that individual who is readily enthusiastic and eager to first, serve others, whose ideas, goals, visions, plans and strategies are in harmony with those of the group, association or nation"* (Nkwocha, 2012, p. 71).

Nkwocha also emphasises cultural insight and local knowledge as beng vital tools for both navigating Nigeria's diverse market and driving economic and social progress. A mutually synergetic and symbiotic relationship naturally starts to exist between the people, the government, the leader, and the entire nation with respect to civic duties and responsibilities. More than merely a guidebook, *Effective Leadership in Nigeria* calls upon Nigerian leaders to embrace a visionary, responsive approach that can create lasting, positive change within communities and organisations across the nation.

Local leadership book	
Title	*Effective Leadership in Nigeria*
Subtitle	Practical Ways to Build Effective, Inspiring, Transformational and Visionary Leadership and Governance in Nigeria
Author	Onyema Nkwocha
Publisher	AuthorHouse
Year	2012
ISBN	1468506781

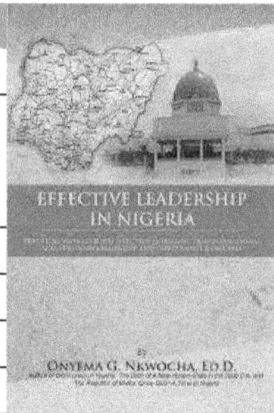

Nigerian leadership YouTube review

Samuel Sanusi, the General Secretary and CEO of the Bible Society of Nigeria, discusses an upcoming leadership conference in Abuja, which will be chaired by former Nigerian President Olusegun Obasanjo. In the video, Sanusi underscores the urgent need for transformational, value-based leadership in Nigeria. He focuses upon foundational principles like justice, integrity, wisdom, and social harmony as being essential values that leaders should embody across all sectors, whether religious, secular, private, or public organisations (Arise TV, 2023, 1:45). For Sanusi, these values are critical for fostering progress and unity within Nigerian society and business organisations. He states, *"If there is justice in the land, everything will fall in line,"* thus underscoring how justice is the cornerstone of societal harmony and effective leadership (Arise TV, 2023, 4:12). Other issues, such as the gender gap, are also undergoing change. Efforts to close this gap and promote female participation within business leadership are being championed by institutions like the Nigerian Stock Exchange (NSE). During an International Women's Day event, Oscar Onyema, the Chief Executive Officer of the NSE, underscored the Exchange's commitment to gender parity by aligning with the United Nations Sustainable Development Goal 5 (gender equality). He noted that the NSE actively supports initiatives that enhance female representation across various sectors, including the boardroom (Channels Television, 2018, 1:25). A recent example of this commitment was the NSE's participation within an educational program that admitted eighty-nine female students, designed to develop future business leaders and create balance in economic opportunities (Channels Television, 2018, 3:33). These initiatives demonstrate how institutions can play a pivotal role in fostering inclusivity and accelerating gender parity in leadership. Onyema concluded by emphasising the importance of pressing for progress in eliminating barriers to female participation within business and leadership. He reiterated that sustained effort and collaboration are necessary to close the persistent gender gap in Nigeria and beyond (Channels Television, 2018, 5:14). In a different video about how leaders should treat others, the speaker, Adesanya, argued that Nigerian leaders need to treat everyone equitably, using varying approaches such as being gentle with some, and more assertive with others to effectively guide them. As they put it: *"You do not deal with people similarly; you deal with people equitably"* (Adesanya, 2013, 0:22). Flexibility is crucial within Nigerian leadership, with successful leaders knowing when to adjust or temporarily 'suspend' certain leadership principles to address specific challenges unique to their environment. Nigerian leaders must navigate diverse cultural and organisational dynamics, demonstrating adaptability whilst upholding core qualities like credibility. This credibility is built on a foundation of competence and character, both of which are essential for earning trust and maintaining effective leadership within Nigeria's complex and hierarchical professional landscape (Adesanya, 2013).

Understanding hierarchy in Nigeria

Hierarchy is a fundamental aspect of Nigerian business culture, where authority and decision-making are traditionally centralised in the upper echelons of organisations. The structured, top-down approach in Nigerian companies reinforces respect for age, seniority, and authority, which, in turn, reflects the strong power distance within the culture, where hierarchy is widely accepted without question (Otiwa et al., 2020). This is evident within Nigerian organisational structures that follow strict chains of command, which serve to create predictability and stability. Historically, Nigerian leadership values were community-centred, with leaders gaining influence through collective achievements and communal respect (Ekekwe, 2011). However, the colonial era shifted this focus towards individual power and wealth accumulation, thus establishing centralised authority as a prominent feature within Nigerian organisations (Ekekwe, 2011). This shift aligns with bureaucratic practises in Nigerian businesses, where authority is often vested in those at the top, who are known as *ogas*, and decision-making roles are typically confined to senior-level figures (Ezirim et al., 2010). The organisational culture within Nigeria's private sector is, therefore, highly formalised, where rules, hierarchy, and specialised roles are integral to maintaining a sense of order and accountability (Ezirim et al., 2010). This is reflected in the CCBS Survey (2024) results, which show that Nigerian leaders place significant emphasis upon education and diplomas. Cultural influences also shape Nigerian leadership styles, particularly with respect to ethnic and familial values that emphasise respect for seniority. The CCBS Survey (2024) lends support to notion of the traditional leader's role being the father of the community, in as far as the majority of the respondents reported that authority comes along with responsibility for employees' wellbeing. The emphasis upon established authority figures across various ethnic groups reflects broader social values that play a crucial role in terms of maintaining hierarchical structures within the business sector (Adekunle & Jude, 2014). The strong emphasis upon hierarchy and strict adherence to established roles has a limitation, which is that it can sometimes limit flexibility and may slow down adaptability within highly competitive environments (Adegboye, 2013). Finally, women's progression to leadership positions in Nigeira is often hindered by these traditional cultural expectations around hierarchy, which serves to confine many women to supportive roles (Ojo & Ajani, 2024). However, with Nigeria being such a hierarchy-dicatated business society, that does not mean women do not have a place within it. Actually, according to Buchholz (2024), Nigeria is now the second highest ranking country in the world where a woman is most likely to be your boss (*oga*). On the other hand, this does not mean that in large Nigerian companies, women are the ones making the decisions. This is evidenced by the fact that women only represent 17% of board chairs in large companies, and within these companies only 7% of the CEOs are women (IFC, 2021).

How Nigerians achieve leadership empathy

Within the contemporary business landscape in Nigeria, cultivating and maintaining sustainable customer-business relationships is crucial, particularly for long-term competitiveness and brand loyalty (Moguluwa & Amadi, 2021). Like elsewhere, emotional intelligence (EI) is also being increasingly recognised as a critical factor for effective leadership in Nigeria, particularly within high-stress sectors such as healthcare. Defined as the capacity to understand, manage, and utilise emotions constructively, EI enables leaders to foster positive work environments and motivate employees, which, in turn, can enhance their job performance (Goleman, 1998; Mayer & Salovey, 1993). Within Nigeria's public healthcare sector, where leaders frequently face challenges like limited resources and workforce disputes, EI has been found to play an essential role in terms of supporting employee performance and workplace cohesion (Oyewunmi et al., 2015). In addition to the service sector, empathy is also a key component of effective leadership within Nigeria more broadly, by virtue of the prevailing cultural norms and values that serve to shape expectations for leadership behaviours. For instance, a 'paternalistic' leadership style, characterised by a combination of guidance and genuine concern for team well-being, is highly valued within Nigeria. This was corroborate dby the results of the CCBS Survey (2024), in as a far as there was broad agreement amongst the respondents over the statement *"Managers should actively spend time ensuring the personal well-being of their team members"*. The fact that leaders must embody a combination of empathy, credibility, and competence was also noted by our interviewee, Emielu, a leadership consultant in Nigeria, who stated: *"A good leader must not only guide their team toward organisational goals but also understand their employees' personal challenges"* (Emielu, 21 November 2024). Moreover, they told us, personal traits such as honesty, integrity, and effective communication are also essential for success in Nigeria. Furthermore, leaders are expected to exhibit vision and a positive influence, along with responsibility and protective behaviour towards their subordinates. This leadership style aligns with Nigeria's diverse ethnic landscape, requiring leaders to display flexibility, cultural awareness, and sensitivity to ethnic diversity within their teams (Lawal et al., 2014; Njoku, 2013). Osunde and Olokooba (2014) further emphasise that Nigerian leaders must be sensitive to the ethnic identities of team members in order to maintain respectful and effective communication. Building upon this, EI is also a critical aspect of empathy-driven leadership within Nigeria's corporate environment. Research by Onabote (2021) indicates that leaders with high EI—characterised by self-awareness, self-regulation, motivation, empathy, and social skills—create supportive and inclusive work environments. This approach positively affects employee engagement, morale, and overall organisational performance. Similarly, Esu (2013) highlights that leaders with high EI foster cooperative workplace dynamics and increase team cohesiveness, ultimately supporting Nigeria's broader national development goals. By building healthier workplace relationships, leaders contribute towards organisational resilience, increased productivity, and the establishment of a more empathetic corporate culture across Nigeria's sectors. Together, these findings illustrate that empathy in leadership is foundational for achieving loyalty, better performance, and cohesion within Nigeria's unique cultural context. From the service sector to manufacturing, empathy-driven leadership and EI have proven essential to fostering organisational success (Esu, 2013; Onabote, 2021).

Paraguay

Federico Hurtado Wiessner, Mohamed Biari, Renske Legebeke, Robin Bartelings,
Samuel Johansson & Zorelly Edam

The Republic of Paraguay (Spanish: *República del Paraguay*; Guaraní: *Tetã Paraguái),* is a landlocked nation situated within the heart of South America that takes its name from the Paraguay River. The derivation of the river's name is believed to come from the *Guaraní* language and means *"the river that gives birth to the sea"* or *"crown of waters"* (Fleck, 2021). The country's landscape is mostly flat, with its highest peak, Cerro Perro, spanning 842 metres, whilst the lowest point, located at the confluence of the Paraguay and Paraná rivers, which are important trade and transport routes, lies at just 46 metres. The nation adopted the colours of the French flag, inspired by the ideals of liberty, equality, and fraternity from the French Revolution (Bethell, 1987). As well as these ideals, religion is also fundamentally important to daily life, with around 90% of the Paraguayan population being Roman Catholic. The Catholic Church's influence is deeply embedded within the culture, and there are many national holidays of especial religious significance. There are two official languages in Paraguay, Spanish and *Guaraní.* Spanish is used in the media, education, and governmental sectors, whilst Guaraní reflects the country's strong indigenous roots.
The organisational culture and business leadership in Paraguay is profoundly influenced by the country's rich cultural heritage and complex history of navigating significant political and economic challenges, which means that the expectations for leaders are deeply intertwined with the values of the Paraguayan people (Meyer, 2013). Integrity and trustworthiness are paramount, as citizens demand transparency and accountability from their representatives. These values are also reflected in the business sector, as informal networks, flexibility, and personal relationships are crucial (Boojihawon et al., 2020). Alongside this, leaders in smaller organisations tend to combine participative and directive styles to respond to evolving local conditions (Kwan Chung & Cardozo, 2018). This chapter builds upon these insights by examining leadership practices through desk-based research, surveys, and interviews with local professionals and leaders, revealing how they navigate and succeed in the Paraguayan business environment.

How Paraguayans characterise leaders?

Historically, Paraguayan leadership has often taken on an autocratic inflection, in as far as senior-level management impose their ideas and beliefs upon employees. This approach is also reflective of a societal preference for strong decisive leadership within Paraguay (Sánchez-Báez et al., 2019). Despite this historical preference, leadership within small- and medium-sized enterprises (SMEs) now primarily follows the situational leadership model, according to Kwan Chung and Cardoso (2018). This model is participatory in nature, and involves leaders and employees engage in the decision-making process together, in order to motivate and instil a sense of shared responsibility across the entire organisation. The situational leadership model in many respects is in accordance with Paraguayan culture, where family and trust are accorded significant importance. This is illustrated in Kwan Chung and Cardozo's (2018) survey-based research, where 62% of their respondents indicated that they had a family connection with the company owner and concluded that relationships are important within the Paraguayan work environment. However, the situational leadership model has been criticised on the grounds that it results in limited employee empowerment, as the participative style stands in contrast to a delegative approach. This point is in line with Yukl's (2002) observations on hierarchical organisational cultures, where centralised control can in some instances lead to better delegation and encourage innovation at the lower levels of the organisational hierarchy. This limitation is further supported by findings in the context of agile distribution strategies, which also emphasise the need for flexibility and responsiveness in leadership to adapt to market demands in Paraguay (Boojihawon et al., 2021). This characterisation of Paraguayan organisations and leaders was corroborated by our interviewee, Richard Ruiz, an expert in organisational coaching and leadership in Paraguay, who explained to us that the country's authoritarian history continues to profoundly shape contemporary workplace dynamics. In our interview, he also underscored a gradual shift towards more transformational forms of leadership in the country, with an attendant focus upon collaboration, transparency, and commitment, particularly within more modern industries in the country (16 November 2024). Moreover, it is crucial to recognise that leadership styles vary significantly across different sectors within Paraguay. For example, the commerce sector tends to exhibit a higher frequency of participative leadership, particularly amongst female leaders, whilst the industrial sector is often characterised by a more directive style, with leaders invariably making decisions on behalf of their employees (Kwan Chung & Cardozo, 2018). Such variation with respect to Paraguayan leadership is in accordance with Sánchez Báez's (2019) findings, which indicate that the organisational culture in Paraguay plays a significant role in shaping leadership practices across different sectors. As aforementioned, leadership in Paraguay has traditionally been dominated by an autocratic style, characterised by centralised authority and decisive leadership. Nonetheless, there is an emergent shift towards a more participatory approach, in an effort to involve employees more within decision-making processes. Notwithstanding the benefits of this shift, it is important to stress that this transition is likely to take time, as the country's autocratic history is deeply ingrained (Kwan Chung & Cardozo, 2018; Sánchez-Báez et al., 2019). Another important quality valued in Paraguayan leaders pertains to their ethical conduct, which requires leaders to be honest and truthful in their interactions with business partners and employees (Soto et al., 2003). High intellect and dignity are also valued attributes within the Paraguayan leadership context, particularly in terms of improving the level of support provided to employees within organisations (Soto et al., 2003). In our interview with her, Maria Esther Cabrali also emphasised the importance of leaders being able to transform problems into opportunities and encourage the development of solutions that yield societal benefit (12 November 2024). Conversely, unethical conduct and violation of the law are two primary reasons for withdrawal of support towards a leader within Paraguayan organisations (Soto et al., 2003). In conclusion, leadership is evolving in Paraguay, particularly within SMEs. Sectoral variations, combined with the way leaders interact and treat their subordinates, also play a critical role in terms of maintaining trust and support within Paraguayan organisations. As a result, the shift towards a more participatory approach is progressing slowly due to deeply embedded traditions.

Survey results and what local respondents say

In order to provide a verifiably accurate depiction of leadership within Paraguay, the CCBS surveys that were administered in both 2023 and 2024 were distributed amongst senior-level professionals working within diverse industries in Paraguay. These surveys served as a pivotal tool through which to gather insights into leadership practices and trends in Paraguay. The responses reveal intriguing patterns that shed light upon the unique leadership ethos in Paraguay. This section examines the most significant of these findings in depth, in an effort to provide a nuanced understanding of the cultural and organisational dynamics that shape leadership in Paraguay. The first noteworthy finding is that a significant proportion of the respondents expressed that managerial decisions are often viewed as definitive, thus reflecting a preference for clarity and consistency in leadership styles (CCBS Survey, 2023). This aligns with the high-Power Distance index score for Paraguay, which means that leaders are expected to make decisive choices that affirm their authority (Hofstede Insights, 2023). This was further corroborated by one respondent, who noted, *"Leaders here* [Paraguay] *often make decisions quickly, but the best ones always circle back to seek team input"* (CCBS Survey, 2023). Despite this sentiment, just under one-third of the respondents emphasised that leaders should remain open to feedback and reconsideration when necessary. The next key finding is that personal well-being emerged as a core focus for leaders, in as far as over half of the respondents stated that it is common for leaders to dedicate time to fostering the well-being of their teams and actively support work-life balance (CCBS Survey, 2023). One participant expressed this focus on employee well-being as follows, *"A good leader knows that a motivated and healthy team performs better"* (CCBS Survey, 2023). This emphasis upon team welfare resonates with the collectivist traits that are inherent to Paraguayan culture, where interpersonal harmony and group well-being often take precedence (Varela et al., 2010). The nature of leadership communication styles also stood out in the survey, as just over one-third of the respondents preferred an approachable demeanour, valuing candid conversations over hierarchical protocols (CCBS Survey, 2023). However, traditional respect for authority remains significant within certain sectors. As one respondent explained, *"Whilst many leaders are moving towards a collaborative approach, the respect for formal titles and roles persists within key industries"* (CCBS Survey, 2024). This duality highlights the evolving nature of leadership within Paraguay, where collaboration and hierarchy coexist within organisations. With respect to the specific traits that are valued in leaders, the majority of the respondents, selected resourcefulness and charisma as being indispensable (CCBS Survey, 2023). Nearly half of the respondents also underscored the importance of intellectual acumen and strong networks, with one remarking, *"A leader in Paraguay must think two steps ahead and know who to call to make it happen"* (CCBS Survey, 2024). These attributes reveal an emphasis upon strategic foresight and the ability to navigate complex social and professional networks, which, in turn, are critical within the Paraguayan business environment. This is further supported by Sánchez-Báez et al. (2019), who emphasise the importance of personal values and organisational culture in driving innovation and decision-making within Paraguayan businesses. Interestingly, there were varying perspectives upon gender equality in leadership. Less than one-quarter of the respondents agreed that men and women have equal opportunities to attain senior-level roles, thus signalling that more progress needs to be made in this area (CCBS Survey, 2023). In relation to this, one respondent remarked, *"Cultural norms are shifting, but there is still a way to go for true parity"* (CCBS Survey, 2024). This finding reflects ongoing societal changes and the gradual dismantling of traditional gender norms within the leadership context. Finally, leadership in Paraguay was seen to balance tradition with adaptability, by virtue of the fact that a significant proportion of the respondents described leaders as being custodians of both organisational goals and cultural values. As one professional concluded, *"Good leadership here is not just about success—it is about inspiring trust and respect across generations"* (CCBS Survey, 2023). This dual role reflects the unique interplay between Paraguay's rich cultural heritage and its aspirations for modern and inclusive workplaces. Scholars like Chung and Cardozo (2018) also emphasise the importance of situational leadership styles in SMEs, where leaders often serve as cultural and operational stewards. These findings thus provide a comprehensive and nuanced understanding of leadership in Paraguay, revealing a blend of cultural richness, emerging inclusivity, and a focus upon team empowerment.

Local leadership analysis

María Esther Cabrali: a Paraguayan Leadership Scholar

María Esther Cabrali, an educator and former national technology specialist within Paraguay, has contributed towards the country's educational centre initiatives like the "one computer per child." Working with Columbia University and the Catholic University of Chile, she has developed multiple leadership skills within the field of education. At the beginning of our interview on 12 November 2024, Cabrali talked about the unique characteristics of leadership in Paraguay, particularly within the educational sector. Specifically, she drew attention to the strong presence of women within leadership roles in this sector. Figures like Dr. Blanca Belar and the late Marta Lafuente were cited as quintessential examples of effective leaders that are constantly conducting research about leadership skills in Paraguay due to their technical expertise and commitment to progress in the country. In response to the question, *"Do you think schools in Paraguay are open to adopting foreign leadership practices, or do they prefer more traditional and local approaches?"*, she opined that many Paraguayan institutions still prefer traditional approaches over adopting foreign leadership strategies (18 November 2024). In addition, she stated that her leadership philosophy is focused upon transforming problems into opportunities. She looks for a leadership approach that is grounded in values like integrity, empathy, and innovation in order to address Paraguay's leadership challenges. She then moved onto explicate that globalisation has brought valuable new perspectives to Paraguayan organisations, which had historically preferred to retain traditional decision-making structures. Furthermore, she discussed examples of successful initiatives, such as, for example, her work on the integration of digital skills within educational programs, which demonstrated the power of collaborative problem-solving (18 November 2024). Regarding this, however, she also told us that the integration of these practices face resistance due to cultural and institutional inertia. As she put it during the interview, "*I think that we are not ready for foreign leadership*" (18 November 2024). In light of this, she called for the development of a gradual, context-sensitive approach that would incorporate foreign leadership models in such a way that ensures they align with local values and traditions. When asked about cultural distinctions that influence leadership styles in Paraguay, Cabrali proceeded to inform us that Paraguayan leaders tend to prioritise social considerations and community well-being over efficiency or profitability (18 November 2024). Finally, whilst contemplating the future of leadership in Paraguay, Cabrali expressed optimism about the potential for change. She underscored the need for leaders to adopt a problem-solving mindset, turning challenges into opportunities and looking for strategies that benefit all citizens in the country. By focusing on long-term societal impact rather than immediate gains, Paraguayan leadership can take care of the complex demands that this rapidly changing world brings. Cabrali concluded the interview by reiterating her belief that effective leadership must balance local cultural values with innovative strategies in order to achieve meaningful progress within Paraguay (18 November 2024).

Richard Ruiz: a Paraguayan Cross-Cultural Trainer

Richard Ruiz, a psychologist and master's degree graduate in cognitive-behavioural psychotherapy, has become a leader in Paraguayan organisational coaching. With experience across Latin America, Ruiz has combined his sales expertise with psychology to help shape leadership practices for the better. His journey began in Mexico, where selling leadership books subsequently ignited his passion for studying the subject. Since moving to Paraguay sixteen years ago, Ruiz has served as Director of the Leadership Centre at the American University of Paraguay, focusing on leadership's transformative potential. At the start of our interview with him, Ruiz (16 November 2024) underscored how Paraguay's historical and cultural context has significantly shaped its business leadership landscape. Many Paraguayans, shaped by decades of authoritarian rule, tend to avoid expressing their opinions openly, out of fear over the potential consequences. As he stated: "*When you are in a dictatorship, people express themselves less*" and "*They do not say what they think because they believe they could be punished*" (Ruiz, 16 November 2024). This hesitancy, in turn, hampers communication within teams, making assertiveness and transparency ongoing challenges. Despite these challenges, Ruiz told us that there has been a gradual shift towards transformational leadership in the country (Ruiz, 16 November 2024). Modern Paraguayan leaders increasingly prioritise collaboration, transparency, and long-term engagement over traditional top-down approaches. However, hierarchical structures nevertheless remain deeply entrenched within certain industries, particularly the agriculture and manufacturing sectors, which Ruiz described as *"very verticalist, very traditionalist"* (Ruiz, 16 November 2024). Within these environments, decision-making is often rigid, with minimal opportunities for dialogue or innovation. One of the most significant challenges that Ruiz encounters in his work is bridging generational gaps within organisations. In relation to this, he explained that senior leaders, accustomed to issuing commands without providing any context, often clash with younger employees who expect dialogue and feedback. To address this, Ruiz (16 November 2024) emphasises coaching strategies that foster mutual understanding, encourage leaders to provide context for their decisions, and cultivate environments in which feedback and dialogue thrive. Accountability has also become a pivotal aspect of Paraguayan leadership. Ruiz (16 November, 2024) underscores the growing implementation of mechanisms such as anonymous reporting and employee feedback tools, which, in turn, promote ethical behaviour and discourage misconduct. These tools place leaders under continuous scrutiny, pushing them to adopt more inclusive and ethical practices. To conclude the interview, Ruiz (16 November 2024) reflected upon global leadership challenges, highlighting the universal nature of these issues. He observed striking similarities in the communication issues faced by teams in Paraguay and those in the U.S. Ruiz believes that the key to addressing these challenges lies in mastering persuasive communication, a concept he explores in his upcoming book, *"The leaders Vehicle"* (Ruiz, 16 November, 2024).

In-country leadership bestseller

One of the bestselling books about leadership is written by Alfred Pajés, a Paraguayan expert in leadership and team management. He has experience coaching individuals and organisations to improve their leadership qualities. *Los Nuevos Poderes del Líder* is his first book, which came to fruition with the support of Ana Nieto Churruca, a renowned Spanish author and founder of Triunfacontulibro.com. This collaboration helped Pajés structure his insights and share them with a wider audience (Casa del Libro, n.d.). In *Los nuevos poderes del líder*, Alfred Pajés shares insights on leadership, which are particularly relevant for Paraguay and other Latin American countries. He makes it clear that modern leadership goes beyond traditional authority and focuses on self-awareness (*darse cuenta*). Self-awareness is fundamental for leaders to understand their own behaviours and emotions, which, in turn, helps them lead effectively. Pajés explains how this process of introspection allows leaders to identify barriers and leverage their strengths, a lesson particularly valuable in the community-driven culture of Paraguay (Pajés, 2022). Another key point Pajés underscores is the importance of emotional connections. Within the Paraguayan context, where personal relationships often outweigh formal rules, leaders must develop empathy and emotional intelligence in order to build trust and foster collaboration (Pajés, 2022). Pajés describes these emotional connections as central to leadership, reflecting the expectations of more 'humane' and emotionally attuned leaders. The book also emphasises resilience and adaptability as essential qualities for Paraguayan leaders, due, in part, to the fact they frequently face challenges such as economic uncertainty or limited resources. Pajés argues that resilience helps leaders overcome obstacles, whilst, simultaneously, inspiring their teams to stay focused on their goals (Pajés, 2022). Finally, Pajés underscores the importance of having a clear vision and communicating it authentically. Paraguayan leaders, especially within environments where innovation is not always prioritised, need to inspire their teams by clearly articulating shared objectives and creating a shared sense of purpose (Pajés, 2022). Authentic communication is not only a tool for motivation, then, but rather also a means through which to extend a leader's positive influence. As Pajés aptly states: *"When we lead, we make the decision to use our talent to guide and support others, putting aside our own selfishness"* (Pajés, 2022, p. 124).

Local leadership book		
Title	*Les Nuevos Poderes del Líder*	
Subtitle	Transfórmate en el mejor líder de tu vida personal, profesional y social	
Author	Alfred Pajés	
Publisher	Self-published	
Year	2022	
ISBN	979-8351713830	

Paraguayan leadership YouTube review

Leadership within Paraguay is a dynamic interplay of historical, cultural, and personal developmental factors. Through interviews with Gabriela Tisdale, a transformational leadership coach, and Richard Ruiz, a psychologist advocating for introverted leadership, this section explores how Paraguayan leadership styles are rooted within the nation's past, whilst, simultaneously, evolving to address contemporary challenges. Their perspectives are contextualised through existing literature on leadership and cultural frameworks in Paraguay. First, Gabriela Tisdale emphasises the transformational power of self-awareness and emotional intelligence in leadership, essential traits in a society navigating systemic challenges like low self-esteem and limited access to leadership training. In an interview with journalist César Benítez, Tisdale notes, *"Leadership starts with yourself… There is no leader who goes out to lead others without first freeing themselves"* (Tisdale, 2024, 03:00). This mirrors global findings that self-reflective leaders excel in building trust and resilience in their teams (Chung & Cardozo, 2018). Drawing from her experience climbing Mount Kilimanjaro, Tisdale recounts how this physical and emotional journey tested her self-leadership. She described the climb as *"a moment of tremendous self-leadership… You start to know yourself"* (Tisdale, 2024, 04:20) which aligns with transformational leadership theory, which posits that adversity can drive personal growth and vision (Basco & Bennedsen, 2019). Tisdale actively addresses Paraguay's historic lack of investment in leadership education in her initiatives, such as the *Fundación Transformación Paraguay* pilot program in over 200 schools, which integrates leadership and values-based education, in an attempt to empower youth to lead with empathy and service. This reflects the findings of Sánchez Báez (2019), who noted that the cultivation of leadership skills amongst young Paraguayans is pivotal for innovation and progress. Tisdale's focus on love and service as leadership foundations echoes servant leadership principles: *"Leadership is about putting others first, and it comes from love"* (Tisdale, 2024, 08:12). The next video to be summarised involves Richard Ruiz, who offers a complementary perspective, advocating for introverted leadership in Paraguay's predominantly introverted society. This is rooted in the cultural influence of the indigenous *Guaraní* tribes and history of authoritarian rule, which suppressed free expression and critical thinking. *"Paraguay is a very introverted country,"* Ruiz notes, citing its *Guaraní* heritage, which fostered reflection and collective values over assertive individualism (Ruiz, 2019, 09:41). This observation aligns with Hofstede Insights' analysis, which places Paraguay high on collectivism and low on assertiveness. Ruiz highlights how these cultural traits, whilst fostering introversion, also serve as a foundation for thoughtful and deliberate leadership. As the country integrates into global markets, these strengths become assets. For example, Ruiz's coaching of Paraguayan executives to become more assertive and effective in international negotiations reflects the growing need for culturally adaptive leadership. Mentorship is crucial in Paraguay's introverted cultural context, in as far as it helps individuals overcome self-doubt and develop leadership confidence, a sentiment supported by Varela et al. (2010), who found mentorship critical in high power-distance cultures like Paraguay. Ruiz's strategy of celebrating incremental successes to build self-efficacy echoes Sánchez-Báez et al. (2019), who emphasise the role of personal validation in fostering innovative leaders. His belief in leveraging Paraguay's cultural strengths highlights how introspection and deliberate action can be effective within both local and international contexts. Both Tisdale and Ruiz address the systemic barriers facing leadership in Paraguay, from low self-esteem to limited access to education and training (Deloitte, 2020). However, their approaches illustrate different, yet complementary, pathways forward. Tisdale's focus is upon transformational and servant leadership champions empathy, resilience, and systemic reform, whilst Ruiz emphasises leveraging cultural introspection and mentoring to empower introverted leaders. Together, their insights align with research highlighting the need for tailored leadership development strategies in collectivist cultures (Varela et al., 2010). Moreover, their work underscores the importance of self-awareness, empathy, and mentorship in cultivating leaders capable of navigating both local challenges and global opportunities. As Paraguay continues to evolve, integrating insights from its unique cultural and historical context with contemporary leadership practices will be critical.

Understanding hierarchy in Paraguay

Hierarchy is a fundamental aspect of Paraguayan business culture, where authority and decision-making are primarily centralised at senior levels within organisations. Reflecting the high power distance common across Latin America, Paraguayan companies maintain a distinct separation between managerial and subordinate roles, with a strong emphasis upon respect for authority and seniority (Hofstede Insights, 2023). This structured, top-down approach fosters predictability and stability, enabling organisations to operate with a clear chain of command and strictly defined responsibilities for all employees (Deloitte, 2020). One of the CCBS Survey (2023) respondents drew attention to this dynamic by stating, *"Leaders here* [in Paraguay] *are often expected to take decisions independently, though younger professionals are seeking more inclusion and dialogue"* (CCBS Survey, 2023). Similarly, another respondent shed light upon the importance of clarity within decision-making in Paraguayan leadership, explaining that employees appreciate leaders who confidently make decisions, whilst, simultaneously, remaining approachable for guidance (CCBS Survey, 2024). Historically, Paraguayan society's hierarchical nature had its roots within both indigenous community traditions and colonial governance structures, which emphasised collective stability and respect for authority. These influences have evolved over time within the business context, embedding a preference for centralised decision-making within Paraguayan organizations (Varela et al., 2010). As one of our interviewees observed, *"In family-run businesses, which dominate the Paraguayan market, leaders are often more flexible and open to informal communication, especially with younger employees. However, in larger organisations, the formality is more pronounced"* (Ferreira, 6 November 2024). Formal communication practices within Paraguayan workplaces further reinforce these hierarchical structures, in as far as employees are expected to approach superiors with deference, reflecting cultural values that prioritise respect for authority figures. However, as Leila Ferreira noted in our interview with them, *"There is a generational shift where younger leaders strive for a more personal connection with their teams, aiming to make relationships more human and understanding"* (6 November 2024). Despite this shift, the traditional emphasis upon respect remains pervasive within Paraguayan organisations, with employees often using formal titles and refraining from challenging authority directly. This adherence to hierarchy minimises ambiguity, providing a clear framework for action and reinforcing organisational cohesion (Deloitte, 2020). For instance, the CCBS survey (2023) revealed that leaders often engage in structured decision-making processes, which are less collaborative but nevertheless highly effective in terms of maintaining stability. As one respondent remarked, *"Having a clear command structure helps prevent confusion and ensures everyone knows their role within the organisation"* (CCBS Survey, 2023). Whilst these formal structures can in some instances restrict open communication, they help to cultivate an environment in which each and every level within the organisation is respected, thus aligning with Paraguay's conservative business values. Yet, personal relationships remain highly valued within Paraguayan business culture. Leaders often cultivate strong interpersonal connections with their teams, which, in turn, fosters loyalty and cooperation. As Ferreira noted, *"Good leaders here are trusted because they take the time to know their employees personally, balancing authority with empathy"* (6 November 2024). The industrial sector in Paraguay, as highlighted by the *Unión Industrial Paraguaya* (UIP), underscores the importance of stability for fostering organisational growth. Whilst traditional hierarchies can slow adaptability within sectors that require rapid change, it supports long-term planning and risk management, which are crucial for companies operating within Paraguay's emerging economy (UIP, 2023). This sentiment was echoed by the respondents in the CCBS Survey (2024), who praised leaders that balanced traditional structures with a willingness to adapt to contemporary challenges.

How Paraguayans achieve leadership empathy

Like many other Latin American countries, Paraguay's culture is largely collectivist rather than individualistic, which, in turn, fosters strong relationships between people (Hofstede Insights, 2023). Nevertheless, the aforementioned traditional hierarchical structures may serve to limit open dialogue, necessitating a conscious effort from leaders to bridge these gaps through empathetic engagement with employees. This aspect of Paraguayan leadership was supported by the results of the CCBS Survey (2023-2024), in as far as a significant proportion of the respondents stated that they do prefer to retain a personal distance from their employees in order to maintain respect. This serves to illustrate the continued existence of hierarchy within Paraguayan organisations. As one of the respondents opined: "*I believe that closeness with collaborators is a great hallmark of leadership in Paraguay. Reach a level of trust sufficient for difficulties to be expressed without limitations in order to find an effective resolution together. Many times, subordinates do not have that trust, which makes them afraid to share their difficulties or stagnations with their superior. This slows down progress on tasks and only creates a distorted bubble of reality.*" This point here from one of the respondents testifies to the importance placed upon trust between employers and their subordinates as well as the consequences when this trust erodes (CCBS Survey, 2023-2024). Initiatives like the Executive Women's Leadership Development Program, conducted by the Inter-American Development Bank in 2022, focus upon strengthening leadership skills from a gender perspective, underscoring the significance of empathy within Paraguayan leadership development (Inter-American Development Bank, 2023). However, the growing awareness of empathy creates opportunities for leaders to cultivate inclusive and supportive environments. The existence of such initiatives that are designed to make leaders more empathetic is important, because in our interview with Richard Ruiz, a psychologist and leadership author, he told us there remains a significant level of verticality within larger Paraguayan companies, which is a hangover from the cultural legacy of the dictatorship where people were not allowed to speak their minds (Ruiz, 18 November 2024). Later in the interview, he also cast light upon the difficulties associated with older and younger generations working together: "*I work here mainly with banks. And what happens? Sometimes*

127

they hire a very high-level manager who has thirty years of experience and comes with a young team and clashes." Consequently, he said, people need more context and more interaction with each other than used to be the case in Paraguayan organisations (Ruiz, 18 November 2024). Similarly, in another interview with an economist, Laila Ferreira, she also noted the difference between the older and younger generations, saying that there is often a sense of closeness to leaders in Paraguay, but that this ultimately depends upon the relative seniority of the leader. Younger people tend to interact more formally with senior leaders but adopt a more personal approach with leaders who are closer to their own age (6 November 2024). Ferreira also observed that this dynamic is evolving as more and more companies train leaders and managers to be empathetic and approachable, particularly towards younger employees who value being listened to (6 November 2024). Whilst employees within Paraguay appreciate managers who are empathetic and responsive, it is important to stress that they also expect them to demonstrate independence and decisiveness. That is to say, employees want to feel heard, but they also value leaders who are confident in their decisions and are not overly reliant upon others (Ferreira, 6 November 2024). This is also reflected in the results of the CCBS Survey (2023-2024) where it was found that being a powerful decision maker and a good listener is what is expected of a Paraguayan leader. Consequently, whilst signs of progress are evident, ultimately this takes place gradually within Paraguayan society. In conclusion, empathetic leadership within Paraguay is deeply rooted in the nation's cultural heritage and historical experiences. By embracing empathy, Paraguayan leaders can build trust, enhance collaboration, and promote a strong sense of community, thereby leading their organisations and society more broadly towards a more inclusive and harmonious future.

Philippines

Masud Mobayyen, Siepan Mirani, Shaed Sarwari, Zain Sarai Edin & Lina Zaal

The Philippines, an archipelagic nation in Southeast Asia with over 7,600 islands in total, is renowned for its rich biodiversity, vibrant culture, and hospitable people (PSA, 2021). This diversity is also espied in the fact that there are over 170 languages and dialects within the country, although Filipino and English are the two official languages. Large ethnic groups like Tagalog, Cebuano, Ilocano, and Bisaya continue to maintain their unique historical customs and traditions, whilst almost four-fifths of Filipinos identify as Roman Catholic, a legacy of centuries of Spanish colonisation of the country. The nation also honours its multicultural heritage through organising annual colourful festivals that blend religious and historical motifs and themes (NCCA, 2020). Economically, the Philippines boasts a mixed economy that primarily comprises agriculture, industry, and service sectors. Agriculture produces staples like rice, coconuts, and sugarcane, whilst the industrial sector focuses on manufacturing and electronic goods. The Business Process Outsourcing (BPO) industry has served to position the country as a global leader, whilst remittances from Overseas Filipino Workers (OFWs) also significantly bolster the country's economy (Candelario & Cáceres, 2022). Centuries of Spanish and American colonisation have had a profound impact upon Filipino society, including, amongst other things, introducing Catholicism, hierarchical social structures, public education, and infrastructural development to the country (Nadeau, 2020; Malloryk, 2021). This historical legacy continues to influence contemporary Filipino business leadership, which embodies cultural principles like *kapwa* (shared identity), *pakikisama* (cooperation), and *bayanihan* (community spirit) (Jocano, 1999; Scroope, 2017). Leaders are expected to be empathetic, community-oriented, and skilled communicators whilst navigating the challenges of globalisation and technological advancement (Gabriel & Mercado, 2020). This chapter explores Filipino leadership through drawing upon academic literature, surveys, and interviews, examining how historical events and cultural values shape leadership practices within the Philippines today.

How Filipinos characterise leaders?

Within the Philippines, leaders are often characterised by their strong moral character, empathy, and effective communication. More specifically, they are often expected to be decisive, humble, and deeply committed to both their families, employees, and communities (Zepp, 2018). Effective communication is particularly significant within the country, in as far as leaders strive to articulate their visions clearly and foster open dialogue with their employees (House et al., 2004). This participative approach encourages collective decision-making and, in turn, enhances community bonds. However, due to the high power distance within the culture in Philippines, there is also an acceptance of hierarchical structures that allows leaders to combine authority with their empathic approach (House et al., 2004). By embodying effective communication and humility within this hierarchical context, Philippine leaders thus uphold important cultural values and enhance their relationships with those they serve. Alongside these aforementioned qualities, Filipino leaders are also distinguished by their ability to balance discipline with compassion, skillfully combining firmness with the provision of support, which, in turn, makes their followers feel both safe and inspired (Kessler & Wong, 2019). This is in line with one of the CCBS Survey (2018) respondents, Ronald Ortiz, from Part General Counsil, who explained:*"As Personal and professional issues are intertwined, both must be considered because employees find it hard to draw a line between personal and the professional"*. Whilst Filipinos have culturally grounded expectations that their leaders should be authorative and decisive in their approach, they also value humility and respect for others. Ultimately, it is this balance between authority and empathy that serves to inspire loyalty and trust amongst employees (Hofstede Insights, 2023). Scroope (2017) also posits that loyalty and reliability are essential traits, as a Filipino leader who keeps their word and stays committed to the workforce earns deep respect and support. Interestingly, there are signs of a generational shift within the Phillippines when it comes to what characterises effective leaders in the country. Gabriel (2020) purports that whilst the older generation of Filipino leaders prioritise tradition, hierarchy, and continuous change, younger Filipino leaders tend to be more focused upon innovation, collaboration, and strengthening their employees within their approach. The divide between these two generations reflects the broader generational difference between old and new management styles within the Philippines, where traditional values like empathy and community continue to shape modern management practices (Gabriel, 2020). According to one of our interviewees, Francis Kong, a Filipino leadership trainer with over twenty years of experience in the field, these shifts reflect a global evolution within leadership, driven by the transition from industrial- to knowledge-based and now technology-driven models. This transformation has also changed attitudes, expectations, and resources, encouraging Filipino leaders to balance traditional values with the new demands of a technology-focused world (8 November 2024). Moreover, there is a deeply rooted expectation that Filipino leaders maintain personal connections with their followers. For example, leaders are encouraged to be present in the daily lives of their subordinates by participating in local events and celebrations. This is because Filipino's value leaders who are authentic and approachable; a leader who becomes too distant or inaccessible can quickly lose the support of those that they lead (Jocano, 1999). This also goes some way to explaining why Filipino leaders are typically strong communicators, who can convey complex ideas in an accessible manner to people from diverse backgrounds, allowing them to build broad support for their decisions (Jocano, 1999a). Respect for tradition is also critically important, in as far as Filipino leaders often honour the wisdom of previous generations, in an attempt to garner support from both younger and older generations of employees (Ki, 2019). This aligns with the findings of the CCBS Survey (2024), in as far as most of the respondents answered "somewhat like me" to the statement, *"As a leader, I prefer to hear criticism in an indirect manner, outside of staff meetings."* Finally, Filipino's view leadership as a means through which to contribute towards society rather than constituting merely a position of power. As a result, leaders often focus upon initiatives that enhance quality of life and promote social growth, embodying a style of servant leadership aimed towards creating a brighter future for those they lead. An example of this would be the implementation of flexible working hours and remote working options, in order to allow employees to maintain a healthy work-life balance, which, in turn, increases their overall job satisfaction and quality of life (Nadeau, 2020).

Survey results and what local respondents say

To gain a deeper understanding of leadership skills and practices within the Philippines, the CCBS Survey (2018-2024) was administered to C-level executives with extensive knowledge and expertise of the organisational culture and prevailing leadership styles in the country. This section summarises the most significant findings that emerged from over 40 respondents, who shared valuable insights into leadership in the Philippines. In order to enhance the generalisability and validity of the findingsm we also drew upon data from two different survey periods (2018-2024). The first key finding is that the majority of the respondents reported that good organisational experience, market experience and technical competence were the main qualities of a good leader in the Phillippines (CCBS Survey, 20q8-2024). This finding is in line with the opinion expressed by one of our interviewees, Vanessa C. Villaluz, a Filipino leadership scholar, who told us.:"*As Asians we look for authority where sometimes this is equated with age when this is not always the case. Where people respect experience as they are older and more knowledgeable*"(27 November 2024). This reflects the deep-rooted cultural connection between age and authority within the Philippines.

Alongside this, the ability to make firm and powerful decisions was also deemed to be a foundational leadership trait by many of the respondents, whils the majority also underscored the significance of being an eloquent speaker for effective leadership in the Phillippines (CCBS Survey, 2018-2024). This is in line with a comment from one of the survey respondents, Hans Roth Montenegro, a COO, who emphasised: "*A leader must be able to inspire, engage, lead with integrity, and always lead from the front*" (CCBS Survey, 2018). Charisma and intellectual ability were also cited as important qualities by the majority of the respondents, whereas only one-third of the respondents stated that having the right family connections was important (CCBS Survey, 2018-2024). As one respondent, Jeramel Burgos, noted with respect to the latter:"*Good political connections or family connections would be important for most companies but not necessarily for a global company*" (CCBS Survey, 2018). Hierarchy and status remain significant factors in leadership in the philippines, as evidenced by the fact that two-thirds of the respondents reported that leaders should be addressed by their titles and positions. As Rina Marquez, a cultural entrepeneur opined:" *Asian culture is big on showing respect. Addressing leaders with their titles is common practice. But if the company is a start-up and is more contemporary in their style, then, it is okay to call the boss by his or her first name*" (CCBS Survey, 2018). This is supported by the fact that fewer than half of the respondents stated that leaders are provided with office space or transportation that is commesurate with their status, thus suggesting that there has been somewhat of a shift in some contemporary work environments (CCBS Survey, 2018-2024). Further insights emerged regarding leadership styles, particularly in terms of firmness and empathy. The next findings is that a significant majority of the respondents noted that leaders remain firm once decisions have been made, whereas only around half placed significant emphasis upon adhering to deadlines, with failure to do so viewed negatively (CCBS Survey, 2018-2024). There were also divergent views on confronting employees in meetings to achieve certain targets. As one business oficer argued:"*Leaders are held responsible for the actions of their subordinates*" (CCBS Survey, 2024). Another important finding is the strong focus upon employee well-being, as a significant number of respondents reported taking time to invest in the personal and professional growth of their subordinates. This empathy-driven approach to leadership is one of the defining characteristics of Filipino leadership, as Myke James, a founder and CEO of a Filipino organisation emphasized:"*The leadership style in the Philippines is a little different in regards to the cultural way of life whereby it is more like a family style relationship in the office...Our leadership style usually comes with more sense of responsibility for employees not only in terms of what happens to them at work, but also helping our employees navigate the personal and family issues whereby allowing them to gain a sense of balance once at work*" (CCBS Survey, 2024). Similarly, Laree Anico, an Executive, stated: "*I think more leaders here if not all are more personal and intentional. At the workplace, there is a family-like atmosphere where employees will feel that they are being valued, so that they will be more motivated to give better work results. It's like creating a safe place where one can bloom*" (CCBS Survey, 2018). In conclusion, leadership in the Philippines blends respect for hierarchy with a strong focus upon empathy and employee well-being. While decision-making can be firm, there is also a deep commitment to supporting staff both personally and professionally.

Local leadership analysis

Vanessa C Villaluz: a Filippino leadership scholar

Vanessa C. Villaluz is a Filipino leadership scholar and a Consulting Director at Ateneo University in Manila. We interviewed her in order to gain additional insights from her knowledge and professional experience into Filipino leadership. She currently works with a centre called the Neo Center for Organisations on Research and Development, which specialises in human resource management, development, organisation, and leadership. As a Consulting Director and leadership scholar with over twenty years of experience in work psychology, leadership has been a prominent focus for her. She contributed towards the launch of a leadership development program at Ateneo University and earned a Ph.D. in 2022, specialising in leadership and work psychology. At the beginning of the interview, when asked about what constitutes the typical business leader within the Philippines, Vanessa responded as follows: "*Social dynamics are very important, and you have to establish rapport with everyone you work with, which does not exempt leaders either*" (27 November 2024). Vanessa elaborated upon this first point by explaining that this is where true influence lies within the Filipino context. She pointed out that the preferred leaders in the Philippines are still god-fearing, firm, and competent, as reflected in the findings from an earlier CCBS

133

Survey (2018). When asked if leadership has changed in recent decades, she replied: *"In terms of leadership, it is not so much that leadership has changed, but rather the domain in which it operates* [that has changed]*"* (27 November 2024). She proceeded to discuss that when the COVID-19 pandemic hit, there was a greater focus within Filipino organisations upon mental health, well-being, and organisational sustainability. These issues must be handled carefully by Filipino leaders, especially with respect to the younger generation of employees who are now entering the labour market (Villaluz, 27 November 2024. Drawing upon her own personal experience, Vanessa explicated that the mentality of the younger generation of employees differs markedly from that of millennials in terms of their consciousness. The younger generation is very adamant about maintaining a strict boundary between their work and personal life, with stress being a critical factor in this respect. In contrast, millennials tend to have a specific goal in mind and strive to complete it. This is where empathy, one of the most important Filipino values, comes into play, Vanesse suggested (27 November 2024). This led to the subsequent question of how age impacts upon leadership in the Philippines. According to Vanessa, the older generation of leaders tends to give out orders in an authoritative manner, whilst their younger counterparts offer their subordinates greater freedom, encouraging creativity and empowerment. Within certain organisations, titles like *'Sir'* or *'Ma'am'* are still used in order to signal authority and rank. When discussing foreign leaders and the challenges they face, Vanessa stated, *"There is a tendency for Filipinos to socialise with each other, and sometimes, even for children's birthdays and family events, you might invite your boss"* (November 27, 2024). This reflects the social dynamics beyond a professional relationship, where a leader is expected to be open, listen to, and understand their subordinates, whether in a professional or personal context. In summary, Vanessa C. Villaluz underscores that Filipino leadership is evolving to prioritise empathy, work-life balance, and strong interpersonal relationships, whilst, simultaneously, remaining rooted in traditional values of authority and competence.

Francis Kong: A Filipino leadership trainer

The next leadership expert we interviewed for the purposes of investigating leadership skills and practices in the Philippines is Francis Kong, who is an accomplished entrepreneur, author, and leadership coach with over twenty years of experience as the Director of Inspire Leadership Consultancy Inc as well as being the founder of Success Options Inc., a company that specialises in publishing and training. His decades of experience, combined with his dedication to personal and professional growth and the fact that he has more than 280,000 LinkedIn followers, makes him an exemplary figure within Filipino leadership. At the start of our interview with him, Kong (8 November 2024) shared his perspective on what precisely defines a Filipino leader and distinguishes them from their counterparts in other countries, both within and outside of the region. He responded by emphasising that it is the combination of Western and Asian influences that ultimately shape leadership styles and practices within the Philippines. More specifically, he proceeded to explain to us, Filipino leaders are more relational, empathetic, and family-oriented than their Western counterparts, valuing above all personal connections and respect for elders (Kong, 8 November 2024). According to Kong, although these characteristics establish workplaces where employees feel supported, they can also pose challenges with respect to balancing professionalism with personal relationships. By getting inspiration from different cultures, Kong has adopted a diverse leadership approach. Specifically, he integrates Japanese principles of continuous improvement and efficiency with the importance Americans place upon structures, systems and clear communication (8 November 2024). Ultimately, it is this balance, Kong believes, that is essential for improving productivity and innovation within Filipino organisations, whilst, simultaneously, maintaining a well-driven workplace. Later in the interview, Kong also ruminated on the evolution of Filipino leadership in recent decades, noting that there was a growing openness towards contemporary practices amongst younger leaders. Inspired by global trends, they are driving change and challenging traditional systems, which older leaders must adapt to in order to stay relevant. Kong concluded the interview by stating: *"Leadership is not just about titles or positions. It is about creating meaningful impact through trust and empathy"* (8 November 2024). By adapting leadership styles to the cultural context of the Philippines, Kong believes leaders can build stronger relationships, improve team dynamics, and create thriving work environments.

In-country leadership bestseller

"Leadership that Matters" is widely regarded as one of the most influential books on leadership within the Philippines. Written by Francis Kong, a renowned Filipino author, speaker, and leadership coach, the book was published in 2017 and has since become a vital resource for individuals and organisations aiming to strengthen their leadership skills. With over twenty years of experience in manufacturing, retail, trade marketing, and corporate consultancy, Kong co-founded Inspire Leadership Consultancy, where he helped guide C-suite leaders. His mission is to share insights that are both relevant and practical, equipping today's Filipino leaders to navigate the challenges they face (Francis,2017).

The book stresses the importance of fostering emotional intelligence, professionalism, and leadership discipline in creating effective teams in the Philippines. Drawing upon real-life scenarios from his own work with aspiring leaders, Kong illustrates key leadership principles. The author argues as one of the central ideas that true competence and confidence are essential. As he puts it: *"And because they are incompetent, they lack the confidence and use their super-inflated ego to mask their weaknesses in terms of skills and knowledge"* (Francis, 2017, p. 150). This can damage both their personal reputation and the organisation, particularly within the local culture where people would rather criticise than confront, which eventually results in demoralisation and disengagement. Kong also stresses the importance of ethics in leadership, acknowledging that it requires significant courage to lead with integrity within the Philippines. Whilst some organisations operate with high ethical standards, others need reform. He asserts that ethical leaders must have the mettle to do what is right, even in challenging circumstances (2017). Transparency, trustworthiness, and leading by example are also key themes in the book. As Kong writes, "Being *a leader carries the responsibility to teach and support his or her people, to act as a role model, and to be ready to serve as well as lead, which has very little difference in between*"(Francis, 2017, p. 149) Ultimately, the book underscores that inspiring leaders involves acknowledging and valuing the efforts of team members and relationship building, which, in turn, will foster growth and adaptability. As the author argues *"The future requires people to learn new skills outside their area of expertise-and good leaders constantly develop themselves and train their people so they can remain relevant and productive"* (Francis, 2017, p, 151). Through this book, Kong provides a blueprint for leadership that fosters growth, adaptability, and long-term success.

Local leadership book		
Title	*Leadership that matters*	
Subtitle	-	
Author	Francis J. Kong	
Publisher	ABS-CBN Books	
Year	2017	
ISBN	9789718161944	

Philippines leadership YouTube review

In addition to academic research and secondary sources, YouTube and other streaming platforms also offer valuable insights into leadership practices within the Philippines. To gain a deeper understanding of Filipino leadership styles, we analysed two YouTube videos that provide culturally nuanced perspectives, moving beyond Western models. The first video is a lecture titled *"Four Leadership Styles in the Philippine Context"* by Attorney Daryl E. Lacdan, which was uploaded on his YouTube channel "Lacdan MD" in 2022. Lacdan is a Filipino entrepreneur, lawyer, and security professional with extensive experience in security management and law enforcement. His channel focuses on educational content related to security, leadership, and legal topics in the Philippines, aiming to educate viewers on practical and ethical aspects of these fields. Within this particular video, he discusses four distinct leadership approaches that are prevalent within the Philippine context: *Pakiramdam* (Empathy), *Takutan* (Fear), Kulit (Persistence), and *Patsamba-tsamba* (Trial and Error). The second video is a webinar titled *"Filipino Psychology and Bridging Leadership in COVID-19 Response,"* presented by Dr. Elizabeth P. De Castro, PhD, and uploaded by the Bridging Leadership Institute in 2020. Dr. De Castro is a former faculty member of the Department of Psychology at the University of the Philippines and an expert in Filipino Psychology (*Sikolohiyang* Pilipino). In this webinar, she shares her insights into the core values of Filipino psychology and examines their relevance to leadership practices, particularly in the context of the COVID-19 response. Regarding the first video, Lacdan's lecture explores the four leadership styles in detail: *Pakiramdam* emphasises emotional intelligence and a deep understanding of team members' needs, fostering a supportive and harmonious environment, which resonates with the Filipino cultural value of *Kapwa* (shared identity), thus underscoring the interconnectedness of individuals within the community, as also discussed by Dr. De Castro in her webinar (Bridging Leadership Institute, 2020, 12:45). *Takutan* relies upon authority and strictness to maintain order and ensure compliance, but over-reliance on it can create a negative and demotivating work environment, potentially hindering open communication and collaboration, which contradicts the collectivist orientation emphasised by Dr. De Castro (2020, 15:30). *Kulit* demonstrates persistence and meticulousness through consistent follow-ups and reminders, enhancing productivity but possibly leading to micromanagement and stifling initiative, which, in turn, may contrast with the value placed upon *Pakiramdam*. *Patsamba-tsamba* embraces flexibility and adaptability, allowing leaders to adjust their approach based on the situation, and can be said to be in accordance with the concept of *Bahala na* (resilience and acceptance of uncertainty) discussed by Dr. De Castro (2020, 20:05), which encourages resourcefulness and a willingness to learn from mistakes. By integrating the insights from both these videos, we can gain a deeper understanding of leadership within the Filipino cultural context. Effective leadership within the Philippines often requires a nuanced approach, drawing upon a combination of styles tailored to the specific situation and the needs of the team. These videos encourage a more holistic and culturally informed understanding of leadership, challenging traditional Western paradigms and promoting greater appreciation for diverse cultural perspectives, highlighting the importance of aligning leadership practices with cultural values to foster effective and harmonious organisational environments in the Philippines.

Understanding hierarchy in The Philippines

The work culture in the Philippines is predominantly characterised by a hierarchical structure, where individuals are integrated into localised hierarchies based on their relationships rather than common attributes like class or occupation. This dynamic, in turn, creates a patron-client relationship that defines many workplace interactions (Vreeland, 1967). The corporate culture is heavily influenced by social traditions that emphasise kinship, a legacy of colonialism, where family connections play a crucial role within various business situations (Selmer, 2007). Traditional Filipino leadership styles prioritise interpersonal relationships and community values, which are reflective of a collective approach to management. The concept of *Pagsangguni*, which means to consult, testifies to the cultural value of seeking and respecting the opinions of others within Filipino culture (Malcolm, 2003). This expectation that leaders will engage in consultation serves to foster a sense of belonging amongst employees. Even within formal settings, Filipino's prefer communication modes that invite persuasion and consultation, further enhancing relational ties (Andres, 1988; Andres, 1991). Gonzales (1997) suggests that corporate cultures often reflect elitism, where the assumption is that higher ranking members are accorded various privileges, and for whom the rules are frequently seen as flexible or subject to exceptions. Despite the emphasis upon collective well-being, a sense of superiority persists amongst Filipino managers, who sometimes perceive themselves as more deserving of respect and rewards than their lower-level employees (Dowling, 1994). Nevertheless, these leaders typically strive to listen to subordinates before issuing directives, in order to maintain a paternalistic image (Malcolm, 2003). The focus upon building trust, loyalty, and respect is a hallmark of Filipino leadership, exemplified by the concept of *Pakkisama*, which involves integrating informal and official matters, blending social interaction with work responsibilities, thereby challenging the boundaries between personal and organisational relationships

(Andres, 1988). Filipino society prioritises collective well-being, demonstrating a strong sense of community. Filipino workers also place value upon *pagtutulungan* (helpful cooperation), which enhances job efficiency and satisfaction. Social acceptance and the fear of rejection also play critical roles in terms of achieving workplace harmony (Marzan, 1984). Within this context, hierarchy is central to workplace culture. Leaders commonly adopt a paternalistic management style, providing clear, direct instructions that employees are expected to follow without question, as open criticism is often avoided to prevent *hiya* (shame). Decision-making tends to be centralised, limiting employee autonomy and emphasising the implementation of leader's decisions through teamwork (Philippine Studies, 2016). According to Jocano (1999), the Filipino value system emphasises *Utang na loob* (debt of gratitude), which significantly influences power dynamics. Individuals who cultivate long-standing relationships and demonstrate loyalty often wield greater influence within organisations. This influence is reinforced by professional experience and educational qualifications, which are critical for gaining power within the workplace. A study by the Philippine Institute for Development Studies (PIDS, 2018) found that employees with advanced degrees and substantial work experience tended to ascend to management roles more rapidly than their peers. However, there remains a metaphorical glass ceiling for women in the workforce, who often struggle to reach senior-level leadership positions despite having the necessary credentials and experience (Esguerra & Kheokao, 2021). As one Filipino cultural entrepreneur stated in the CCBS Survey (2018), there are certain organisations that reserve senior-level leadership positions only for men based on the belief that *"Women are emotional"* and that only men are trustworthy leaders. Finally, the influence of political networks and connections significantly shape power dynamics, particularly within larger organisations and high-level government roles. These networks provide access to resources and opportunities that can further enhance an individual's standing within the organisation (PIDS,2020).

How the Filipinos achieve leadership empathy

Within the Philippines, leadership empathy is a defining characteristic that is influenced by cultural, familial and community values that emphasise care, appreciation, and mutual support. Filipino leaders often adopt a paternalistic management style, wherein empathy is crucial to fostering trust and trustiness (Selvarajah, 2020). According to Selvarajah's (2020) study, Filipino leaders prioritise empathy by creating strong emotional bonds with their employees. In so doing, leaders become empathic by cultivating and maintaining a supportive work environment in which there is a lot of trust and integrity. By actively engaging with their team and exhibiting genuine interest in the well-being of their employees, these leaders can create a sense of security and motivation amongst their employees, directly enhancing employee satisfaction and productivity (Selvarajah, 2020). Building upon the significance of empathy, emotional intelligence also plays a critical role with respect to Filipino leadership skills and practices, in as far as it complements leaders' ability to manipulate strain, build trust, and enhance collaboration within their teams. Studies show that Filipino leaders who exhibit immoderate emotional intelligence can also effectively navigate stressful situations, build more potent relationships with their employees, and establish a greater supportive work environment (Tolentino, 2022). A study by Undung and De Guzman (2009), for example, emphasises how empathy, as a key part of care-driven leadership, ensures that leaders can better understand and respond to the emotional needs of their employees. By recognising these emotional needs, leaders can offer the right support, which, in turn, improves the overall level of team performance. This approach not only aligns with Filipino cultural values of a strong relational and community bonds, but rather also strengthens the ethical foundations of an organisation (Undung, 2009). Empathy enhances a more collaborative and learning work environment, leading to greater organisational success and employee satisfaction. This can be achieved when leaders take clear actions to understand their own employees. For instance, one of our interviewees, Mr. Francis Kong, a leadership consultant and author, shared his approach to demonstrating empathy: *"To show empathy to my employees, I respect their time, listen to different opinions, and provide a safe space for open conversation. Instead of punishing mistakes, I guide them to learn and improve, reward good performance, and work together to align expectations and grow"* (Kong, 8 November 2024). The results of the CCBS Survey (2018-2024) that was administered to Filipino executives also testify to the importance of empathy within Filipino leadership, in as far as most of the respondents agreed with the statement *"Managers should actively spend time ensuring the personal well-being of their team members"*. This demonstrates that Filipino leaders recognise the importance of caring for employees on a personal level, and, in fact, view it as an essential part of their role as leaders. By prioritising the well-being of their employees, leaders cultivate an environment that shows trust and support, reinforcing strong emotional bonds that improve team morale and productivity.

Sierra Leone

*Sarah Havinga, Thimo Loos, Annerina Tuijnman, Dean van Eikeren,
Roos Hafkamp, Direnç Kaygusuz*

ɔltɛm wok fɔ in wanwɔd pis, fridɔm ɛn prɔsperiti (Always work for her unity peace, freedom and prosperity) is one of the lines in the national anthem of Sierra Leone, written in Krio. The country is situated on the southwest coast of West Africa and has a population of 8.6 million. Sierra Leone is a country with several languages spoken across different regions. The official language is English, which is used in government, legal matters, and education (Smith, 2024). Krio, a Creole language derived from English and various African languages, is the lingua franca spoken by the vast majority of the population and, as such, facilitates communication across different ethnic groups (Yakpo, 2023). Whilst English is predominantly used within the business sector, especially in formal settings and international trade (Sengova, 1987), Krio also plays an important role in more informal business dealings and day-to-day *toktok* (conversation), (Yakpo, 2023).

Sierra Leone's national pledge also encompasses the core values that leaders are expected to uphold in the country. Leadership is not solely about economic success, but rather also about fostering social harmony and contributing towards national growth and prosperity. Responsible leadership means advancing the collective well-being of all citizens, rather than focusing on personal or narrow interests. These guiding values ensure leadership aligns with broader national goals of unity, development, and inclusiveness, reflecting a commitment to responsible and virtuous leadership, which is grounded in values of justice, care, and accountability (Cameron, 2011). Dr. Modupe Taylor-Pierce sums this up in four main qualities in his book about business leadership within Sierra Leone: *"Integrity, Courage, Vision, and Passion. These are four minimum qualities required for good leadership."* (2022, p. 229). The following chapter investigates business leadership in Sierra Leone, specifically by exploring how culture impacts upon leadership skills and practices.

How the Sierra Leoneans characterise leaders?

Within Sierra Leone, leadership is profoundly influenced by traditional values, historical legacies, and the nation's diverse cultural fabric. Leadership styles within large organisations as well as the public sector are often underpinned by a hierarchical and centralised approach, where authority is respected, and decisions are typically made by senior-level management (Bessiama, 22 November 2024). This dynamic is predicated upon the cultural emphasis on respect for elders and authority figures, which itself is grounded in the country's indigenous governance systems where chiefs and traditional leaders hold significant influence (Fanthorpe, 2001). However, leaders in small and medium-sized enterprises (SMEs), which are of critical importance to Sierra Leone's economy, have been observed as adopting more participative approaches. This participative style aligns with the cultural norm of *padi padi* (a Krio term for close friendship and collaboration), where leaders engage employees in discussions and the decision-making process, thus reflecting the communal spirit that is deeply embedded in Sierra Leonean society. As one of our interviewees, Alicious Bessiama, (22 November 2024), noted: *"Leaders here are very polite in how they interact with their teams and stakeholders,"* an approach that serves to foster trust and cooperation between leaders and their employees. In appreciation of the interdependence between people and bonds within the community, leaders in this society also tend to include employees when making decisions. This participative style corresponds to the collectivist trend in Sierra Leonean society, where mutual assistance and collaboration are valued (Jackson, 2004). This characterisation of leadership within Sierra Leone was also corroborated in the findings of the CCBS Survey (2024), where many of the respondents reported that building consensus, inclusiveness, and respect for different opinions were an integral part of their own leadership behaviour. As one of the respondents explained, the important dimension of community-based decision-making is something embedded within their own leadership: *"Leaders often seek input and approval from a wide range of stakeholders before making decisions, reflecting the country's collective culture and history of traditional community decision-making processes"* (CCBS Survey, 2024). Emerging leaders, particularly amongst the younger generation, are increasingly advocating for leadership styles that promote innovation, employee engagement, and adaptability. Influenced by global trends and the need to address contemporary challenges, these leaders are seeking to integrate traditional values with contemporary management practices (Richards, 2006). This generational shift in leadership skills and practices was also noted by our second interviewee, Ibrahim Kebe, a Sierra Leonean scholar, who, in response to a question about if leadership had changed in the country over the years, answered: *"You now have a very young population compared to the last two to three decades. The age group in the country is now a youthful population. It tells you that leaders have to adjust the way they manage their employees now"*. He proceeded to explain further: *"Now it is more focused upon understanding people, meeting them, and getting closer to younger people because you cannot manage people if you do not understand them."* (12 November 2024). This shift reflects a growing recognition of the benefits of transformational leadership for achieving sustainable development and economic resilience. Improving communication and fostering empathy are also deemed to be critical for addressing these challenges. Although three-quarters of our survey respondents reported that they value leaders who ensure their team's well-being, there nevertheless remains a gap in interpersonal skills, as highlighted by the limited focus on listening and trust-building in the survey responses (CCBS Survey, 2024). In our interview with them, Dr. Ibrahim Kebe stressed the importance of cultivating a 'symbiotic' relationship between leaders and employees, advocating for open communication and closer engagement to build trust and accountability (12 November 2024). However, there can sometimes be cultural resistance to such change, which can further complicate leadership. This was illustrated by Dr. Ibrahim Kebe, when he explained that foreign managers often struggle with local resistance to deadlines and risk-taking, as many Sierra Leonean organisations prefer stability over disruption (12 November 2024). However, examples such as Dr. Gilpin's leadership at Rokel Commercial Bank, where hierarchical structures were flattened to foster greater collaboration, show to demonstrate the potential for adaptive leadership to enhance organisational performance. Indeed, the survey respondents also emphasised the importance of traits such as visionary thinking and decision-making ability within leadership. These findings underline the need for leadership development programs that focus on strategic thinking, empathy, and adaptability, whilst, simultaneously, respecting cultural traditions (CCBS Survey, 2024). In summary, leadership in Sierra Leone embodies a blend of traditional respect for authority and evolving practices that emphasise participation and innovation. Effective leaders bridge the gap between these values and the demands of a changing global environment, fostering both community cohesion and organisational performance.

Survey results and what local respondents say

The CCBS Survey (2024) was conducted in order to gather primary research and gain insights into business leadership styles and practices within Sierra Leone. This survey allowed C-level executives and other highly qualified professionals with in-depth knowledge of Sierra Leonean business leadership to share their perspectives. The following section discusses the most notable results emerging from the survey. The first significant finding is that organisational experience, technical competence, and market expertise were the top three factors cited as the primary reasons employees look up to their leaders in Sierra Leone (CCBS Survey, 2024). The importance placed upon expertise in Sierra Leonean leadership was illustrated by one of the survey respondents, Emmanuel Lavalie, who remarked: *"The leadership style and skills of Sierra Leoneans is more about the ability to be resilient and manage finance well, to build trust between the team and the funders"* (CCBS Survey, 2024). Another noteworthy result is the strong adherence to formal hierarchical structures within Sierra Leone, which was illustrated by the fact that the majority of the respondents agreed that it is both important for subordinates to address leaders by their titles or positions within the organisation, and that employees are not allowed to address their leaders by their first names. As one respondent from Frinong Citi explained, *"Di Lida dem lek rekspect,"* (*"the leader likes respect"*) (CCBS Survey, 2024), thus underscoring the importance of maintaining the hierarchical order. The survey also shed light upon how leaders in Sierra Leone treat adherence to deadlines. A significant proportion of the respondents agreed that failing to meet a deadline is seen as equivalent to failure, which serves to illustrate the high level of importance placed upon timeliness and accountability within Sierra Leonean workplaces (CCBS Survey, 2024). Another key result pertains to leadership empathy. The overwhelming majority of the respondents strongly agreed that managers should actively dedicate time to ensuring the personal well-being of their team members, thus indicating a strong emphasis upon relational leadership within Sierra Leone. As Isaac Kargbo noted, *"In Sierra Leone, leadership is often characterised by a strong emphasis upon community and consensus-building, with leaders typically valuing respect for tradition, familial ties, and collaboration, which can distinguish it from more individualistic leadership styles found in other countries"* (CCBS Survey, 2024). Interestingly, the survey also revealed mixed perspectives regarding which leadership styles prevail in the country. Whilst a notable proportion of the respondents observed that leaders encourage a degree of competition within their teams to drive results, the majority emphasised that collaboration and harmony are critical to success. This is reinforced by one of the respondents,

Augustine Martin Martinez, who shared, *"There are a couple of leadership styles that manifest a great sense of community resilience guided by social and political odds. For example, collective decision-making, where local chiefs and elders of the community bring traditional wisdom into modern governance"* (CCBS Survey, 2024). Finally, the survey shed light upon how leaders approach innovation and criticism within their organisations. A significant number of respondents reported that leaders in Sierra Leone often prefer to approach innovation with a resourceful mindset. As a CEO from Freetown put it, *"Leaders in Sierra Leone often approach innovation with the mindset of 'doing more with less,' focusing on using available resources and maximising local potential to address community needs"* (CCBS Survey, 2024).

Local leadership analysis

Ibrahim Kebe: an Sierra Leonean leadership scholar

An interview was conducted with Dr. Ibrahim Alusine Kebe, a lecturer at the Institute of Public Administration and Management (IPAM) in Sierra Leone and a PhD. research scholar specialising in Business Administration and Change Management. With over six years of teaching experience, Dr. Kebe has also served as the Deputy Head of Department, managing both administrative and academic functions. Within this role, he frequently interacts with students, faculty, and staff. Dr. Kebe began the interview by reflecting upon the distinct characteristics of Sierra Leone's leadership style, emphasising that the nation is *"a high power distance country"* in which leaders are seen as figures of authority and, as such, deserving of respect. As he himself put it, *"Leaders are like demigods...you do not get to question them too much because if you do, they think you are not fit for the position"* (Kebe, 12 November 2024). This hierarchical perspective, deeply rooted in the cultural norms of Sierra Leone, profoundly shapes the behaviour of both leaders and employees. Discussing the evolution of leadership in Sierra Leone, Dr. Kebe highlighted the impact of the country's youthful population and technological advances. He stated: *"The age group in the country is now a youthful population...leaders have to adjust the way they manage their employees"* (Kebe, 12 November 2024). They proceeded to further explain that social media and other platforms are forcing leaders to adopt more adaptable and engaging approaches. Next, Dr. Kebe addressed the challenges faced by foreign managers in Sierra Leone, particularly concerning cultural differences in work ethic as well as attitudes toward time. In relation to these points, he remarked, *"Foreign managers...are crucial about respecting time and deadlines, but for us as Sierra*

Leoneans, we do not respect time" (Kebe, 12 November 2024), adding that efforts to enforce stricter time management are often perceived as overly rigid or demanding. These insights underscore the cultural nuances that influence leadership practices within Sierra Leone. Dr. Kebe concluded by stressing the need for leadership approaches tailored to Sierra Leone's unique cultural context. More specifically, he advocated for the development of African-centric leadership literature, stating, *"We need contemporary African leadership textbooks that speak to the African context…many of the leadership practices we apply are from the West, and there are differences when you try to apply them"* (Kebe, 12 November 2024). His reflections provide valuable insight into the interplay between tradition and modernity within Sierra Leonean leadership.

Alicious Bessiama: a Sierra Leonean cross-cultural trainer

Alicious Bessiama is a dedicated youth activist and founder of the Sunrise Movement, Sierra Leone, an organisation that focuses upon climate change, agriculture, leadership, and youth empowerment. His journey into leadership began in 2021, driven by the high unemployment rate within Sierra Leone. After graduating from university and struggling to find a job, he chose to establish his organisation to create opportunities for young people. He has been a leader since his school days and remains committed to empowering Sierra Leonean youth through collaborative and impactful initiatives. As Bessiama (22 November 2024) put it at the beginning of our interview with him, *"Leadership has been part of me… from my secondary school to university days and until now"*. In his leadership philosophy, Bessiama highlighted a cultural emphasis upon respectful communication. He noted, *"Leaders here are very polite in how they interact with their teams and stakeholders,"* a practice that serves to foster trust and cooperation between leaders and their employees (Bessiama, 22 November 2024). Specifically in relation to Sierra Leonean business leadership, Bessiama described that leaders are varied but often innovative, forward-thinking, and inspiring. He proceeded to highlight the shift from traditional leadership methods to more modern approaches, with digital technology playing a significant role in driving this historical shift in leadership practices. For example, online business practices and electronic transactions are coming to replace older, labour-intensive systems. Despite such progress, Bessiama (22 November 2024) noted that leadership in Sierra Leone retains a strong hierarchical nature. He proceeded to emphasise that hierarchy is *"recognised and highly respected,"* although he also acknowledged that *"some leaders misuse the trust placed in them"*. Bessiama explained that age plays a crucial role in terms of the organisational hierarchy within Sierra Leone, with elders often commanding deference and shaping decisions within professional settings. Later in the interview, Bessiama addressed how Sierra Leone's leadership style differs from other cultures. Specifically, he praised the politeness and communication style of leaders, which fosters mutual respect. However, he acknowledged variations in managerial attitudes, with some exercising excessive authority whilst others adopt more collaborative approaches (Bessiama, 22 November 2024).. Effective leaders, according to him, build trust through consistent communication, accountability, and respect. As he put it: *"Trust is built through keeping your words and being accountable"* (Bessiama, 22 November 2024), thus emphasising the importance of integrity within leadership. In summary, Alicious Bessiama embodies the evolving leadership culture of Sierra Leone. His work reflects the country's blend of traditional respect for hierarchy and modern efforts to promote inclusivity and innovation. By emphasising trust, empathy, and empowerment, he aligns with Sierra Leone's communal ethos, whilst, simultaneously, addressing challenges within business leadership.

In-country leadership bestseller

Dr. Modupe Taylor-Pearce, a seasoned Sierra Leonean entrepreneur and academic, uses his work *Business Bomba* to empower Sierra Leoneans with essential knowledge for building successful, sustainable businesses. His mission stems from a desire to see an economically transformed Sierra Leone. In *Business Bomba*, he presents a 'cookbook' approach, designed to systematically lead aspiring entrepreneurs through each aspect of starting, growing, and stabilising a business within Sierra Leone. By sharing his practical experience, Taylor-Pearce seeks to reduce the high failure rate amongst new businesses and help foster a wave of entrepreneurs who can create meaningful job opportunities within the country. Leadership in Sierra Leone's business landscape faces unique challenges, including economic instability and a lack of resources and guidance. However, leaders armed with the right knowledge and strategic mindset can turn these challenges into opportunities. Above all, Taylor-Pearce emphasises the value of resilience, risk tolerance, and initiative—qualities essential for success in Sierra Leone's emerging but challenging market. They stress that Sierra Leone requires leaders with integrity, passion, vision, and courage in order to transform the nation. Effective leadership, he argues, involves honesty, resilience, and the ability to inspire trust. He underscores the need for entrepreneurial innovation and job creation, stressing that good leadership is essential for both addressing Sierra Leone's systemic challenges and unlocking its potential. These insights align with Sierra Leone's cultural values, which prioritise community, respect for authority, and collective progress. However, leadership in the country often struggles with issues like corruption and a lack of accountability. In response, Taylor-Pearce calls for leaders who embody integrity and have a clear vision for development, leveraging the nation's communal and resilient spirit. By fostering trust and responsibility, such leaders can harness Sierra Leone's cultural emphasis upon collective success to drive entrepreneurship, growth, and societal transformation.

Local leadership book	
Title	*Bussiness Bomba*
Subtitle	A step-by-step guide to creating a successful and sustainable business in Sierra Leone
Author	Dr. Modupe Taylor-Pearce
Publisher	Lulu publishing services
Year	2022
ISBN	978-1-312-78476-5

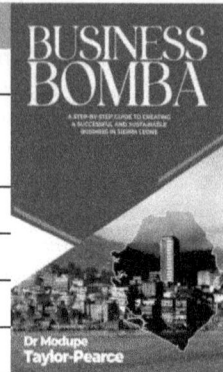

Sierra Leone leadership YouTube review

In addition to academic sources, YouTube provides direct access to leadership insights, including interviews with prominent Sierra Leonean leaders. These videos highlight progressive leadership rooted in accountability, community welfare, and ethical decision-making. Dr. Modupe Taylor-Pierce Jr., an influential leader and educator, emphasises that effective business leadership in Sierra Leone is not about exerting authority but rather about benefiting both organisations and stakeholders. As he puts it, *"When leaders make wise decisions, their people's lives are improved"* (Taylor-Pierce, 2022, 5:04). This principle reflects the expectation for Sierra Leonean leaders to act as custodians, ensuring sustainable success, whilst, simultaneously, taking moral responsibility for their choices. Taylor-Pierce then proceeds to highlight the role of coaching in fostering leadership growth. Rather than traditional advisory roles, coaching in Sierra Leone focuses upon collaboration, with coaches acting as a *"thought partner"* to help leaders navigate challenges. *"A coach supports you in thinking through those thorny issues... without telling you what to do"* (Taylor-Pierce, 2022, 12:36). This approach encourages reflective and innovative decision-making, which are vital for navigating the complexities of contemporary business. He further stresses the importance of lifelong learning, urging leaders to reject the *"graduation mindset,"* which assumes education ends with formal degrees, arguing instead that *"Lifelong learning is essential for leaders to stay relevant,"* as knowledge must evolve to remain applicable. By embracing peer-sharing environments and continuous self-improvement, leaders in Sierra Leone can cultivate adaptability and drive progress within competitive environments. The values of vision, trustworthiness, and community orientation are pivotal to Sierra Leonean leadership. Vision provides clear direction, trustworthiness fosters confidence and reliability, and a focus on community ensures leadership decisions are inclusive. Taylor-Pierce summarises this as follows, *"Vision is what gives leadership its direction, trustworthiness builds confidence, and focusing on community makes leadership meaningful"* (Taylor-Pierce, 2022, 24:07). President Julius Maada Bio also reflects these ideas in his leadership philosophy. In an interview at the United Nations General Assembly, he emphasised the critical role of youth in leadership, stating, *"The youth are not just the leaders of tomorrow; they are the leaders of today"* (Bio, 2024). This statement underscores his commitment to empowering younger generations to actively participate in decision-making processes. For Bio, strong leadership begins with equipping youth with the skills and confidence to shape the future. Education, therefore, plays a foundational role in his vision for Sierra Leone. He remarked, *"Investing in education is investing in our future"* (Bio, 2024, 02:35), highlighting the need to create a leadership pipeline of capable, forward-thinking individuals by prioritising access to quality education as a key driver of leadership development. In a podcast hosted by Terrence Taylor, he emphasises trust, adaptability, and proactive engagement as vital traits for effective leadership in Sierra Leone. He advises, *"Show up for every opportunity created for you"* (Taylor, 2024), stressing the importance of building social capital and embracing opportunities. Taylor's reflections reinforce the value of collaboration, listening, and inspiring action. These qualities, he argues, allow Sierra Leonean leaders to remain connected to those they serve whilst navigating challenges with resilience. Another key element Taylor addresses is the value of intentional collaboration. He describes leadership as a process of empowering others, not through directive authority but rather by creating spaces where teams can innovate and succeed together. Listening, he notes, is a vital skill for: *"*[Sierra Leonean] *Leaders who listen do not just hear problems—they identify opportunities for growth"* (Taylor, 2024, 06:54). This ability to listen deeply and respond meaningfully helps Sierra Leonean leaders inspire action and remain connected to their teams and communities.

Understanding hierarchy in Sierra Leone

Relationships in Sierra Leone are deeply people-oriented, with community and mutual aid forming the foundation of social interactions. This cultural emphasis upon inclusivity fosters a low level of hierarchical distance, where decisions are often communal, and consideration is given to everyone's input irrespective of their rank (Taylor-Pearce, 2023). Consequently, open dialogue and group cohesion are also encouraged (Doberstein, 2016). Notwithstanding this, Sierra Leone does also display attributes that are reflective of a high power distance culture, in as far as authority figures are highly respected, and hierarchical structures dominate. This is illustrated by the fact that one of our interviewees informed us that Sierra Leonean leaders are often viewed as 'demigods' whose authority is rarely questioned, thus reflecting the societal value placed upon titles and hierarchy (Kebe, 12 November 2024). Sierra Leonean society is therefore an interesting blend of low and high power distance (Oshodi, 2019). Communal systems promote inclusivity, whilst traditional respect for authority ensures hierarchical structures remain intact, especially within formal settings. This duality shapes business operations, where respect for authority coexists with harmony-driven collective decision-making (Oshodi, 2019). Further evidence for such duality comes from Dr. Kebe, who also stressed that *"some leaders exercise a lot of authority and sometimes humiliate their subordinates, whilst others foster a more collaborative and respectful environment"* (Bessiama, 22 November 2024). Respect for elders plays a crucial role in this regard, with senior leaders often regarded as custodians of experience. Although some scholars have noted that participative forms of decision-making are slowly emerging in the country, traditional deference to seniority remains vital (Taylor-Pearce, 2023). Dr. Ibrahim Alusine Kebe also discussed this in our interview with them, noting that some leaders prioritise hierarchical titles over financial incentives even, thus, once again, underscoring the cultural significance of recognition (12 November 2024). Similarly, Mr. Alicious Bessiama stated, "*hierarchy is something that is recognised and highly respected, but it also has limitations because some leaders misuse the trust placed in them*" (Bessiama, 22 November 2024). He also emphasised that "*age is held in very high esteem,*" with elders in Sierra Leone afforded deference both professionally and socially (Bessiama, 22 November 2024). Age stratification also influences leadership, creating a blend of traditional and modern practices (Taylor-Pearce, 2023; Kebe, 12 November 2024). Leaders are expected to foster trust and cohesion, aligning with Sierra Leone's communal ethos. As Bessiama observed, "*leaders who build trust and respect do so through mutual communication and accountability*" (Bessiama, 22 November 2024). Open-door policies and storytelling—a cultural hallmark—are common tools that are used to inspire and connect teams (Oshodi, 2019; Kebe, 12 November 2024). However, entrenched patriarchal norms continue to restrict women's leadership opportunities, as men still dominate decision-making roles within business and politics, whilst women are confined to the domestic sphere, especially in rural areas. Those women who are in leadership positions thus frequently face resistance and exclusion (Moline et al., 2022). Dr. Kebe explained how communal values can both support and hinder progress, as traditional attitudes clash with modern gender equality ideals (12 November 2024). The 2022 Gender Equality and Women's Empowerment (GEWE) Act introduced a 30% quota for female political candidates, equal pay, extended maternity leave, and increased representation within larger companies. Whilst this Act is groundbreaking, mixed perceptions about equality persist. This was evidenced in the results of the CCBS Survey (2024) where only one-third of the Sierra Leonean respondents strongly agreed with the statement that men and women have equal leadership opportunities, whilst one-third disagreed with this. In conclusion, Sierra Leone's business culture reflects a blend of traditional respect for elders and emerging participative practices. Whilst authority remains influential, there is growing advocacy for inclusivity and equal representation within leadership for women.

How Sierra Leoneans achieve leadership empathy

Given the integral role that business leaders in Sierra Leone play in terms of both social and economic development, they face significant demands that in turn require exceptional forms of emotional intelligence and resilience. Specifically, Sierra Leonean leaders must navigate complex environments characterised by economic scarcity, historical injustices, and the need for collective healing from recent conflicts (Jackson, 2004). These challenges necessitate empathy, community-oriented values, and adaptability in order to achieve business success, whilst, simultaneously, fostering unity and development in harsh conditions. As Johnson et al. (2021) note, these traits enable leaders to address social issues affecting the workforce and economy, and serve to position them as central to driving sustainable development. An example of this is the First Lady of Sierra Leone, Dr. Fatima Maada Bio, who promotes inclusive governance and socioeconomic equality, embodying relational and collective leadership models emphasising collaboration and empathy (Pearce & Conger, 2003; Cummings et al., 2018). Within the healthcare sector, for example, leaders must balance compassion with resourcefulness to tackle ethical dilemmas and resource shortages. Whilst these challenges are indeed specific to this sector, the resilience

151

and adaptability required reflect broader leadership qualities that are essential across industries in Sierra Leone (Johnson et al., 2021). Dr. Ibrahim Alusine Kebe, one of our interviewees, also emphasised the importance of empathy and engagement specifically in relation to building trust, stating, *"You have to get closer to employees, understand them, and talk with them... The more you understand people, the more you are able to manage them effectively"* (12 November 2024). Our second interviewee, Alicious Bessiama, also underscored the importance of respectful communication for fostering both cooperation and trust within teams. She noted, *"Leaders here are very polite in how they interact with their teams and stakeholders,"* thus emphasising that this politeness is not just a personal trait but rather a reflection of Sierra Leone's collectivist traditions. These traditions prioritise harmony, mutual respect, and the careful maintenance of relationships, which are deemed to be vital for both effective leadership and long-term collaboration. Ultimately, this approach enables leaders to navigate complex interpersonal dynamics, whilst, simultaneously, reinforcing a sense of unity and shared purpose. Leadership frameworks emphasise adaptability and ethical decision-making as critical skills, particularly within high-stakes contexts like one sees in Sierra Leone (Johnson et al., 2021). Within Sierra Leone, ethical decision-making often involves prioritising fairness in resource allocation, ensuring transparency in team interactions, and addressing systemic challenges such as corruption through integrity-driven leadership practices. By demonstrating these values, leaders build trust and accountability within their teams and communities. Hence, resilience and principled leadership are vital for navigating this complex environment (Kebe, 12 November 2024).. The Sierra Leonean emphasis upon communal well-being shapes leadership practices, in as far as leaders have to act as stewards of collective welfare, aligning with transformational principles. This feature of Sierra Leonean leadership was also highlighted in the CCBS Survey (2024), specifically in relation to the fact that many of the respondents reported that leaders prioritise employee well-being and engage closely with their teams to build trust and support (CCBS Survey, 2024; Kebe, 12 November 2024). The responses from Sierra Leonean managers who participated in the survey testify to the pervasive influence of collectivist traditions upon leadership, which emphasise relationships, humility, and understanding (CCBS Survey, 2024; Cartwright, 1978). Ultimately, Sierra Leonean leadership is rooted in compassionate and inclusive governance, prioritising collective well-being and fostering social cohesion and equality through visionary, community-oriented leadership (Curry et al., 2012).

Suriname

Amaury Adriana, Emmilia Ekezie, Je-mell Foen-A-Foe, Ajay Jaggoe,
Sebastiaan Svechtarov & Nathania Van-Lare

The *Republiek Suriname* (Republic of Suriname), the smallest independent country in South America, has a population of just over 600,000 residents. This multi-cultural country comprises a diverse group of ethnicities and a wide variety of languages and religions (Surinaamse Overheid, 2023). Prior to gaining *Srefidensi* (independence) in 1975, Suriname was a Dutch colony (Demarest & Veenendaal, 2021). Therefore, Dutch remains the official language of the country along with *Sranang Tongo* (UNDDR, 2022). The phrase *"Stre de'f stre wi no sa frede, Gado de wi fesiman"* (*"There is a fight to fight, we shall not be afraid, God is our leader"*) from Suriname's national anthem (Urumaxi Anthems, 2020, 1.35), embodies the nation's collective courage, pride, unwavering faith and sense of belonging (Menzo, 2012). This sentiment of unity can also be espied in the country's participation in CARICOM (the Caribbean Community). Suriname greatly benefits from this strong trade relationship with regional partners (United Nations, 2022). Historically, the country has been reliant upon its natural resources, particularly bauxite, oil, and gold mining, but over time its economy has been shaped by its rich mineral wealth and river systems. Despite the potential wealth from their natural resources such as oil, Surinamese economy remains unstable and imbalanced (Khemraj & Pasha, 2024). According to Shankar (2021), this instability is exacerbated by external factors, such as globalisation or crises, that companies in Suriname must adjust to. In an era marked by such rapid change and uncertainty, the role of leadership has become more complex and demanding than ever before. Contemporary leadership in Suriname often reflects a traditional hierarchy, with clear distinctions between management levels and roles. Moreover, leaders are expected to navigate a landscape shaped by technology, evolving markets, and a globalised economy and culture (Soerjdan, 2022). Therefore, leadership styles also need to keep evolving and adapting to create successful business management styles for the future generations to come (Shankar, 2021). This chapter examines leadership skills and practices in Suriname, drawing on primary and secondary research data.

How the Surinamese characterise leaders?

In Suriname, characterisations of what precisely constitutes an effective business leader can differ based on generational differences, values, and ethnicity. According to the respondents in the CCBS Survey (2024), most of the large companies in Suriname are ran in an autocratic leadership style, where hierarchy and respect are deeply valued. This approach is also reflected within the communication style that leaders adopt towards their subordinates. In Suriname, direct communication is common within the business environment (CCBS Survey, 2024). This communication style is captured in the local saying *'Taki reti, a no asranti'* (*"Saying the truth is not rude"*) (Surinaams Erfgoed, n.d.). Within the context of small and medium-sized enterprises (SMEs), which are a vitally important part of the Surinamese economy, various leadership styles can be observed (Soerdjan, 2022). One predominant style is a transactional leadership approach, where leaders focus upon specific tasks and short-term objectives. Northouse (2021) posits that this style is used within multiple sectors, including the sales sector. For example, a manager could tell their team to reach a specific sales goal in a week, and if they achieve this goal then they are rewarded with a bonus, and if they do not there will be a follow-up evaluation onto how improve (Northouse, 2021). This approach is usually directive, hierarchical and prioritises efficiency and clarity in roles (Soerdjan, 2022). Another key characterisation of the leadership style in Suriname is that it is relationship-based. This is perhaps unsurprising given that Suriname is commonly known for having a 'culture of being', which is predicated on the notion that cultivating and maintaining good relationships with others is vital. Consequently, values related to work and accomplishments are less important in Suriname than more developed countries in Europe and North America, for example, where there is a dominance of the 'culture of doing' (Smith, 2022). According to our interviewee, Ir. Jean-Pierre Polanen, a management consultant, lecturer and writer, the reason for this is that Suriname is a small society where everyone knows each other both on a private and professional basis (8 November 2024). This makes it easy to build relationships and know how to treat others at work. This perspective is also supported by the results of the CCBS Survey (2024), where it was found that managers in Suriname frequently prioritise the personal well-being of their colleagues. However, this dynamic is not without its drawbacks. It can also lead to several challenges, including, amongst other things, favouritism, and nepotism, resulting in unequal treatment within the workplace (Polanen, 8 November, 2024). Surinamese people often pursue a good time with family, co-workers or friends, further emphasising this aforementioned culture of being (Smith, 2022).

This feeling of '*gemeenschapzin*' (The feeling of connectedness) is also significant when doing business in Suriname. There is a great deal of networking and relationship building that one must undertake prior to actually collaborating and talking about business and numbers (MacDonald, 2016). This is why having relationships and connections in Suriname is also useful, as this opens the door for opportunities. An example of this was given by Eddy Jahrap, who was a former politician and the first director of one of the biggest companies in Suriname called Staatsolie. He was encouraged by a local manager to go to informal events. Going to these events eventually led him and his team to get a US$ 2 million loan to finance their project (Jharap, 2012). Today, Surinamese leaders face several challenges in the business and political sectors. They must adapt to a rapidly changing global market, which, in turn, requires flexibility and innovation, particularly in SMEs and larger companies. To achieve this, leadership styles also need to develop (Soerdjan, 2022; Shankar, 2021). The younger generation in Suriname is the driving force behind this evolution, because they are more open to change, particularly when it comes to moving away from older traditions and values, which might be less common or less readily embraced by older generations (Waalring, 2013). Waalring (2013) points out that the younger generation in Suriname is more focused upon a participative leadership style, where leaders are open to feedback. This is important given that research shows that participative leadership, which encourages employees to express their opinion, and transformational leadership, which motivates through a shared vision, contribute towards enhanced employee motivation (MacDonald, 2016; Soerdjan, 2022). Overall, leadership in Suriname is primarily hierarchical with a direct communication style, albeit there appears to be somewhat of a shift occurring as a result of the younger generation of leaders coming to the fore in the country.

Survey results and what local respondents say

To gather insight and information about current trends in Surinamese leadership skills and practices, 72 C-level executives with leadership skills from a variety of Surinamese companies participated in the CCBS Survey (2024). This section focuses on five key findings that emerged from the analysis of the survey data, which are discussed in turn below. The first key finding emerging from the survey underscores the significance of formal titles and recognition within Suriname. More than half of the respondents reported that subordinates should address them by their titles (CCBS Survey, 2024). This formality reflects a high power distance culture, where titles carry weight as symbols of respect (Hofstede, 2019). As one participant, a Manager at an Air Freight company, explained: *"In Suriname*

155

a significant amount of leadership is owned through names and faces" (CCBS Survey, 2024). This emphasis upon formal recognition underscores the value placed on hierarchy and structured authority within Surinamese workplaces and culture more generally. Moreover, the data revealed that leaders within larger organisations are often provided with office space and transportation that is commensurate with their position within the company, thus further highlighting their elevated status. Secondly, the survey demonstrated that accountability and punctuality are highly valued qualities within Surinamese leadership. A significant proportion of the respondents stated that missing a deadline is considered to be a failure, thus underscoring a disciplined approach in which reliability is closely tied to professionalism (CCBS Survey, 2024). This strict stance upon time management reinforces a culture in which leaders set high expectations for both themselves and their teams, emphasising that meeting deadlines is crucial to maintaining organisational discipline (CCBS Survey, 2024). Interestingly, some of the respondents were proponents of a more flexible approach, advocating for a second chance to resolve issues and improve outcomes. This balance between strict accountability and occasional flexibility is thus suggestive of a nuanced approach within Surinamese workplaces, where high standards are upheld, yet room is allowed for solutions that may benefit the organisation in the long term. Thirdly, Surinamese leaders demonstrate a strong commitment to team welfare, with the majority of the respondents indicating that ensuring team members' well-being is a key part of their role (CCBS Survey, 2024). One respondent, a General Director at a producing company, stated: *"In Suriname you have to keep in mind the different cultures and races. People can be very sensitive and the way the leader guides, coaches or direct their subordinates can be very different"* (CCBS Survey, 2024). This person-centred approach aligns with transformational leadership values, which prioritise empathy and care. Another participant who is a consultant-trainer expressed: *"Usually direct and focused on the growth of both employees and the organisation"* (CCBS Survey, 2024). Furthermore, the survey revealed that many Surinamese leaders stand firm on their decisions, emphasising that they do not easily change a decision once it has been made (CCBS Survey, 2024). As one respondent, a Director at a Manufacturing company, noted: *"In Suriname, we are still mostly using the classic command and control leadership style."* (CCBS Survey, 2024). This rigidity reflects a respect for authority and tradition within leadership, reinforcing the perception that revisiting decisions can be seen as a lack of strength. The remaining respondents all stated, *"A no mi"* (not like me) in response to whether they change decisions, thus indicating that decisiveness and consistency are highly valued (CCBS Survey, 2024). Finally, a notable aspect of Surinamese leadership is the tendency to maintain professional boundaries, with a small proportion of leaders preferring to retain personal distance from their employees to preserve their authority (CCBS Survey, 2024). This practice underscores respect for hierarchy, with clear boundaries between leaders and employees being maintained. One respondent expressed that Surinamese leadership remains hierarchical, due to prevailing cultural norms of respect for authority that are instilled from an early age. This respect extends into the workplace, where employees uphold a professional distance from managers in order to show respect for these traditional values (CCBS Survey, 2024). In conclusion, the data from the CCBS Survey (2024) revealed that Surinamese leaders respect traditional authority whilst strongly valuing team well-being. They focus on accountability, consistency in decision-making, and formal recognition, whilst, simultaneously, maintaining a relational approach that prioritises employee welfare. This balance reveals a nuanced leadership style in which traditional values blend with a gradual shift towards people-centred practices, allowing Surinamese leaders to navigate both local expectations and global trends.

Jean-Pierre Polanen: a Surinamese leadership scholar

The first expert on Surinamese leadership that we interviewed in Jean-Pierre Polanen. Ir. Polanen has an MBA and is currently working in Hungary as an Operations Manager, Management Consultant and University lecturer. He actively contributes to Suriname by being a guest lecturer at the Anton de Kom University and being the co-founder and board member of Wi Tru Sranan, which is a national foundation for Unity, Values and Norms in Suriname (Polanen, 8 November 2024). He has also written the following books: *"Transform Your World"* (2020) and *"The Soul of a Nation"* (2024). At the start of the interview, Ir. Polanen stated that his career path not only helped him gain experience in Surinamese leadership styles, but also internationally, as he worked abroad with his then employer Nestlé in countries like Japan, the Netherlands and France (8 November 2024). During his experience abroad in France and the Netherlands, he noticed multiple resemblances and differences between these leadership styles and Surinamese leadership styles. These differences and resemblances primarily pertained to the degree of openness and vulnerability of leaders. In his experience, French leaders are not as open and vulnerable as Dutch leaders. Surinamese leaders can be situated somewhere in the middle of this spectrum but bear a stronger resemblance to French leaders, as they are quite distant from their subordinates when it comes to exhibiting vulnerability and transparency. He elaborated upon this further by stating: *"People are a little more cautious about making themselves vulnerable as a leader. That also has to do with the culture"*.

In response to a question about what the typical leadership styles are in Suriname, Ir. Polanen responded, somewhat interestingly, that there is not really one specific leadership style in Suriname, due to the ethnic diversity, demographic shifts, and evolving leadership trends. These trends centre on improving and developing leadership within Suriname and are primarily being driven by the younger generation (8 November, 2024). This has resulted in a division between old and new leadership styles. The old leadership style is very hierarchical, and there is no space for contradicting the leader. There is also an unequal distribution of welfare and power, which, in turn, makes a lot of leaders quite arrogant. Conversely, Ir. Polanen informed us, the emerging leadership style focuses more on HR methods, with teambuilding and the well-being of the team taking on increased importance (8 November, 2024). Managers ask for feedback and use this to improve themselves and their team. This new leadership style is a necessity in as far as Suriname is characterised by an unequal distribution of wealth within society at large. This unequal treatment is also difficult to overcome as Suriname is a small society where connections and networks already exist, thus making opportunities for outsiders scarce. Ir. Polanen concluded the interview by explicating that the main way to address this inequality is for the new generation of leaders to empower the Surinamese people. As he put it: "*A young generation of Surinamese must develop themselves as leaders and role models in order to achieve a transformation in society*".

Dirk Currie: a Surinamese cross-cultural trainer
The second leadership expert we interviewed is Dirk Currie, who is currently the Manager at Your Leadership Toolbox (YLT) Consultancy. Currie has held various significant positions in Suriname, including being the former CEO of Telesur and a board member at Wi Tru Sranan. This helped him gain extensive experience in business leadership. Moreover, as the chairman of the Lotjes Huis, an orphanage in Suriname, Currie has demonstrated a strong commitment to youth welfare. His role as a leadership consultant and trainer has provided him with insights into many companies and a wide range of leadership styles. At the start of the interview, Currie reflected upon what defines a 'typical' Surinamese leader, sharing an interesting observation that his own leadership style is very different from what he has seen and experienced in Suriname (Currie, 15 November 2024). According to Currie, many Surinamese leaders tend to be highly direct in their approach, and, as such, often lack emotional intelligence. This problem, he explained, derives from the fact that most leaders in Suriname have not been formally trained for leadership roles. Leadership courses are uncommon and there is a common belief that individuals with Higher Education degrees are

automatically qualified to lead, even if they lack the practical skills required for effective leadership. Currie encapsulated this issue through the following phrase "*Koni ne poer dong,*" which means that being highly educated does not equate to wisdom (15 November 2024). Next, he proceeded to discuss that many leaders from the older generation rely on strict and controlling leadership styles, which he believes does little to motivate subordinates. In fact, Currie pointed out that these approaches often create a culture of fear, as many leaders are resistant to being questioned or challenged. He underscored the importance of emotional intelligence and a coaching-based leadership approach, whilst also stressing the need for flexibility, as effective leaders must be able to adapt their style to suit different situations (15 November 2024). Despite these challenges, Currie expressed optimism about the emergence of a younger generation of leaders. Influenced by social media and global leadership trends, younger professionals are more ambitious and less willing to accept old-fashioned ways, which poses challenges for older leaders who are often unprepared to guide these individuals. Currie also addressed the role of bureaucracy in leadership, acknowledging that although strict procedures and rules can be useful in some circumstances being overly firm is not effective in every situation. He believes that many Surinamese leaders struggle because they fail to balance rules with flexibility. As he put it: *"There is no room, no space left for people to come up with new ideas".*
In order to drive meaningful change, Currie advocated for a shift away from the belief that academic qualifications alone make someone a competent leader. Rather, he recommended focusing upon practical skills and embracing coaching-based leadership practices. Currie has incorporated these principles into his own work by prioritising competence and emotional intelligence over degrees when assessing leadership potential. He concluded the interview with an inspiring statement: *"Leiderschap begint bij het sturen van je eigen leven,"* which means that leadership starts by taking control of your own life.

In-country leadership bestseller

The established author Jean-Pierre Polanen, who was born in Paramaribo, Suriname and grew up in both Suriname and the Netherlands, has written two books on leadership and values in Suriname, which were recommended by one of the respondents of the CCBS Survey (2024). Further research on Jean-Pierre Polanen led to the discovery of his second bestseller, *The Soul of a Nation – A Journey into the past, present and future of Surinamese Values.* The book was independently published in 2024 with the purpose of understanding Surinamese values and helping leaders to contribute towards both the well-being and wealth of Suriname. In this book, Jean-Pierre writes about the values that Surinamese citizens have on an individual level, the values that they experience in Suriname and the values that are needed for the future. Examples of these future values are honesty, unity, sustainability, collaboration, and long-term perspective. Leaders in Suriname should use these values and apply them to their organisational values and company culture. As he himself notes: "*Employers can have a strong positive socialisation impact on their employees by creating a company culture based on positive core-values*" (Polanen, 2024, p. 86). According to Polanen (2024), leadership is not limited to politics; it also applies to the business world. This suggests that leaders in companies have the potential to drive societal change by actively promoting and implementing it. For example, employees can promote these values within the broader society by inspiring their friends and families. To change or adapt organisational values, leadership is needed, because leaders should guide their subordinates. The prevailing leadership style in Suriname, both historically and at the present juncture, is an autocratic leadership approach, where change can often be difficult. The younger generation in Suriname appears to favour a more participative leadership style, emphasising new values: unity, collaboration, and a long-term perspective, with employees who are good listeners and have a solution- and decision- oriented manner. Consequently, this book helps ambitious leaders in Suriname to adapt to a changing economy, whilst, simultaneously, applying their Surinamese values (Polanen, 2024). In conclusion, Ir. Polanen thinks that promoting social values, such as collaboration and unity, can help develop the individual and collective well-being of Suriname, as social values have the power to unite and inspire, especially when presented and promoted by a leader that people can look up to.

Local leadership book	
Title	*The Soul of a Nation*
Subtitle	*A Journey into the Past, Present and Future of Surinamese Values*
Author	Jean-Pierre Polanen
Publisher	Independently published
Year	2024
ISBN	979-8873429585

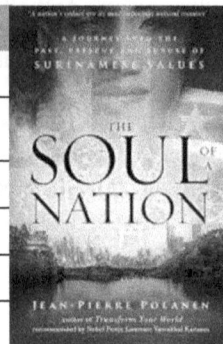

Suriname leadership YouTube review

The first video features Rudy Verdamme interviewing Dutch-Surinamese learning and development specialist Bryan Walker about leadership development in Suriname. Verdamme started his YouTube channel to share information on how professionals can work in a development-oriented manner. The purpose of this interview was therefore to conduct research on how business development occurs within the Surinamese context. At the beginning of the video, Walker emphasises that leadership within Suriname is deeply rooted in cultural values, particularly the strict upbringing of children, where respect for authority is essential. He connects this cultural norm to the business environment, noting that whilst hierarchical structures are prominent, they do not necessarily require leaders to adopt a purely authoritarian approach. As Walker stated in the interview: *"You can have a hierarchical position, as a [leader] you have a hierarchical position, but that does not mean that your way of training and managing has to be hierarchical"* (Walker, 2021, 2:07). Later in the video, Walker endorsed this view by explicating that if leaders in Suriname were to adopt a coaching leadership style, then this would benefit themselves, their direct employees and ultimately maybe even society. This perspective is also supported by the former director of the Suriname Leadership Academy (SLA), who, in an interview with Surinamese news channel Sun Web TV regarding the sixth edition of the SLA, emphasised the importance of relational leadership. In the video, he stated: *"A good relationship between managers in the workplace is how you look at it, because you can lead and you are a leader, but you can also receive guidance from the people you have under you"* (Malone, 2023, 4:06). This view underscores the potential value of reciprocal guidance and suggests that effective leadership in Suriname should strive to balance hierarchical respect with a more adaptive management style. The SLA really wants this narrative to proliferate within Suriname, by hosting leadership courses. In response to a question about how leadership and the views of SLA can grow within Surinamese society, Malone (2023) discussed that planning is key. He elaborated upon this by saying that organisations can incorporate change by planning and budgeting courses with SLA that help develop leadership in Suriname. The concluding video is an interview on STVS's *"Mmanteng Taki"* (Morning Talks) featuring JCI Suriname National President Gillian Pooters and SLA National Director Malcolm Asin during the seventh annual JCI Suriname Leadership Academy. They discuss the importance of nurturing truthful leaders, emphasising the saying *"Jong geleerd, is oud gedaan"* (*"What is learned in youth, is carried into old age"*) (Pooters, 2024, 0:41). The academy's theme, *Leadership and Diversity*, focuses on equipping participants with skills for leadership roles whilst fostering collaboration and inclusivity within Suriname's diverse society.

Pooters stresses the need for unity and leveraging each other's strengths to grow collectively up the economic ladder (Pooters, 2024).

Understanding hierarchy in Suriname

The hierarchical structure of Surinamese organisations has undergone significant changes following the military coup of 1980 and the restoration of democracy in 1985 (Ramsoedh, 2017). Currently, this structure is still deeply rooted within both political and corporate sectors, stemming from historical influences, including the establishment of military-civilian governance that emphasised top-down forms of control (Veenendaal, 2020). These political events have also profoundly influenced the prevailing business leadership styles within Suriname, particularly within larger companies. In Surinamese SMEs, leadership is characterised by a combination of transactional and informal transformational styles (Soerdjan, 2022). SMEs dominate the economy by relying on a directive, hierarchical approach that emphasises authority and power, thus demonstrating a strong preference for transactional leadership. Whilst elements of informal transformational practices are present, they tend to lack formal structure in the organisational framework. According to Dirk Currie (15 November 2024), who has accumulated extensive experience over the years as a consultant working with various companies and conducting leadership style assessments, leadership within many organisations in Suriname often gravitates towards a dominant style. He argues that this inclination is partly driven by a fear amongst leaders that if they empower their subordinates that this may result in those individuals surpassing them in terms of expertise and competence (Currie, 15 November 2024). This perspective aligns with the work of Soerjdan (2022), who also argues that a more dominant and hierarchical leadership style predominates in Suriname. According to Soerdjan (2022), most SMEs have adopted these leadership practices to remain competitive in an ever-evolving market. This tendency towards informally structured transactional leadership is further reinforced by Surinamese cultural attitudes towards power inequality, which exhibits a high Power Distance Index (PDI) of 85, thus indicating that hierarchical practices are widely accepted, and employees are more likely to comply with authority (Hofstede, 2019). Moreover, in high PDI cultures like Suriname, employees may be hesitant to challenge authority or provide input due to fear of potential repercussions, thus further reinforcing the hierarchical framework within these organisations. For example, employees might avoid offering suggestions in meetings, based upon their expectations that decisions will be made solely by senior-level management (Dai et al., 2022). The results of the CCBS Survey (2024) also corroborate this depiction of Surinamese leadership, in as far as in contrast to employees in some countries who address leaders by their first names, Surinamese leaders favour a more traditional approach that supports established structures and roles, reinforcing authority and respect (CCBS Survey, 2024). Furthermore, the majority of the respondents reported that leaders are likely to directly address their subordinates in meetings to ensure that goals are met, in addition to encouraging competition amongst team members to achieve better results (CCBS Survey, 2024). Within SMEs, the presence of a hierarchical leader, where decision-making is centralised in the hands of a single leader, often results in employees experiencing a sense of detachment from their leader. This was corroborated by one of our interviewees, who informed us that, traditionally, leaders in Suriname have a certain level of detachment from their employees and keep a safe distance, in order to avoid making themselves vulnerable (Polanen, 8 November 2024). The results of the CCBS Survey (2024) also support this observation, as one of the respondents, a Finance Manager, stated that within the public sector it is noticeable that there is a large distance between leaders and employees. Additionally, this participant endorsed the view that leadership styles are more authoritarian, relying more on the effort of employees than focusing on building relationships (CCBS Survey, 2024). In contrast, the private sector is showing a growing awareness of 'servant leadership,' in which empathy and the well-being of people is centralised (CCBS Survey 2024). This demonstrates that transactional leadership plays a key role in many organisations in Suriname, especially within the public sector where the power gap between leaders and employees is larger than in the private sector.

How the Surinamese achieve leadership empathy

Considering the ethnic diversity within Suriname society as well as its business environment, empathy plays a pivotal role in terms of promoting an inclusive workspace (Östlund, 2020). An important characteristic of some Surinamese leaders is that they ordinarily have close interpersonal relationships with their subordinates (Mac Donald, 2016). The multi-ethnic population in Suriname benefits from empathetic leadership practices that respect cultural differences, helping to reduce prejudice and bias within the workspace. This characterisation of Surinamese leaders is also supported by the results of the CCBS Survey (2024), in as far as all of the respondents agreed with the statement that managers should actively spend time ensuring the wellbeing of their team members by improving relations, enhancing services, and addressing societal issues related to inequality. As indicated by one of our interviewees, Jean-Pierre Polanen, a business scholar, Surinamese leaders can create positive relationships by earning respect from their subordinates, instead of expecting it (8 November 2024). Jean-Pierre Polanen proceeded to inform us that Surinamese leaders can achieve this by listening to their team and by taking their personal needs and situations in to account. An example of this is that the Surinamese economy is not at its strongest right now, which means that some people might need to work two jobs to earn additional income to be able to afford daycare for their children. A manager could take this into account and help think of solutions that best fit the needs of their employee (Polanen, 8 November 2024). Although these aforementioned discussions indeed suggest that Surinamese leaders are willing to take responsibility for the well-being of their employees, it is important to stress that in return for this they expect loyalty and respect from them. As Mac Donald (2016) suggests, this means that Surinamese leaders are both caring and supportive, whilst, simultaneously, also being demanding, authoritarian and disciplinary. In a similar vein, in our interview with the leadership consultant Sharmila Ramadhin (15 November 2024), they informed us that empathetic leadership is not always the norm in Suriname, as many leaders struggle with practicing empathic listening. Surinamese employees often view their leaders primarily as authoritative decision-makers and problem-solvers, rather than fostering a culture in which employees take the initiative themselves. However, interestingly, the results of the CCBS survey (2024) suggest that employees expect their leaders to be powerful decision makers but also good listeners. This indicates that change is needed. According to the leadership consultant Dirk Currie, who we interviewed, leaders in Suriname often spend more time with their co-workers at the office than with their families at home. Yet, workplace problems are common and frequently overlooked. Currie questions: *"Why don't we do anything? Why don't we know what is wrong?"* (15 November 2024). In Suriname, there is often a lack of meaningful engagement between leaders and employees. However, leaders who prioritise empathy actively endorse diversity initiatives that promote inclusivity within the workplace. By doing so, they create an environment where employees from diverse cultural and ethnic backgrounds feel valued and understood, which, in turn, supports team cohesion and reduces conflicts borne from cultural misunderstandings (Östlund, 2020). The way a leader motivates their team is by ensuring that employees from different backgrounds feel valued and understood. Mac Donald's (2016) research shows that Surinamese employees who have a directive leader are more likely to have a low level of motivation, whilst two-thirds of highly motivated people in Suriname have participative leaders. The importance of this participative approach is also supported by Soerdjan (2022), who argued that transformational leadership in Suriname, which is connected to participative leadership, stimulates individual needs, motivation, and team building. According to one of our respondents, it appears that there is an increasing shift towards more participative and empathetic forms of leadership in Suriname. As Anushka Sonai, President at Creative Technology Hub Caribbean (2024), noted: *"In Suriname, the leadership style varies by generation. Older leaders are more authoritative and hierarchical, whilst younger leaders focus on collaboration, inclusivity, and consensus-building, creating a more community-oriented approach."*

Syria

*Nassim Ait Chrif, Nardi van Leeuwen, Amel Loukili, Rick Baas,
Max Streefkerk & Jaimy loupias*

As the Arab poet Al-Mutanabbi once said, "إذا رأيت أسنان الأسد مكشوفة، فلا تظن أن
الأسد مبتسم." (*"If you see the lion's teeth exposed, do not assume the lion is
smiling"*). This saying serves as both a good reminder of the strength and
resilience of Syria, or the Syrian Arab Republic as it is officially known, and
metaphor for the current state of Syria and its business landscape. Despite the
manifold challenges and adversities, the Syrian people have undergone
historically, its people have shown incredible strength, especially within the
business sector (Turkmani & Mehchy, 2022). Located at the centre of ancient
trade routes, Syria has a long history of trade and entrepreneurship. It shares its
borders with Turkey, Iraq, Jordan, Israel, Lebanon, and the Mediterranean Sea,
which makes it an important location for regional commerce (Fakih & Ibrahim,
2016). Prior to the war, Syria had a growing economy with a GDP of around 55
billion Euro, driven by agriculture, oil, and tourism. Even though this conflict has
caused profound difficulties, Syrians continue to demonstrate strong business
leadership skills, especially within small businesses and trade. Alongside their
aforementioned resilience, they also exhibit tremendous creativity as well as an
ability to adapt during tough periods. Entrepreneurship has always been a key part
of Syria's culture, with traders once leading global trade on the famous Silk Road.
Syrian businesses also possess inimitable skills that help them navigate challenges,
such as flexibility, innovation, and a focus upon building strong relationships.
Important skills in the Syrian business world, where leaders must often deal with
uncertainty and risk. By being strategic and adaptable, Syrian business leaders
manage to find opportunities in challenging times (Megheirkouni, 2016). This
chapter explores Syrian management features and practices by drawing upon
academic research and survey and interview data with local professionals and
experts in the field of Syrian business leadership.

How do Syrians characterise leaders?

Business leaders in Syria are characterised by a blend of strategic adaptability, resilience, and cautious alignment with political power. The complex environment in Syria, historically marked by conflict and economic challenges, profoundly impacts upon both how business leaders operate and what qualities and traits are most valued (Megheirkouni, 2016). Syrian business leaders, particularly those within the elite networks that have connections to the prevailing political regime, are regarded as strategic and adaptable by the populace and their employees (Haddad, 2012). This was illustrated by one of the respondents of the CCBS Survey (2024), who stated: *"Leadership in Syria requires not only making decisions but understanding and navigating personal connections"*. According to Megheirkouni (2016), business leaders in Syria display a wide array of skills, such as, for example, strategic thinking, adaptability, and problem-solving. These traits are particularly essential for navigating the volatile business environment in Syria, where political instability and economic sanctions often pose significant risks for all involved.

In light of these challenges, Syrian leaders must therefore exhibit tremendous flexibility and resilience in their day-to-day approach in order to manage their businesses amidst such challenges, and invariably focus upon maintaining stability and continuity within their operations (Siham, 2013). Moreover, the Syrian business community is composed of various groups, all of whom have different strategies for navigating the challenging economic landscape. For instance, the 'integrated' business elite are closely aligned with influential networks, leveraging their connections in order to gain access to contracts and opportunities that are in accordance with the prevailing economic power structures (Cadmus, 2020). Loyalty and alignment with authority are highly valued traits within this group of Syrian business leaders. Leaders who are deemed to be loyal, whether to family, community, or political allies, often gain trust and support, which are vitally important within a culture that values strong social connections. How the power structures will develop after the fall of the Assad regime remains to be seen. Conversely, there are other business leaders who operate with greater independence, a group which often includes expatriates or those with diversified investments abroad. This particular group of leaders focus upon maintaining flexibility and neutrality within their approach, in an effort to allow them to adapt their strategies to protect and grow their businesses regardless of external economic or political shifts (ETH, 2013). Consequently, these types of leaders who operate internationally or have less direct political affiliations are expected to maintain a degree of neutrality and discretion in their approach (ETH, 2013). This balancing act performed by Syrian leaders reflects the broader Syrian cultural values of exercising caution when navigating relationships and maintaining harmony, which, in turn, allows leaders to protect their businesses even under uncertain political conditions. Despite the advantages of staying aligned with the regime, business leaders in Syria are often criticised for prioritising their own interests over broader societal needs (Cadmus, 2020). Whilst they are viewed as influential within the economic landscape, their focus upon maintaining personal and familial wealth has led to accusations of corruption and nepotism. Such practices are seen as detrimental to the development of the broader business environment and economic fairness in Syria (Cadmus, 2020). In summary, Syrian business leaders are characterised by their adaptability and strategic acumen, which are shaped by the need to navigate a challenging political and economic environment. Whilst they possess the skills to manage businesses effectively under pressure, their close ties to political power and reliance upon the overthrown Assad regime loyalty reveal a vulnerability within their leadership approach.

Survey results and what local respondents say

The CCBS Survey (2017-2024) was administered to C-level Syrian business leaders in order to learn from their knowledge and expertise and gain insight into business leadership practices and dynamics in Syria. In order to enhance both the generalisability and validity of the findings, we combined survey data from two different periods of collection (2017-2024). The most significant findings emerging from the survey will be discussed in turn within section. The first noteworthy result is that the respondents emphasised that there was a preference in Syria for leaders who exhibit "*calm authority*" combined with the ability to "*distribute energy equally*" amongst their teams, especially in environments with limited resources (CCBS Survey, 2017-2024). As one respondent described, "*Leadership in Syria requires not only making decisions but understanding and navigating personal connections*" (CCBS Survey, 2017-2024). Consequently, leaders are expected to balance authoritative decision-making with empathetic forms of engagement, in order to ensure the well-being and motivation of their teams and foster a supportive atmosphere (CCBS Survey, 2017-2024). This was illustrated by one respondent, who reported that leaders in Syria "*actively ensure the well-being of their team members,*" thus underscoring the critical role of personal investment within leadership there. The second significant finding revealed by the survey is that respect for hierarchy is deeply ingrained within Syrian organisations. This is evidenced by the fact that leaders are often addressed formally, thus reflecting the cultural emphasis placed upon authority and professionalism. However, interestingly, this cultural respect for hierarchy does not negate the importance of approachability. Rather, as one respondent noted, *"The balance between authority and approachability defines effective Syrian leadership"* (CCBS Survey, 2024). This was corroborated by another survey respondent, who informed us that Syrian leaders should not only be decision-makers but rather also motivators who *"make everyone feel welcome and at ease"* (CCBS Survey, 2024). This expectation that Syrian leaders must personally engage with their employees sets high standards for leadership in Syria, where the ability to connect with employees on a personal level is deemed to be just as vital as making strategic decisions. Gender equality within the context of business leadership within Syria was a source of considerable debate amongst the different respondents. For example, whilst some expressed optimism about increasing opportunities for women within Syrian organisations, others pointed to persistent societal and cultural barriers. As one respondent remarked, "*Leadership roles are still influenced by traditional views, making it harder for women to reach senior positions despite gradual improvements*" (CCBS Survey, 2024). This diversity of thought reflects the ongoing tension between progress and entrenched cultural traditions. Another respondent reported that leadership in Syria *"is about much more than just making decisions; it's about understanding and navigating the intricate balance between respect, authority, and personal connections"* (CCBS Survey, 2024). This complex perspective underscores how Syrian leadership must intertwine professional responsibilities with deeply rooted cultural dynamics. Generational differences also surfaced as a key theme in the survey. Specifically, it was reported that older leaders tend to favour cautious and traditional management styles, shaped by their prior experiences, and have a preference for control, whereas their younger counterparts advocate for the introduction of more flexible and contemporary approaches. This evolution reflects broader shifts in organizational culture as younger Syrians enter the workforce and challenge established norms. As these generational perspectives converge, Syrian leadership continues to evolve, blending traditional values with modern expectations. The unique balance between calm authority, personal engagement, and adaptability makes leadership in Syria both a challenging and rewarding role (CCBS Survey, 2017-2024).

Local leadership analysis

Lana Alkoubaytari: a Syrian cross-cultural trainer
Lana Alkoubaytari, a leadership coach and consultant, drew upon her extensive knowledge and experience to offers us deep insights into the challenges and nuances of managing teams within Syria's unique cultural and business

environment. To begin the interview, she explained how the organisational culture in Syria is characterised by informal, friendly relationships between leaders and their employees. As Alkoubaytari explained: *"The bond between managers and their team members is more familial than formal, which may present a challenge for foreign managers accustomed to professional boundaries"* (20 November 2024). They proceeded to inform us that Syrian employees are typically expected to follow instructions from managers without question, in as far as workplaces are generally hierarchical with limited opportunities for democratic interactions, something that can also prove challenging for foreign managers who are used to a more collaborative approach (Alkoubaytari, 20 November 2024). Next, Alkoubaytari moved onto discuss challenges with Syria's education system, which has been severely impacted by the ongoing conflict, explaining that graduates often lack essential skills such as presentation abilities or problem-solving, which are critical within professional settings, and hinder their performance in job interviews or technical assessments (20 November 2024). Alkoubaytari also pinpointed specific cultural habits that may pose difficulties for foreign managers operating in Syria, namely the cultural resistance to flexible working hours in Syria. Hence, even when foreign managers attempt to introduce flexible or hybrid work models, they often face resistance from senior management. This lack of adaptability to contemporary work practices can make it challenging for foreign leaders to implement necessary changes within a dynamic international business environment. As Alkoubaytari (20 November 2024) notes, *"Foreign managers must be culturally aware and adapt their leadership styles to the informal nature of Syrian workplaces"*. Despite these challenges, Alkoubaytari stresses that Syrian employees are hardworking and adaptable once they trust their leaders. *"Syrian employees are eager to work under foreign leadership because they associate it with higher education and professionalism,"* she said. They value the opportunity to learn from managers with international experience and are open to adopting new methods, albeit initial resistance to change is common. *"Employees may resist new practices initially, but once they see the benefits, they quickly adapt"* (Alkoubaytari, 20 November 2024). For example, companies like SyriaTel, which integrate foreign leadership and international practices, have created professional, structured work environments that blend local and global approaches successfully. Within larger, structured companies such as SyriaTel, conflict resolution is formal and professional, which is important according to Alkoubaytari (20 November 2024), who explained that clear policies ensure respectful communication and that *"raising one's voice is forbidden,"* with formal complaints and penalties for violations. Alkoubaytari told us that this is in marked contrast to smaller or less formal Syrian companies, where conflicts are often handled informally and some managers retaliate against employees who file complaints, thus creating a culture of fear and mistrust (20 November 2024). Moreover, these types of Syrian companies often lack the infrastructure, training, and professional values seen at SyriaTel, which, in turn, leads to inconsistent handling of workplace issues and less emphasis upon employee well-being or fairness. To conclude the interview, Alkoubaytari provided several key insights for foreign managers aiming to succeed in Syria. Understanding informal relationships between managers and employees is crucial, and foreign managers must adapt their leadership styles to respect this cultural norm, whilst, simultaneously, setting clear boundaries. Change should be introduced gradually, as employees may initially resist but adapt once they come to see the benefits. Trust is also a significant asset, Alkoubaytari informed us, because Syrian employees tend to admire foreign managers with proven expertise, which can foster collaboration. By keeping these factors in mind, foreign managers can thus navigate Syria's unique workplace challenges, build stronger relationships with their teams, and foster a productive and positive work environment (Alkoubaytari, 20 November 2024).

Omar Ali: a Syrian leadership expert
Omar Ali is a barbershop manager in the Netherlands, who is originally from Damascus, Syria. Prior to emigrating to the Netherlands, he observed his father's twenty-year-long leadership career in Syria, which, in turn, inspired him to pursue management himself. In our interview (16 November 2024) with him, Omar began by discussing his own leadership journey and underscored notable differences between Syrian and Dutch business leadership styles and practices. The most significant difference, according to Ali, is that Syrian leadership often places a heavier burden of responsibility upon managers, who are expected to oversee every aspect of their organisation's operations (16 November 2024). Omar explained that in Syria, managers hold significant levels of authority, and there is altogether less room and possibility even for workers to challenge or discuss leaders' decisions, in contrast to the much more open and collaborative approach one discerns within the Netherlands. Omar (16 November 2024) proceeded to explain that respect for leaders in Syria is profoundly influenced by age and experience, in as far as older individuals are often regarded with higher esteem as a direct consequence of their perceived wisdom and expertise. This contrasts starkly with Dutch organisations, where respect tends to be earned through one's performance and skill rather than one's age. When asked about which qualities, traits and behaviours are valued in Syrian leaders and why this is the case, Omar (16 November 2024) stated that, above all, honesty and fairness are essential qualities for Syrian leaders to possess, in as far as these qualities help to cultivate

and maintain a sense of trust with one's employees and raise team morale. In conjunction with this, he also shared with us that empathy, a value emphasised by his father, is highly important for managing conflicts and understanding the needs of teams in Syria, which is why he now incorporates this within his own role as a manager in the Netherlands. Despite these aforementioned differences between Syrian and Dutch business leadership skills and practices, Omar (16 November 2024) acknowledged that Syrian leadership values, such as, for example, community and family, play a significant role in shaping workplace dynamics. Leaders are expected to treat their employees fairly, maintain strong interpersonal connections, and act with integrity in order to build trust within their teams. Later in the interview, Omar also discussed the challenges that foreign managers may encounter when working in Syria, particularly with respect to understanding local cultural norms and navigating the hierarchical structures within the country. In order to succeed, he specifically advised that foreign leaders should focus upon building trust, fostering personal relationships, and learning about Syrian customs and traditions. Omar (16 November 2024) concluded the interview by stressing the importance of ethical, empathetic, and culturally informed leadership, especially when seeking to bridge Syrian and Western styles of leadership. He underscored that whilst Syrian leaders often face greater pressure and responsibility, their focus upon social harmony and fairness creates a supportive and respectful work environment.

Syrian Leadership Social Media Review

Within Syria, discussions about business leadership skills and practices on social media platforms offer insights into local values and practices, which are influenced by a blend of historical, cultural, and political factors. Broadly speaking, the content found on social media platforms about Syrian business leadership reflects the need for strong, authoritative leadership, but also indicates an emerging focus upon collaboration and empowerment within certain circles. One notable voice on Syrian business leadership is Dr. Fadwa al-Khalil, a leadership coach and academic. Through her Facebook and Instagram pages, Dr. Fadwa al-Khalil emphasises the importance of empathy and integrity within Syrian leadership. In one of her posts, she writes, "*A true leader in Syria must understand the challenges of their people, be close to them, and lead with compassion*" (Al-Khalil, 2023). This perspective suggests that there has been a shift from traditional, top-down leadership styles towards a more inclusive approach in which emotional intelligence and understanding come to be seen as key traits of a successful leader in the country. Another key figure on Syrian business leadership online is Rasha Ibrahim, an entrepreneur and advocate for women's leadership, who frequently discusses

Syrian leadership in the context of empowerment and social responsibility. On her LinkedIn, Instagram and YouTube platforms, Ibrahim stresses (2023) that leadership in Syria is evolving, especially with respect to women's position in business. On the other hand, Samir Al-Mohammad, a Syrian business consultant, adopts a more traditional approach in his social media posts, particularly on X (formerly Twitter). Al-Mohammad argues that effective leadership within Syria must balance decisiveness with discipline. He mentions, "*In our culture, a leader must be strong and assertive—showing clarity in decisions and a firm hand in action*" (Al-Mohammad, 2023). His stance is more aligned with the traditional view of leadership in Syria as an authoritative role, which remains dominant within many sectors of Syrian society. These contrasting views—emphasising compassion, empowerment, and decisiveness—serve to illustrate the diversity of leadership philosophies within Syria today. Whilst some advocate for more modern, collaborative forms of leadership, others maintain that strong, centralised authority is necessary for addressing the country's ongoing challenges.

Understanding hierarchy in Syria

Syria's political and social system is highly centralised, which is to say that most power has been concentrated at the top by a small group of people, mainly the Assad family and the Ba'ath Party. The government uses the army and security services to keep control over the country and make sure people are loyal to the state (Hinnebusch, 2023). Even though Syria is in the midst of a civil war, this structure helped the government to maintain control within many areas (Tokmajyan, 2023). With the rapid Hayat Tahrir al-Sham operation, it is to be seen how this will develop in the coming years. Until recently, the Ba'ath Party controlled politics, and the president had considerable power. The Assad family had ruled Syria for decades, using security forces and the army to maintain their position of authority and power. Making arrangements with local warlords and business leaders in order to secure control over areas (Hinnebusch, 2023). The government uses a mixture of rewards, such as, for example, money or business opportunities, and threats to make sure the aforementioned leaders support them (Khatib, 2024). The Syrian government's centralised form of control also tends to directly influence the business environment, in turn, creating a highly structured and deeply hierarchical culture, characterised by an 'integrated' business elite who has to demonstrate loyalty to the state and strategically align with powerful political figures in order to achieve business success (Cadmus, 2020). Prior to the war, the government controlled many sectors and used their economic influence to reinforce this loyalty amongst the 'integrated elite.' However, even within the current fragmented economy, loyalty is still essential, and business leaders are often rewarded or punished based on their political alignment, thus impacting upon their business operations and decision-making process (Hinnebusch, 2023). This goes some way to explaining why loyalty, social relationships, and alignment with authority are highly valued traits amongst Syrian business leaders.

This was illustrated by one of the respondents of the CCBS Survey (2024), who reported: "*Leadership in Syria requires not only making decisions, but understanding and navigating personal connections*". Within the organisational cultures in Syria, a hierarchical approach is strongly emphasised, thus mirroring the country's political structure. Employer-employee relationships are often formal, and decision-making power is concentrated at the top, which reflects Syria's cultural norms around authority and respect (Hinnebusch, 2012). This was corroborated by one of our interviewees, Lana Alkoubaytari, a leadership coach, and consultant, who told us that Syrian employees are typically expected to follow instructions from their leaders without question, because organisations are generally hierarchical and pose limited opportunities for democratic interactions (20 November 2024). Similarly, our second interviewee, Omar Ali, who grew up in Syria and whose father had twenty years of leadership experience in the country, also noted that there is heavier burden of responsibility upon Syrian leaders, who are expected to oversee every aspect of their organisation's operations. This, in turn, means that managers hold significant levels of authority, and there is altogether less room and possibility even for workers to challenge or discuss leaders' decisions (16 November 2024). One way to make sense of this is by drawing upon Hofstede's power distance dimension, which posits that in countries that score high on this dimension, such as Syria, employees are less likely to challenge superiors and tend to follow top-down instructions closely, valuing loyalty and stability (Hofstede, 1980). Such environments promote bureaucracy and careful communication, where respect for authority is a key cultural value that helps to maintain organisational harmony. As aforementioned, the government's relationships with certain 'integrated' business elites enable centralised control over resources, which, in turn, further encourages a controlled and top-down management style within many companies. This form of governance and business management reflects Syria's collectivist values, where loyalty to authority and alignment with social hierarchy are highly valued (Khatib, 2024). Within Syrian businesses, hierarchy is intertwined with collectivist values, where loyalty, respect, and familial ties play an essential role. In contradistinction to individualistic societies, Syria's business culture emphasises loyalty and respect towards superiors, and personal connections frequently influence career progression and decision-making (Cadmus, 2020). In summary, Syrian business leaders must operate within a tough environment characterised by economic instability, changing markets, and political affiliations. Hence, it is crucial for Syrian business leaders to be decisive decision makers, resilient, flexible and cultivate personal relationships with the political elite. As the business world changes, however, leaders in Syria need to continue to adapt in order to ensure success for future generations of leaders (Shepherd & Saade, 2020).

How Syrians Achieve Leadership Empathy

Within Syria, empathy is a vital leadership skill, shaped by the country's complex social and political landscape. Given the manifold challenges Syrian has faced, both historically and at the present juncture, leaders have become adept at utilising empathy in order build trust and foster unity within their teams (Ali, 16 November 2024). By prioritising mutual support, they, in turn, create a supportive work environment that is essential for maintaining stability, particularly during difficult times (Avolio & Luthans, 2006). Syrian business leaders, particularly those within elite networks connected to the regime, that is, the so-called aforementioned 'integrated' leaders, are seen as strategic and adaptable (Haddad, 2012). Alongside these aforementioned qualities, a further core leadership attributed required within the Syrian context is authenticity, which plays a crucial role in terms of building trust with potential business partners as well as employees (Al-Haddad & Kotnour, 2015). In fact, Syrian leaders understand more than most the importance of being transparent, open, and self-aware. This is because in contexts such as Syria where trusts in institutions can be low, embracing honesty and transparency helps leaders to cultivate and maintain genuine connections with their teams (Al-Haddad & Kotnour, 2015). The importance of these qualities within the context of Syrian leadership were also corroborated by one of our interviewees, who stated that honesty was a vitally important trait for Syrian leaders to possess in as far as it helps to raise team morale and build trust with one's employees (Ali, 16 November 2024). Hence, by being honest and authentic with those that they lead, Syrian leaders thus help to break down barriers and foster a shared sense of unity within their organisations (All-Haddad & Kotnour, 2015; Ali, 16 November 2024). Non-verbal forms of communication are also critically important in this regard; within the Syrian context, maintaining eye contact and actively listening to employees are two powerful ways through which Syrian leaders achieve leadership empathy and engage with their employees, as these subtle but nevertheless meaningful gestures help to build trust and convey respect. Research has demonstrated the significance of non-verbal cues within Middle Eastern leadership specifically, in as

175

far as such actions can have a profound impact upon strengthening relationships (Hall, 1976). Emotional intelligence is also a critical factor in Syrian leadership. As leaders are better able to manage their own emotions and understand the emotions of others. In a high-stress environment like Syria, it enables leaders to address conflicts with care and empathy, ensuring they respond to their teams' needs thoughtfully (Chung et al., 2023). Additionally, Syrian leaders often use positive reframing to build resilience within their teams. This involves approaching challenges from an optimistic perspective, which helps maintain morale in difficult situations. The importance of emotional intelligence was also underscored by one of our interviewees, who based on observing his father who had twenty-years of leadership within Syria, shared with us that empathy is highly important for managing conflicts and understanding the needs of teams in Syria (Ali, 16 November, 2024). This characterization of Syrian leaders as empathic was also supported by the results of the CCBS Survey, where it was reported that leaders actively spend time ensuring the wellbeing of their team members. As one respondent put it, *"Leadership in Syria requires not only making decisions but understanding and navigating personal connections"* (CCBS Survey, 2024). Consequently, leaders are expected to balance authoritative decision-making with empathetic forms of engagement, in order to ensure the well-being and motivation of their teams and foster a supportive atmosphere (CCBS Survey, 2017-2024). One explanation for this is that Syrian business leadership is deeply rooted within Syrian cultural values that emphasise collective responsibility and prioritise the well-being of the community over individual goals. This community-centred approach helps build trust and collaboration, creating a supportive work environment. This is in accordance with research on leadership in the Middle East region which shows that this collective mindset serves to strengthen relationships within teams, further promoting a culture of empathy and cooperation (Hofstede, 1980). In summary, then, empathy within Syrian leadership is grounded in a distinct combination of authenticity, emotional intelligence, non-verbal communication, and a deep commitment to preserving community values, which, in turn, enable Syrian leaders to foster strong, supportive teams that are resilient in the face of tremendous adversity.

Bibliography

Bibliography

Εασε (ενωση ανωτατων στελεχων επιχειρησεων). (2017, June 2). Η ηγεσία μέσα από τα μάτια των ηγετών [Video]. YouTube. https://www.youtube.com/watch?v=XPimUnFwZSs

Εκδόσεις Κάκτος. (2024, 2 oktober). The Timeless Leaders - εκδόσεις Κάκτος. https://www.kaktos.gr/product/leadership-lessons-from-ancient-greece/

Abarca, N., Majluf, N., & Rodríguez, D. (1998). Identifying management in Chile. *International Studies of Management & Organization*, 18–7. http://dx.doi.org/10.1080/00208825.1998.11656732

Abubakar, I., Dalglish, S. L., Angell, B., Sanuade, O., Abimbola, S., Adamu, A. L., Adetifa, I. M. O., Colbourn, T., Ogunlesi, A. O., Onwujekwe, O., Owoaje, E. T., Okeke, I. N., Adeyemo, A., Aliyu, G., Aliyu, M. H., Aliyu, S. H., Ameh, E. A., Archibong, B., Ezeh, A., . . . Zanna, F. H. (2022). The Lancet Nigeria Commission: investing in health and the future of the nation. The Lancet, 399(10330), 1155–1200. https://doi.org/10.1016/s0140-6736(21)02488-0

Adegboye, M. (2013). The Applicability of Management Theories in Nigeria: Exploring the Cultural Challenge. In University of Lagos, International Journal of Business and Social Science, 4(10), 205–206 [Journal-article]. https://ijbssnet.com/journals/Vol_4_No_10_Special_Issue_August_2013/26.pdf

Adekunle, A. S., & Jude, A. I. (2014). Cross-Cultural Management Practice: The Impact on Nigerian Organization. European Journal of Business and Management. https://www.iiste.org/Journals/index.php/EJBM/article/view/11759

Ahmed-Ghosh, H. (2003). A History of Women in Afghanistan: Lessons Learnt for the Future. Journal of International Women's Studies, 4(3), 1-14.

Aizpurua-Iraola, J., Rasal, R., Prieto, I., Comas, D., Bonet, N., Casals, F., Calafell, F., & Vásquez, P. (2023). Population analysis of complete mitogenomes for 334 samples from El Salvador. *Forensic Science International Genetics*, 66, 102906. https://doi.org/10.1016/j.fsigen.2023.102906

Alfaro, L., Larangeira, C., & Costas, R. (2024). El Salvador: Launching Bitcoin as Legal Tender. *Harvard Business School*. https://www.hbs.edu/faculty/Pages/item.aspx?num=62068

Al-Haddad, S., & Kotnour, T. (2015). Integrating the organizational change literature: A model for successful change. *Journal of Organizational Change Management*, 28(2), 234-262

Ali O. (2024). [MS Teams] interview. 16 November

Alilat, S., Demmouche, N., & Université Constantine- Abdelhamid Mehri. (2022). L'élaboration d'une cartographie des déterminants du profil de l'entrepreneur. *Revue Humaines & Sociales des Sciences. 8* (2), 871–886).

Al-Khalil, F. (2023). The role of empathy in leadership. Facebook

Al-Mawred Al-Thaqafi (Culture Resource), Bokrouh, M., Ettijahat. Independent culture, & Kassab, A. (2014). *Cultural policies in Arab countries: A comparative study.* ARCP.

Alvarenga Jule, L. E. (2001). La situación económico-laboral de la maquila en El Salvador: Un análisis de género. Santiago de Chile: Unidad Mujer y Desarrollo.

Andres, T. D. (1988). *Managing people by Filipino values.* https://www.google.rs/books/

Andres, T. D. (1991). *Human resource management in Philippine* setting. https://www.google.rs/books/

Anonymous (2024). [MS Teams] interview. 8 November.

Anonymous, M. (2024, 2 November). [Teams] Interview. 20 November.

Arise News. (2024, October 8). Nigeria: Effective Leadership And National Stability- Samuel Sanusi [Video]. YouTube. https://www.youtube.com/watch?v=ywAR7TDer0o

Ariyibi, O. (2024). Interview Cross Cultural trainer.

Azadi, R. R., & Siddique, A. (2022, 4 October). "Nothing Left to Lose": Afghan women refuse to be silenced in face of Taliban violence, restrictions. RadioFreeEurope/RadioLiberty. https://www.rferl.org/a/afghanistan-women-resistance-taliban/32065187.html

Badia, A. (2011). *Leadership in Dominican Enterprises*. Santo Domingo Press.

Bases de las Relaciones Laborales en El Salvador (n.d.). Universidad Centroamericana José Simeón Cañas.

Becker, T. H. (2011). Doing business in the new Latin America: keys to profit in America's next-door markets. *Choice Reviews Online*, 48(10), 48–5779. https://doi.org/10.5860/choice.48-5779

Bedggood, G., & Benady, I. (2016). *Dominican Republic - culture smart!: The essential guide to customs and culture*. Dreamscape Media.

Benzaim, S., & Djermane, R. (2017). Strategic Management Culture & Foreign Partnership: Algerian-Foreign Companies case. *La Revue Des Sciences de Gestion*, 285-286, 103–104. https://www.cairn.info/revue-des-sciences-de-gestion.htm

Berreziga, A., & Meziane, A. (z.d.). La culture entreprenuriale chez les entrepreneurs algeriens. *Colloque National Sur : Les Stratégies D'Organisation Et D'Accompagnement Des PME en Algérie*, 1–3.

Betances, E. (2004). The Catholic Church and Political mediation in the Dominican Republic: A Comparative perspective. *Journal of Church and State*, 46(2), 341–364. https://doi.org/10.1093/jcs/46.2.341

Bethell, L. (1987). *The independence of Latin America*. Cambridge University Press.

Bonetti, L. (n.d.). Leadership is not synonymous with popularity but with conviction [LinkedIn post]. December 2024. https://www.linkedin.com/ligia-bonetti

Boojihawon, D.K., Richeri, A., Liu, Y., & Chicksand, D. (2021). Agile route-to-market distribution strategies in emerging markets: The case of Paraguay. *Journal of International Management*, 27, 100740. https://doi.org/10.1016/j.intman.2020.100740

Bouchetara, M. (2024). [MS Teams] interview. 12 November.

Boukhezer-Hammiche, N., & Mehdi, F. A. (2022). Le profil du dirigeant et l'internationalisation des entreprises algériennes. Cas des entreprises de la région de Bejaïa. *Les Cahiers Du Cread*, 38(2), 113–142. https://doi.org/10.4314/cread.v38i2.5

Branine, M. (2001). Human resource management in developing countries. In P. S. Budhwar & Y. A. Debrah (Reds.), *Routledge*(Vols. 155–172). Routledge & Cardiff University. http://ndl.ethernet.edu.et/bitstream/123456789/38927/1/19%202001.pdf#page=19

Bridging Leadership Institute. (2020, April 17). Filipino Psychology and Crisis Leadership [Video]. YouTube. November 8, 2024, from https://www.youtube.com/watch?v=8sog9LhzxDE

Broome, B. J. (1996). Exploring the Greek mosaic: A guide to intercultural communication in Greece. Intercultural Press.

Brunner, N. (2023, 21 September). The Power of Latino Leadership, second edition, revised and updated: Culture, Inclusion, and Contribution ¡Ahora! by Juana Bordas, Berrett-Koehler, Inc. QRCA.

Buchholz, K. (2024, April 26). Where Women Are Most Likely To Be Your Boss [Infographic]. Forbes. https://www.forbes.com/sites/katharinabuchholz/2024/04/23/where-women-are-most-likely-to-be-your-boss-infographic/

Cabrali, M. E. (2024). Video interview 12 November

Cabrera, J. (2017). Economic Transformation in the Dominican Republic. *Caribbean Journal of Development Studies*, 18(3), 112-125.

Cadmus. (2020). *The Syrian Chambers of Commerce in 2020: The Rise of a New Business Elite*. European University Institute

Cameron, K. (2011). Responsible leadership as virtuous leadership. *Journal of Business Ethics*, 98(S1), 25–35. https://doi.org/10.1007/s10551-011-1023-6

Canales, A. (2024) Teams interview. 12 November.

Candelario, C. M. C., & Cáceres, M. K. (2022). Integrative review of workplace health promotion in the business process outsourcing industry: Focus on the Philippines. *Public Health in Practice*, 3, https://doi.org/10.1016/j.puhip.2022.100250

Cartwright, J. R. (1978). *Political leadership in Sierra Leone*. University of Toronto Press.

Casa del Libro. (n.d.). *Ana Nieto Churruca*. https://www.casadellibro.com/libros-ebooks/ana-nieto-churruca/51595

CCBS Survey. (2017-2020). *Global Leadership Survey*. SurveyMonkey: Amsterdam University of Applied Sciences.

CCBS Survey. (2021-2024). *Global Leadership Survey*. In Qualtrics: Amsterdam University of Applied Sciences.

Ceballos, J. G. (2014). *Chile país del vino*. Google Books.

Center for International Stabilization and Recovery at JMU (CISR), & Keane, J. (2008). Algeria. *Journal Of Mine Action*, *11*(2). https://commons.lib.jmu.edu/cisr-journal/vol11/iss2/31

Channels Television. (2018, March 8). CEO NSE Oscar Backs More Leadership Role For Nigerian Women |Business Morning| [Video]. YouTube. https://www.youtube.com/watch?v=RDDjFZSVyGI

Charla "Liderazgo Estratégico en Chile" - Jaime Riquelme. (2018, August 6). [Video]. Youtube. https://www.youtube.com/watch?v=kO3QKchMyaQ

Charlas Motivacionales Latinoamérica. (2024, June 18). Felicidad en el trabajo - Santiago Vázquez - [Video]. YouTube. https://www.youtube.com/watch?v=_liymb-gWsA

Chatterjee, G. E. (2018). Leadership styles and outcome patterns for the nursing workforce and work environment: A systematic review. *International Journal of Nursing Studies*, 85, 19–60. https://doi.org/10.1016/j.ijnurstu.2018.04.016

Chatzivamvaki, P. (2016, January 21). Leadership styles and organizational performance in Greek enterprises. Home. https://repository.ihu.edu.gr/xmlui/handle/11544/12424

Chekkal, M. (2024). [MS Teams] interview. 8 November.

Cherak, M. (2024). Effect of Leadership Style on Organizational Commitment in Algeria. *American Journal Of Leadership And Governance*, *9*(2), 64–76. https://doi.org/10.47672/ajlg.2147

Chete, L., Adeoti, J., Adeyinka, F. M., & Ogundele, O. (2014). Industrial Development and Growth in Nigeria : Lessons and Challenges. https://www.semanticscholar.org/

Chile, de la autoridad al liderazgo - Maven Lomboy. (2020, 9 April). [Video]. https://www.youtube.com/watch?v=WmFmTRQZskM

Chotkan, R. (2009). Female entrepreneurship: Surinamese women acting entrepreneurial. [Master's thesis, University of Twente].

Chowdhury, A. M. R., Alam, M. A., & Ahmed, J. (2006). Development knowledge and experience - from Bangladesh to Afghanistan and beyond. Bulletin of the World Health Organization, 84(8), 677–681. https://doi.org/10.2471/blt.05.028332

Chung, C. K. K., & Cardozo, S. (2018). Estilo de liderazgo situacional predominante en las Micro y Pequeñas Empresas de Asunción, Paraguay. *Academo Revista De Investigación En Ciencias Sociales Y Humanidades*, *5*(2), 117–126. https://doi.org/10.30545/academo.2018.jul-dic.4

Civilnet. (2021, 25 January). *Secret advantages for diasporas & foreigners doing business in Armenia*. [Video]. YouTube. https://www.youtube.com/watch?v=K0SzPn4QNpg&t=28s

Civilnet. (2022, 3 August). *Realizing the potential of Armenian entrepreneurship*. [Video]. YouTube. https://www.youtube.com/watch?v=EEjKB1GCP2Q&t=191s

Comunidad Mujer, PNUD, & UN, P. (2018). Una Década De Cambios Hacia La Igualdad De Género En Chile (2009-2018): Avances Y Desafíos.

Conger, J. A., & Pearce, C. L. (2003). *Shared leadership: Reframing the hows and whys of leadership* (1st ed.). Sage Publications.

Constantino, R. (1975). *The Philippines: A past revisited*. Tala Publishing Services. https://www.researchgate.net/publication/

Contributor. (2020, August 7). Ramon S. Ang: Today's ideal Filipino leader. Asian Journal News. from https://asianjournal.com/business/business-news/ramon-s-ang-todays-ideal-filipino-leader/

Córdova Macías, R., FUNDAUNGO, Cruz, J. M., Seligson, M. A., & United States Agency for International Development. (2013). The Political Culture of Democracy in El Salvador and in the Americas, 2012: Towards Equality of Opportunity.

Creanza, P. P. (2024). Institutions, Trade, and Growth: The Ancient Greek Case of Proxenia. The Journal of Economic History, 84(1), 1–39. doi:10.1017/S0022050723000505

Currie, D. (2024). [Teams] interview. 15 November.

Curry, L., Taylor, L., Chen, P. G.-C., & Bradley, E. (2012). Experiences of leadership in healthcare in sub-Saharan Africa. Human Resources for Health, 10(1), 33–33. https://doi.org/10.1186/1478-4491-10-33

Dai, Y., Li, H., Xie, W., & Deng, T. (2022). Power distance belief and workplace communication: The mediating role of fear of authority. International Journal of Environmental Research and Public Health, 19(5), 2932. https://doi.org/10.3390/ijerph19052932

Dardano, G. F., (2024). [Teams] interview. 21 November

De La Sota, P., & Zaino, A. (2018). Personalismo in Latin American Leadership: A Comparative Study. Latin American Journal of Business.

Dedola Global Logistics. (2024). Port of Piraeus Shipping Solutions: Dedola Logistics. Dedola Global Logistics. https://dedola.com/ports/port-of-piraeus-greece/

Deep Leadership. (2023, 4 November). The Power of Latino Leadership with Dr. Juana Bordas [Video]. YouTube.

Dìaz, N. (2019). Las 12 Preguntas. Biblioteca Nacional Pedro Henrìques Ureña.

Díez Cabral, M. (2024). FITUR 2024: Leadership and partnerships. LinkedIn. December 5, 2024. https://www.linkedin.com/in/manuel-diez-cabral-810a3b108/recent-activity/all/

Doberstein, C. (2016). Designing collaborative governance decision-making in search of a "collaborative advantage." Public Management Review, 18(6), 819–841. https://doi.org/10.1080/14719037.2015.1045019

Dowling, J. M. (1994). Transactional analysis in Philippine organizations. In C. D. Ortigas (Ed.), Human resource development: The Philippine experience (p. 116). https://books.google.rs/books/

Dupree, N. H. (2002). Cultural Heritage and National Identity in Afghanistan. Third World Quarterly, 23(5), 977–989. http://www.jstor.org/stable/3993399

Dy, M. B., Jr., & Others. (1994). Values in Philippine culture and education. Cultural Heritage and Contemporary Change Series III. Asia, 7. https://www.crvp.org/publications/Series-III/III-7.pdf

Ekekwe, E. (2011). Nigeria: Leadership and Development. AuthorHouse

Ekorinthos. (2024, 18 June). EKorinthos - Thomas Katakis The Timeless Leaders Leadership Lessons From Ancient Greece. eKorinthos. https://ekorinthos.gr/

El Mestari, S. (2022). Leading from the Middle: Investigating the Roles of Algerian Academic Middle Leaders in Three Universities [Thesis].

El Salvador - United States Department of State. (2023, 7 December). United States Department of State. https://www.state.gov/reports/2022-report-on-international-religious-freedom/el-salvador/

Elkinser. (2011, April 5). How to do Business in Afghanistan [Video]. YouTube. https://www.youtube.com/watch?v=xOhHmn0Qda0

Emmanuel Emielu, E. (2024). Interview scholar.

Emploitic Algérie. (2020, 14 June). Webinar Conseils carrière : Le leadership [Video]. YouTube. https://www.youtube.com/watch?v=Mwb1Pb1KdQs

Erumebor, W. (2017). How to revive Nigeria's neglected leather industry. https://www.ajol.info/index.php/epr/article/view/165278

Esguerra, W. S. I., & Kheokao, J. (2021). Beyond boundaries: Redefining gender roles in Philippine workspaces. AB English Language Program, College of Arts and Sciences, St. Paul University Manila, Philippines, 475–478. https://wpuat-commarts.utcc.ac.th/

Esta Noche Mariasela. (2023, July 25). *Dominicana se Transforma, una iniciativa de Raul Burgos y la fundación de Liderazgo John C. Maxwell* [Video]. YouTube. https://www.youtube.com/watch?v=Ap0eu2UgH0c

Esu, B. B. (2013). Emotional Intelligence: Pathway to Improved Leadership Capacities in Nigeria. Journal Of Sociological Research, 3(2). https://doi.org/10.5296/jsr.v3i2.3004

ETH. (2013). Syria's Business Elite: Between Political Alignment and Economic Interest.

Ezirim, C. B., Nwibere, B. M., & Emecheta, B. C. (2010). Organizational culture and performance: the Nigerian experience. International Journal of Business and Public Administration, 7(1), 40.

Fakih, A., & Ibrahim, M. (2016). The impact of Syrian refugees on the labor market in neighboring countries: rmpirical evidence from Jordan. *Defence and Peace Economics*, 27(1), 64-86

Fanthorpe, R. (2001). Neither citizen nor subject? 'Lumpen' agency and the legacy of native administration in Sierra Leone. *African Affairs*, 100(400), 363–386. https://doi.org/10.1093/afraf/100.400.363

Ferozi, S., & Chang, Y. (2021). Transformational leadership and its impact on employee performance: focus on public employees in Afghanistan. Transylvanian Review of Administrative Sciences, 49-68. https://doi.org/10.24193/tras.63E.3

Ferreira, L. (2024). Video interview 6 November

Fiore, L. V. (2024, November 20). Lucía Vilariño Fiore on LinkedIn: [Español bajo] I am proud to be a mentor in the Organización de. . . . https://www.linkedin.com/posts/

Fleck, E. C. D. (2021). Paraguay Natural Ilustrado by José Sánchez Labrador SJ: Between the American Experience and Exile. *HoST-Journal of History of Science and Technology*, *15*(2), 121-148.

Flores-Hernández, E. R., Rodero-Cosano, M. L., & Perla-Cartagena, A. E. (2022). Complexity of family businesses in El Salvador: a structural equation model. *Sustainability*, 14(11), 6773.

Forbes. (2024, September 25). *Sierra Leone leading by example: President Bio on youthful leadership and Africa's global future* [Video]. YouTube. https://www.youtube.com/watch?v=dp_Q4VpRxt0

Future Armenian, (2019, September). Tech and entrepreneurial ecosystem mapping. *Report*. https://futurearmenian.com Tech-and-Entrepreneurial-Ecosystem-Mapping.pdf

Gabriel, A. G., & Manalo, G. M. (2020, March 23). How do millennial managers lead older employees? The Philippine workplace experience. *SAGE Open*, 10(1). https://doi.org/10.1177/2158244020914651

Galanaki, E., & Papalexandris, N. (2017). Demographic challenges for the future business leader: evidence from a Greek survey. Evidence-Based HRM: a Global Forum for Empirical Scholarship, 5(3), 297–310. doi:10.1108/ebhrm-03-2017-0019

García, P., & Peña, M. (2016). Unique Resources of the Dominican Republic: Tobacco and Larimar. *Caribbean Business Review*, 14(2), 56-72.

Gerber, M., & Hoffman, R. (2015). The Mediterranean diet: health, science and society. British Journal of Nutrition, 113(S2), S4–S10. doi:10.1017/S0007114514003912

Gill, R., & Negrov, A. (2021). Perspectives on leadership development in post-Soviet Eurasia. *International Journal of Cross-Cultural Management*, 21(3), 409–429. https://doi.org/10.1177/14705958211051551

Giousmpasoglou, C. (2014). Greek management and culture. European Journal of Cross-Cultural Competence and Management, 3(1), 51. https://doi.org/10.1504/ejccm.2014.063403

Global Entrepreneurship Monitor (2020). *Global Entrepreneurship Monitor Armenia national report 2019/2020*. Ameria Management Advisory. https://ameriaadvisory.am GEM-EnglishFinal.pdf

Goleman, D. (1998). Working with emotional intelligence. Bantam Books.

Gómez, R., & Martínez, C. (2015). *Hispaniola: A Shared Island with Unique Stories*. Santo Domingo: Editorial Caribe.

Gonzales, R. L. (1994). Corporate culture modification. In C. D. Ortigas (Ed.), *Human resource development: The Philippine experience*. https://books.google.rs/books/

Gustavo, B. (n.d.). El nuevo liderazgo dominicano: Un modelo caribeño que inspira. LinkedIn. December 7, 2024. https://www.linkedin.com/

Haddad, B. (2012). *Business networks in Syria: The political economy of authoritarian resilience*. Stanford University Press

Haddam, F., Bouabdallah & LLC Research Lab. (2022). Journal of the Linguistic Situation vs Education in Post-colonial Algeria. In *Revue Plurilingue : Études Des Langues, Littératures Et Cultures, 6.1* 83–90

Hall, E. T. (1976). *Beyond culture*. Anchor Books

Haran, F. (2015). Leaders and followers: European pre-understanding and prejudice in the Greek financial crisis. https://biopen.bi.no/bi-xmlui/handle/11250/2377378

Harutyunyan, M., & Malfeito-Ferreira, M. (2022). The rise of wine among ancient civilizations across the Mediterranean Basin. *Heritage*, 5(2), 788–812. https://doi.org/10.3390/heritage5020043

Hassan, A. R., & Lituchy, T. R. (2016). Leadership in Nigeria. Palgrave Macmillan US eBooks (pp. 89–106). https://doi.org/10.1057/978-1-137-59121-0_7

Hastings, E. (2023, March 30). The power of Latino leadership in the multicultural future. Crestcom Intern.

HETCO| Hellenic Trade Council. (2020, January 21). Logistics & Transport - HETCO: Hellenic Trade Council. HETCO: Hellenic Trade Council. https://hetco.org/logistics-transport/

Hinnebusch, R. (2012). Syria: From authoritarian upgrading to revolution? *International Affairs*, 88(1), 95-113

Hinnebusch, R. (2023). 'Great power competition in Syria: from proxy war to sanctions war. *Syria Studies Journal*, 15(1), 1-51

Hofstede Insights. (2023, October 16). Country Comparison. Retrieved from https://www.hofstede-insights.com/country-comparison/

Hofstede, G. (1980). *Culture's consequences: International differences in work-related values*. Sage Publications.

Horak, S. (2021). Aristotelian Business Ethics. In: Poff, D.C., Michalos, A.C. (eds) Encyclopedia of Business and Professional Ethics. Springer, Cham. https://doi.org/10.1007/978-3-319-23514-1_1282-1

House, R. J., Hanges, P. J., Javidan, M., Dorfman, P. W. & V. Gupta (2004). *Culture, Leadership, and Organizations: The GLOBE Study of 62 Societies*. Sage Publications.

House, R. J., Hanges, P. J., Javidan, M., Dorfman, P. W., & Gupta, V. (Eds.). (2004). Culture, leadership, and organizations: The GLOBE study of 62 societies. Sage Publications.

Hovsepyan, L. (2024, July 18). *Employee engagement and leadership in the U.S. and Armenia*. Linkedin. https://www.linkedin.com/pulse -vc8sc/

Huidobro, V. (2008). HRM in Chile: the impact of organisational culture [Research Paper]. *Research Paper*.

Human resource management in developing countries. (2001a). In P. S. Budhwar & Y. A. Debrah (eds.). Routledge. http://ndl.ethernet.edu.et/bitstream/123456789/38927/1/19%202001.pdf#page=19

Ibneatheer, M.U., Rostan, P., & Rostan, A. (2021). Internal processes in decision-making (mental, emotional, cultural, ethical and spiritual) of Afghan business leaders. PSU Research Review, 7(1), 33-50.

Ibrahim, R. (2023). Women leadership in Syria: New perspectives. Instagram.

Iguisi, O. (2014). Indigenous Knowledge Systems and Leadership Styles in Nigerian Work Organisations. International Journal of Research in Business and Social Science, 3(4), 1–13. https://doi.org/10.20525/ijrbs.v3i4.107

Impulsa Tu Liderazgo RD. (2023). Ser un buen líder implica guiar a otros, pero ser extraordinario va más allá [Instagram post]. November 2024. https://www.instagram.com/impulsatuliderazgoRD

Jackson, M. (2004). *In Sierra Leone*. Duke University Press.

Jackson, T. (2004). *Management and change in Africa: A cross-cultural perspective*. Routledge.

James, G. (2023). *Introduction to Armenia*. Google Books. https://www.google.nl/books/edition/Introduction_to_Armenia/6xXAEAAAQBAJ?hl=nl&gbpv=1

Jharap, E. (2012). De weg van Staatsolie. Het verwerven van technische en management expertise. Acadamic Journal of Suriname, 3, 267-275. ISSN 207903456

Jiménez, A. (2010). Santo Domingo: The First City of the Americas. *Historical Review*, 22(1), 45-67.

Jocano, F. L. (1997). *Filipino value systems: A cultural definition*. Punlad Research House https://books.google.rs/books/about/Filipino_Value_System.html?id=ebcuAQAAIAAJ

Jocano, F. L. (1999a). *Working with Filipinos: A cross-cultural encounter*. Punlad Research House.

Jocano, F. L. (1999b). *Management by culture: Fine-tuning modern management with Filipino cultural values*. Punlad Research House.

Johnson, O., Sahr, F., Begg, K., Sevdalis, N., & Kelly, A. H. (2021). To bend without breaking: A qualitative study on leadership by doctors in Sierra Leone. *Health Policy and Planning*, 36(10), 1644–1658. https://doi.org/10.1093/heapol/czab076

Jordán, R., Garay, M., Cristian Santos, Guillermo Trujillo, Equipo Vertical Capital Humano, & Omar Céspedes - Disomce, diseño + innovación. (2014). *Liderazgo Real de los fundamentos a la práctica* (Segunda).

Journal of The Linguistic Association of Nigeria. (n.d.). https://jolan.com.ng/index.php/home

Kaifi, Mujtaba, B. A., Bahaudin G. (2010). Transformational Leadership of Afghans and Americans: A study of Culture, Age and gender. https://www.scirp.org/pdf/jssm20100100019_17680537.pdf

Kallmer, B. (2024, 5 January). Latin America Erupts: Millennial Authoritarianism in El Salvador | Journal of Democracy. Journal Of Democracy. https://www.journalofdemocracy.org/articles/latin-america-erupts-millennial-authoritarianism-in-el-salvador/

Kammweiler, J., & Ruiz, R. (2019). *Introverted leadership and cultural influence in Paraguay*. [Video]. YouTube. https://www.youtube.com/watch?v=GY-qND2DRuE

Kanneh, L., & Haddud, A. (2016). Performance management in Sierra Leone public sector organisations. *International Journal of Public Sector Performance Management*, 2(4), 411–429.

Karageorgiou, G., & Selwood, D. (2020, December 16). Successful companies live up to this ancient Greek ideal. Harvard Business Review. https://www.helleniscope.com/2020/

Karapetyan, G. (n.d.) *The Hidden Side of Success*. Newmag. https://newmag.am/-side-of-success

Kasali, S. (2024, 13 February). Nigeria has no problem but its inhabitants — Oba of Lagos. Tribune Online. https://tribuneonlineng.com/nigeria-has-no-problem-but-its-inhabitants-oba-of-lagos/

Katakis, T. (z.d.). Thomas Katakis. CEOWORLD Magazine. https://ceoworld.biz/author/thomas-katakis/

Kazantzakis, N. (1966). Travels in Greece. Oxford, England: Bruno Cassirer. Lee, D. (1959). Freedom and culture. American University.

Kermani, H., Badis, N., University of Algiers 3 -Ibrahim Soltane Chibout, & University of Khenchela -Abbes Laghrour. (2024). Exploring the connection between emotional intelligence and strategic leadership: Perspectives from Medium-Sized Enterprises in Algeria. *Remittances Review*, 9(2), 3683–3695. https://doi.org/10.33282/rr.vx9i2.190

Khadil, I. (2024). [MS Teams] interview. 12 November.

Khatib, L. (2024). Autocracy, Iran, and Religious Transformation in Syria. *Syria Studies Journal*, 15(2), 1-21

Khemraj, T., & Pasha, S. (2024). Structural change and sectoral interconnectedness in two resource-abundant economies. Resources Policy, 88, N.PAG.

Khzrtian, S., & Samuelian, T. (2012). The Armenian culture of negotiation: Research approaches. *Negotiation Journal*, 14(3), 221-240. https://boon.am/

Kobayashi Cabrera, A. (2012). Liderazgo organizacional en Chile: un estudio de los discursos de gerentes del área de recursos humanos de empresas en Santiago, Chile (By L. Godoy Catalán; G. Guajardo Soto, Trans.). https://repositoriobiblioteca.udp.cl/ST3152.pdf

Kolachi, N. A., & Heğeş, N.-E. (Reds.). (2019). The 15th International RAIS Conference on Social Sciences and Humanities. In *PROCEEDINGS*. International RAIS Conference on Social Sciences and Humanities. https://ssrn.com/abstract=3505285

Kong, F. (2024). [Teams] interview. 8 November

Kong, F. J. (2017). *Leadership that matters*. https://www.amazon.co.uk/

Kori-Siakpere, U., Gokeme, O., Omale, R. O., Aniah, A. R., Ojukwu, P. M., & Okache, M. O. (2024). The Impact of Linguistic Diversity on Intercultural Communication in Nigerian Organizations: A Review. Deleted Journal, 2(2), 25–33. https://doi.org/10.54536/jir.v2i2.3174

Koubaytari, L. (2024). [MS Teams] interview. 20 November.

Koutoula, D. G. (2022). Leadership and emotional intelligence for managers in Greek public organizations and in international organizations: Aristotle's Relevant Legacy in Nicomachean Ethics. In M. Rammata, Master Thesis. https://dspace.lib.uom.gr/

Lacdan, M. D. (2022, October 10). Anu-ano ba ang mga istilo ng pamumuno (Styles of leadership)? [Video]. YouTube. November 8, 2024, from https://www.youtube.com/watch?v=qDPWVGFmpAY

Laidouci, M. (2024). [MS Teams] interview. 13 November.

Larras, C. & Kareche Meriem. (2022). L'intelligence émotionnelle, un trait de leadership influençant la performance de l'entreprise. Cas d'étude: HENKEL Algérie. *Revue Innovation*, 12(1), 355–372.

Lawal, A., Ajonbadi, H., & Otokiti, B. (2014). Leadership and Organisational Performance in the Nigeria Small and Medium Enterprises (SMEs). https://www.semanticscholar.org/

Liebl, V. (2007). Pushtuns, Tribalism, Leadership, Islam and Taliban: A Short view. Small Wars and Insurgencies, 18(3), 492–510. https://doi.org/10.1080/09592310701674481

Littrell, R. F., (2013). Influence of values on preferred leader behaviour in Chile and Mexico. In *Journal of Management Development* (Vols. 32–32, Issue 6, pp. 629–656) [Journal-article]. https://doi.org/10.1108/JMD-04-2013-0055

Mac Donald, S. (2016). De relatie tussen leiderschap en motivatie in Suriname. [Unpublished master's thesis, Erasmus Universiteit Rotterdam].

Malakyan, P. (2016). Anthropology of leadership: An Armenian perspective. Academia. https://www.academia.edu/68158850/Anthropology_of_Leadership_An_Armenian_Perspective

Malcolm, D. (2003). *Consultative leadership in the Philippines*. https://www.google.co.uk/books/edition/

Malone, D. (2023, August 28). Zesde editie Suriname Leadership Academy georganiseerd [Video]. YouTube. https://youtu.be/OOyYEgQKM10

Manara Magazine Editorial Team. (2023, 23 May). 'Files from Exile' Interview Series with Female Leaders from Afghanistan - Manara Magazine. https://manaramagazine.org/files-from-exile-interview-series/

Manchanda, N. (2019). The Graveyard of Empires: Haunting, amnesia and Afghanistan's construction as a burial site. Middle East Critique, 28(3), 307–320. https://doi.org/10.1080/19436149.2019.1633745

Martin, W. (2017). Leadership: Outdated Theories and Emerging Non-traditional Leadership [Thesis, Northcentral University].

Martirosyan, R. (2014). Family Business in Armenia. *Erenet Profile, 9*(1), 24-30. https://citeseerx.ist.psu.edu/document

Megheirkouni, M. (2016). Leadership behaviours and capabilities in Syria: An exploratory qualitative approach. *Journal of Management Development*, 35(5), 636-662

Menzo, M. (2012). Ethnic Group Boundaries in Multicultural Suriname: A study on language use, ethnic boundaries, core values and national identification among Creoles and Hindustanis in Suriname [Thesis, Louvain School of Management]. https://arno.uvt.nl/show.cgi?fid=127779

Moguluwa, S., & Amadi, C. (2021). Empathy and customers loyalty in business-to-business relationship: a case of Airtel Nigeria's business partners. https://www.semanticscholar.org/

Mohsen., Ahsanullah., Sharif., Omer. (2020). Employee participation in decision making and its effect on job satisfaction. https://mpra.ub.uni-muenchen.de/102471/1/MPRA_paper_102471.pdf

Monsutti, A. (2007). War and Migration: Social Networks and Economic Strategies of the Hazaras of Afghanistan. Routledge.

Montek S. Ahluwalia, Eduardo Aninat, Leszek Balcerowicz, Mario I. Blejer, Kwesi Botchwey, Fernando Henrique Cardoso, Kemal Dervis, Alejandro Foxley, Yegor Gaidar, Rima Khalaf Hunaidi, Lawrence H.

Summers, John Williamson, & Zhou Xiaochuan. (2005). Development Challenges in the 1990s: Leading Policymakers Speak from Experience. In T. Besley & R. Zagha (Eds.), *A Copublication of the World Bank and Oxford University Press.*

Montesino, A. (2002). Leadership and Communication Styles in the Dominican *Republic. Caribbean Journal of Business and Culture.*

Montesino, M. (2003b). Leadership/Followership similarities between people in a developed and a developing country: the case of Dominicans in NYC and Dominicans on the island. *Journal of Leadership & Organizational Studies,* 10(1), 82–92. https://doi.org/10.1177/107179190301000107

Moriano León, J. A., Topa Cantisano, G., & Lévy Mangin, J.-P. (2009). Leadership in Nonprofit Organizations of Nicaragua and El Salvador: A Study from the Social Identity Theory. *The Spanish Journal of Psychology,* 12, (2),667–676). http://www.redalyc.org/articulo.oa?id=17213008026

Mortimer, R. A., Cambridge University Press, & JSTOR. (1970). The Algerian Revolution in Search of the African Revolution. *The Journal Of Modern African Studies,* 363–387. https://www.jstor.org/stable/158849

Mujtaba, B. (2019). Leadership and management philosophy of "Guzaara" or cooperating to "Get along" in South Asia's Afghanistan. https://essuir.sumdu.edu.ua/handle/123456789/72828

Mujtaba, B. G., & Kaifi, B. A. (2010). An inquiry into eastern leadership orientation of working adults in Afghanistan. Journal of Leadership Studies, 4(1), 36–46. https://doi.org/10.1002/jls.20153

Mujtaba, B. G., Senathip, T., & Sungkhawan, J. (2021). Task and Relationship Orientation of Professionals in Afghanistan and Thailand. Business Ethics and Leadership, 5(2), 6-20. https://doi.org/10.21272/bel.5(2).6-20.2021

Muñoz, C. (2022, September 25). *Liderazgo para crecimiento organizacional | Carlos Muñoz* [Video]. YouTube. https://www.youtube.com/watch?v=Fx-D-xazBBU

Nadeau, K. (2020). *The history of the Philippines (2nd ed.).* Google Books.

Nem Singh, J. T. (2012). States, Markets and Labour Unions: The Political Economy Of Oil And Copper In Brazil And Chile [PhD dissertation]. *University of Sheffield, United Kingdom.* https://etheses.whiterose.ac.uk/3392/1/JT_Nem_Singh_PhD_Thesis.pdf

Njoku, M. G. C. (2013). Leadership strategies for Nigeria. Management Strategies Journal, 22(4), 57–62. http://www.strategiimanageriale.ro/papers/130405.pdf

Nkwocha, O. (2012). Effective Leadership in Nigeria: Practical Ways to Build Effective, Inspiring, Transformational and Visionary Leadership and Governance in Nigeria. AuthorHouse.

Northouse, P. (2021). Leadership: Theory and practice. SAGE Publications.

Nwagbara, U., Kamara, H. Y., London School of Commerce (LSC), & London School of Commerce (LSC). (n.d.). Corporate social responsibility (CSR) leadership and poverty reduction: The case of Nigeria and Sierra Leone. Economic Insights – Trends and Challenges, IV–LXVII(No. 2/2015), 21–30.

Nwankwo, I., Heussen-Montgomery, E., & Jordans, E. (2019). Leadership and Culture in Corporate Organizations in Nigeria. https://www.semanticscholar.org/

Ojo, M. A., & Ajani, E. O. (2024). Changes in the Role and Status of Women in the Nigerian Baptist Convention, 1914–2021. Religions, 15(9), 1079. https://doi.org/10.3390/rel15091079

Ojokuku, R. M., Odetayo, T. A., & Sajuyigbe, A. S. (2013). Impact of Leadership Style on Organizational Performance: A Case Study of Nigerian Banks. American Journal of Business and Management, 2(1), 202. https://doi.org/10.11634/216796061706212

Ojukwu, E (2020). Culture as an instrument of Nigeria's Afrocentric foreign policy: The FESTAC 77 Example. Nigerian Journal of African Studies, 2(1)

Omar, B., & Khamsa Larguo. (2017). The Impact of Cultural Values on the Performance of Small and Medium-Enterprises (Case Study of Managers in Bechar, Algeria). *International Journal Of Business And Administrative Studies,* 3(6), 217–228. https://doi.org/10.20469/ijbas.3.10003-6

Omilo. (2023, 16 May). 10 important Greek Proverbs. Omilo. https://omilo.com/nl/10-important-greek-proverbs/

Onabote, G. (2021). Emotional Intelligence and Leadership Performance in Manufacturing Organizations in Lagos State, Nigeria [Thesis]. In Walden University, M. Zelihic, B. Forsyth, M. Sharifzadeh, & S. Subocz, Walden University.

Oolasunkanmi. (2023, 29 October). Sanwo-Olu congratulates oba Akiolu at 80. Lagos State Government. https://lagosstate.gov.ng/

Östlund, P. (2020). The power of friendship, can friendship between ethnic groups reduce prejudices in multi-ethnic Suriname? Uppsala Universitet. https://www.diva-portal.org/

Osunde, O., & Olokooba, S. M. (2014). Managing Diversity in the Workplace: Legal and Theoretical Perspectives in Nigeria. Managing Diversity in the Workplace: Legal and Theoretical Perspectives in Nigeria - ProQuest, 7(6), 1–6.

Otiwa, J., Edet, E. S., & Adomokhai, S. S. (2020). Hofstede's Cultural Dimensions and implications for entrepreneurial development in Nigeria. Journal of Management & Entrepreneurial, 2(1). https://www.researchgate.net/

Oyewunmi, A. E., Oyewunmi, O. A., Ojo, I. S., & Oludayo, O. A. (2015). Leaders' Emotional Intelligence and Employees' Performance: A Case in Nigeria's Public Healthcare Sector. International Journal of Human Resource Studies, 5(3), 23. https://doi.org/10.5296/ijhrs.v5i3.7854

Pajés, A. (2022). Los nuevos poderes del líder.

Palla, K., (2024, 29 November). [Zoom] Interview. 29 November

Pamir, E., Waheedi, A.H., & Habib, K.A. (2023). Some Aspects of Pashtun Culture. Randwick International of Social Science Journal.

Papalexandris, N, & Galanaki, E. (2017). Demographic challenges for the future business leader: evidence from a Greek survey. Evidence-based HRM: a Global Forum for Empirical Scholarship. 5. 00-00. 10.1108/EBHRM-03-2017-0019.

Papalexandris, N. (1997, November). Issues and prospects of internationalization among Greek SME's. Paper presented at the 24th International Small Business Congress, Taipei, Taiwan.

Papalexandris, N. (2007). Greece: From ancient myths to modern realities. In J. S. Chhokar, F. C. Brodbeck, & R. J. House (Eds.), Culture and leadership across the world: The GLOBE book of in-depth studies of 25 societies (pp. 767–802). Lawrence Erlbaum Associates.

Papalexandris, N., & Galanaki, E. (2012). Connecting desired leadership styles with ancient Greek philosophy: Results from the GLOBE research in Greece, 1995–2010. In G. P. Prastacos, F. Wang, & K. E. Soderquist (Eds.), Leadership through the Classics (pp. 339–350). Springer.

Papatheodorou, A., & Arvanitis, P. (2023). The economic impact of tourism on Greece's GDP: A 2023 assessment. Journal of Tourism Economics, 29(3), 412-425.

Pasarly, S. (2023, 23 November). The Leadership Evolution: Why today's world needs more bosses. [Video]. YouTube. https://www.youtube.com/watch?v=YZRvoZXDXFM

Perspectiva Laboral El Salvador (2011). Organización Internacional del Trabajo.

Philippine Institute for Development Studies. (2018). Career progression and educational impact on management roles. from https://www.pids.gov.ph/

Poghosyan, G. A. (2021). Armenian family. Between tradition and modernity. Sotsiologicheskie Issledovaniya, 10, 106–115. https://doi.org/10.31857/s013216250015319-3

Polanen, J. (2024). [Zoom] interview. 8 November.

Polanen, J. (2024). The Soul of a Nation – A Journey into the past, present and future of Surinamese Values. Jean-Pierre Polanen.

Pooters, G. & Asin, M. (2024, 20 June). 7e editie van de JCI Suriname Leadership Academy opkomst [Video]. YouTube. https://youtu.be/N56D9cp2Ya0

Publishers, B., & Bordas, J. (n.d.). The Power of Latino Leadership, second edition, revised and updated. https://bkconnection.com/books/title/

Putz, C. (2022, June 21). What are the social and political values of the Afghan people? The Diplomat. https://thediplomat.com/2022/06/what-are-the-social-and-political-values-of-the-afghan-people/

Ramadhin, S. (2024). [Teams] interview. 15 November.

Ramsoedh, H.(2017). Post-Colonial Trajectories in the Caribbean (1st edition). Routledge. https://doi.org/10.4324/9781315552248

Rarick, C., Winter, G., Falk, G., Nickerson, I., & Barczyk, C. (2013). Afghanistan's Younger, Elite and Educated Population: A Cultural Assessment and Possible Implications for the Economic and Political Future of the Country. Global Journal of Management and Business Research Administration and Management, 13(4),

Republic of Sierra Leone. (n.d.). African Commission on Human and Peoples' Rights.

Richard, C. J. (1995). The founders and the classics: Greece, Rome, and the American enlightenment. Harvard University Press.

Richards, P. (2006). Young men and violence in Sierra Leone and Liberia. In C. Christiansen & H. Vigh (Eds.), *Navigating youth, generating adulthood: Social becoming in an African context* (pp. 39–59). Nordic Africa Institute.

Rivera, L., & Torres, J. (2013). Cultural Fusion in the Caribbean: The Dominican Republic's Identity. *Hispaniola Studies*, 10(4), 34-50.

Rodriguez, J. K., (2009). HRM in Chile: the impact of organisational culture [Research paper]. *Employee Relations, 31–31*(3), 276–294. https://doi.org/10.1108/01425450910946479

Ruiz, R. (2024). Video interview 16 November

SAFETY4SEA. (2023, October 2). 2023 SAFETY4SEA Athens Forum: Keynote speakers. [Video]. YouTube. https://www.youtube.com/watch?v=9jFP9OOjA9U

Sánchez Báez, E.A. (2019). Valores personales de los empresarios, cultura organizacional y clústers: impacto en la innovación de las pymes en Paraguay. (Tesis Doctoral Inédita). Universidad de Sevilla. https://hdl.handle.net/11441/8819

Sanchez, C. M. (2000). Motives for corporate philanthropy in El Salvador: Altruism and political legitimacy. *Journal of Business Ethics*.

Sánchez, E., & Rodríguez, H. (2014). Leadership Values in the Dominican Republic: A Cultural Perspective. *Latin American Leadership Quarterly*, 7(1), 89-102.

Sánchez-Báez, E. A., Fernández-Serrano, J., & Romero, I. (2019). Organizational culture and innovation in small businesses in Paraguay. *Regional Science Policy & Practice*, 12(2), 233–247. https://doi.org/10.1111/rsp3.12203

Sargsyan, K. N., Kirakosyan N. L. (2021) *Management and leadership Armenian business*. Cyberleninka. https://cyberleninka.ru/article/n/menedzhment-i-liderstvo-v-armyanskom-biznese/viewer

Saydee, F. (2023, 28 September). Getting to know Afghan Newcomers: Considerations for culturally aware communication. Switchboard. https://www.switchboardta.org/getting-to-know-afghan-newcomers-considerations-for-culturally-aware-communication/

Sayes, C. E. & Universidad Católica de El Salvador. (2015). Aplicación del liderazgo de las jefaturas de las pequeñas y medianas empresas (PYMES) de la Zona Occidental de El Salvador. *Anuario de Investigación*, 4, 263–264.

Schmalenbach, C., Monterrosa, H., Larín, A. R. C., & Jurkowski, S. (2022). The LIFE programme – University students learning leadership and teamwork through service learning in El Salvador. *Intercultural Education*, 33(4), 470–483. https://doi.org/10.1080/14675986.2022.2090689

Schneider, B. R. (2009). Hierarchical market economies and varieties of capitalism in Latin America. *Journal of Latin American Studies*, 41(3), 553–575. https://doi.org/10.1017/s0022216x09990186

Seguel, C. C. (2015). Ciudades satélites periurbanas en Santiago de Chile: paradojas entre la satisfacción residencial y precariedad económica del peri urbanita de clase media. *Revista INVI*, 30(85), 83–110. https://doi.org/10.4067/s0718-83582015000300003

Segundo, M. G., G. (2022). Leadership and Culture: What Difference Does It Make? In Regent Research Roundtables Proceedings (pp. 104–119). Regent University School of Business &Leadership.

Sellidj, Y., Lounaci, A., & Bouchetara, M. (2023). The Motivational Factors of Necessity Entrepreneurship in Algeria. *Management Of Organizations Systematic Research*, *89*(1), 103–121. https://doi.org/10.2478/mosr-2023-0007

Selmer, J. (2007). *Kinship in Philippine business practices*. https://www.google.co.uk/books/edition/Culture_and_Management_in_Asia/HXkBAwAAQBAJ

Selvarajah, C. M. (2020, June 8). Profiling the paternalistic manager: Leadership excellence in the Philippines. *Asia Pacific Business Review*, 26(4), 425-452. https://doi.org/10.1080/13602381.2020.1770467

Semerdjian, R. (2024). [MS Teams] Interview. 23 November.

Sengova, J. (1987). The national languages of Sierra Leone: A decade of policy experimentation. *Africa*, 57(4), 519–530. https://doi.org/10.2307/1159897

Shankar, B. (2021). Het Interdependentiebewust Leiderschap voor duurzaam construeren. Anton de Kom Universiteit van Suriname.

Shaw, D. (2022). Plato on Leadership. In: An Ancient Greek Philosophy of Management Consulting. Contributions to Management Science. Springer. https://doi.org/10.1007/978-3-030-90959-8_7

Siegel, G. (2024). Leadership reflections: Family, resilience, and community [Instagram post]. December 2024. https://www.instagram.com/gwendolynsiegel

Siham, A. (2013). *The Role of the Syrian Business Elite in the Syrian Conflict: A Class Narrative*. Leiden University.

Smith, G. (2022). The Tribal Characteristics of the Suriname Society. ResearchGate. https://www.researchgate.net/publication/372935734

Smith, J. D. (2024). On the absence of certain island effects in Mende. *Languages*, 9(4), Article 131.

Soerdjan, L. (2022). Enhancing the Role of Leadership in Small and Medium Size Enterprise Performances in Suriname. Acadamic Journal of Suriname, 13, 1-20. ISSN 207903456.

Soto, C., Bareiro, L., & Soto, L. (2003). Mujeres y hombres líderes: Vivencias y opiniones de la población. República del Paraguay, Secretaría de la Mujer. https://biblioteca.clacso.edu.ar/Paraguay/cde/20121022051937/lideres.pdf

Spahie, K. M. & Consejo Nacional de la Cultura y las Artes. (2017). Reflexiones, debates y propuestas en torno al patrimonio en Chile. In Sonia Montecino Aguirre, Rosario Mena Larraín, & Alejandra Alvear Montecino (Eds.), *Tramas de la diversidad*. https://www.cultura.gob.cl

Stonenews. (2024, August 7). Greece: A significant gateway from Asia to Europe. StoneNews.eu. https://stonenews.eu/greece-a-significant-gateway-from-asia-to-europe/

Suriel, A. J. y Escalante, J. L. (2023). Competencias emocionales y su relación con el liderazgo efectivo: un acercamiento desde las directoras educativas de la República Dominicana. *Cuaderno de Pedagogía Universitaria*, 21 (41), 52-63.

Surinaamse Overheid. (2023, July 1). Herinterpretatie tradities en cultuur van cruciaal belang voor natievorming. Overheid van de Republiek Suriname. https://gov.sr/

Taraday, J. (2024). *Business traditions and mentality: Business culture in Armenia*. REAB. https://reab.pro/en/info/business-traditions-and-mentality/business-culture-in-armenia

Taylor, T. (2024, November 10). *Leadership in Sierra Leone* [Audio podcast episode]. In T. Taylor (Host), *Terrence Taylor Podcast*. Spotify

Taylor-Pearce, M. (2022). *Business Bomba: A step-by-step guide to creating a successful and sustainablebusiness in Sierra Leone*. Lulu Publishing Services.

Taylor-Pearce, M. (2023). *Leadership made in Africa: An anthology of leadership articles and perspectives for practitioners*.

Tenreiro, S. (2024). [Video]. Instagram Reel. https://www.instagram.com/reel/C-Y5eqgp1fd/?igsh=Y3k1eGhvOXM0NXBo

Ter-Mkrtchyan, A. (2008). *Project Management Styles in Armenian Public Organizations*. American University of Armenia. https://dspace.aua.am/xmlui/

Thanailaki, P. (2021). Familiocracy in the Greek Business Elite Class: Endogamy and Other Cultural Traits. In: Gendered Stereotypes and Female Entrepreneurship in Southern Europe, 1700-1900. Palgrave Macmillan. https://doi.org/10.1007/978-3-030-66234-9_2

The Power of Latino Leadership by Juana Bordas (Chile 1964-66) – Peace Corps Worldwide. (n.d.).

Thinkers50. (2022, January 27). *Thinkers50 2022 Radar LinkedIn Live with Modupe Taylor-Pearce* [Video]. YouTube. https://www.youtube.com/watch?v=9OxYUejwqv0&t=1447s

Tokmajyan, A. (2023). Mechanisms of Domination: State Violence and Local Intermediaries in Syria. *Syria Studies Journal*, 15(2), 1-41

Tolentino, F. C. (2022). Emotional intelligence and experiences: Their relationship to teaching performance. *AIDE Interdisciplinary Research Journal*, 3(1). https://ejournals.ph/article.php?id=18278

Torres, A. M. N. (2024, November 11). Ana María Núñez Torres on LinkedIn: #businessschool #management #leadership #highereducation #ucsh #chile. https://www.linkedin.com/posts/

Tribuna Paraguay. (2024). *Liderazgo en Paraguay | Tribuna*. Retrieved from https://www.youtube.com/watch?v=DdZd3wmIguU

TurismoRD. (2020, January 31). República Dominicana mantiene liderazgo de crecimiento del PIB en la región | @MTurismoRD [Video]. YouTube. https://www.youtube.com/watch?v=k6Wp8njGUo8

TurismoRD. (2023). Strategic leadership driving Dominican tourism [YouTube video]. Retrieved December 2024, from https://www.youtube.com/user/TurismoRD

Turkmani, R., & Mehchy, Z. (2022). *Building resilience in Syria*.

Udegbe, S. E. (2012). Impact of business communication on organizational performance in Nigerian companies. Australian Journal of Business and Management Research, 2, 16–26. http://ajbmr.com/articlepdf/aus_20_35i2n1a3.pdf

Umana, M., (2024). [Teams] interview. 15 November

Undung, A. B. Y. (2009, May 28). Understanding the elements of empathy as a component of care-driven leadership. *Journal of Leadership Studies*, 3(1), 19-28. https://doi.org/10.1002/jls.20092

Unión Industrial Paraguaya. (2023). Análisis de la estructura productiva y el crecimiento industrial en Paraguay. UIP. https://uip.org.py/doc/dia-de-la-industria-paraguaya-2023/

United Nations Office for Disaster Risk Reduction (UNDRR). (2022, 10 June). Disaster Risk Reduction in Suriname, Situational Analysis 2022.

United Nations Sustainable Development Group. (n.d.). Algeria: Boosting youths' social inclusion, entrepreneurship, and global citizenship. United Nations Sustainable Development Group.

United Nations. (2022, 12 July). CARICOM and United Nations recommit to achieving the SDGs in the region. https://easterncaribbean.un.org/en/

University of Business Learners. (2021, 7 November). Leadership | Lecture # 1 | Rana University, Kabul Afghanistan [Video]. YouTube. https://www.youtube.com/watch?v=pOFYJcvmqAM

Ureña-Espaillat, H. J. (2024). Microsoft Teams interview. 24 April

Ureña-Espaillat, H. J., Peñalver, A. J. B., Conesa, J. a. B., & Córdoba-Pachón, J. (2022). Knowledge and innovation management in agribusiness: A study in the Dominican Republic. *Business Strategy and the Environment*, 32(4), 2008–2021. https://doi.org/10.1002/bse.3233

Urumaxi Anthems. (2020, February 29). National Anthem of Suriname - "God Zij Met Ons Suriname" [Video]. YouTube. https://www.youtube.com/watch?v=M2KbaQBXz_g

Useem, M., Kunreuther, H., & Michel-Kerjan, E. (2015). Leadership dispatches. Stanford Business Books.

Van Gelder, E. (2017, December 2). Niet Bollywood, maar Nollywood: de filmindustrie waarvan je nooit hebt gehoord. NOS.

Vanessa, V. (2024) [Teams] interview. 27 November.

Varela, O. E., Salgado, E. I., & Lasio, M. V. (2010). The meaning of job performance in collectivistic and high power distance cultures: Evidence from three Latin American countries. *Cross Cultural Management: An International Journal*, 17(4), 407-426. https://doi.org/10.1108/13527601011086603

Vargas, F. (2019). Baseball and National Identity in the Dominican Republic. *Journal of Sports and Society*, 15(2), 78-95.

Vazquez, P., Carrera, A. and Cornejo, M. (2020), "Corporate governance in the largest family firms in Latin America", Cross Cultural & Strategic Management, Vol. 27 No. 2, pp. 137-163. https://doi.org/10.1108/CCSM-11-2018-0194

Vedovato, C. (1986). *Politics, foreign trade, and economic development: A study of the Dominican Republic.* Croom Helm.

Veenendaal, W. (2020). Democracy in small states: Persisting against all odds. Oxford University Press. https://books.google.nl/books

Veenendaal, W., & Demarest, L. (2021). How population size affects power-sharing: a comparison of Nigeria and Suriname. Contemporary Politics, 27(3), 271–291. https://doi.org/10.1080/13569775.2020.1855739

Vreeland, H. (1967). *Hierarchical structures in Filipino society. Area Handbook for the Philippines*. November 1, 2024, from https://www.google.co.uk/books/edition/Area_Handbook_for_the_Philippines/Qm8sAAAAYAAJ

Waalring, R. (2013). Opvoeden in Suriname. Stichting Bevordering Maatschappelijke Participatie. https://www.stichtingbmp.nl/cms/projecten/

Wahab, W., & Bangash, K. K. (2021). Inclusive Leadership with Relation to Employee Engagement: Mediating Role of Psychological Empowerment. Kardan Journal of Economics and Management Sciences. https://doi.org/10.31841/kjems.2021.102

Walker. B. (2021, February 28). Bryan Walker getuigt van leiderschapsontwikkeling in Suriname [Video]. YouTube. https://youtu.be/YVo5SAAvax0?list=LL

Weaving Influence. (2023, March 21). The Power of Latino Leadership *Webinar* with Dr. Juana Bordas [Video]. YouTube. https://www.youtube.com/watch?v=rndc_Ct7d6k

WebTV de l'université de Bejaia. (2016, 20 June). *"Le leadership" par Dr Rachid AMOKRANE Part 1* [Video]. YouTube. https://www.youtube.com/watch?v=-82ExZT9ctk

World Trade Press (2010). Dominican Republic Women in Culture, Business & Travel: A Profile of Dominican Women in the Fabric of Society.

Yakpo, K. (2023). Two types of language contact involving English Creoles: Why Krio (Sierra Leone) has evolved more towards English than its relative Pichi (Equatorial Guinea) towards Spanish. *English Today*, 39(1), 12–23.

Yegyan, N. (2018). Cultural dimensions of Armenians based on Hofstede's theory and their subsequent implications of doing business in Armenia. American University of Armenia. https://dspace.aua.am/xmlui/

Yukl, G. (2002). Leadership in organizations. Prentice Hall

Zepp, R. A. (2018, January 10). Perceptions of good and bad leaders by Philippine teachers. Journal of Management and Strategy. https://www.researchgate.net/publication/323316020

Zhamakochyan, A., Hakobyan, L. (2013, July 29). *Armenia's value orientations in the context of inter-cultural researches*. Noravank Foundation. http://www.noravank.am/eng/articles

Zivkovic, S. (2022). Empathy in Leadership: How it Enhances Effectiveness. In 80th International Scientific Conference on Economic and Social Development and 10th International OFEL Conference [Conference-proceeding].